AGAINST RELIGION

Also by Christos Yannaras

Elements of Faith

The Enigma of Evil

The Freedom of Morality

On the Absence and Unknowability of God

Orthodoxy and the West

Person and Eros

Postmodern Metaphysics

Relational Ontology

Variations on the Song of Songs

CHRISTOS YANNARAS

AGAINST RELIGION

THE ALIENATION OF THE ECCLESIAL EVENT

Translated by
Norman Russell

HOLY CROSS ORTHODOX PRESS
Brookline, Massachusetts

Published by Holy Cross Orthodox Press
50 Goddard Avenue
Brookline, Massachusetts 02445

ISBN-13 978-1-935317-40-1
ISBN-10 1-935317-40-7

Originally published in Greek as *Enantia stē thrēskeia*, Ikaros, Athens, 2006.

On the cover:
Pollock, Jackson (1912–1956) © ARS, NY. The Flame, c. 1934–38. Oil on canvas mounted on fiberboard, 20 1/2x30" (51.1 x 76.2 cm). Enid A. HauptFund.
© Pollock-Krasner Foundation / Artists Rights Society (ARS), New York
The Museum of Modern Art, New York, NY, U.S.A.
Digital Image © The Museum of Modern Art/Licensed by SCALA / Art Resource, NY

Library of Congress Cataloging-in-Publication Data

Giannaras, Chrestos, 1935-
[Enantia ste threskeia. English]
Against religion : the alienation of the ecclesial event / Christos Yannaras ; translated by Norman Russell.
pages cm
Includes bibliographical references and index.
ISBN 978-1-935317-40-1
1. Religion. I. Title.
BL48.G4913 2013
200--dc23

2013003533

Contents

Chapter 1

Religiosity

1.1. *An Instinctive Need . . .*

Religiosity is a natural human need, a need that is innate and instinctive within us.

The needs we call natural, innate, and instinctive are those that are not controlled by reason and the will. They are embedded in us as imperative demands, within the functioning of our biological being.

Psychologists summarize the drives that determine humanity's psychosomatic structure as two basic instincts: they speak of an *instinct of self-preservation* and an *instinct of self-perpetuation*. Religiosity may be seen as a manifestation of the instinct of self-preservation. It belongs to the reflexes that have developed in human nature (our automatic, involuntary psychosomatic reactions) so as to ensure survival.

Religiosity is analogous to hunger, thirst, the fear of illness and pain, or terror in the face of death. Why? A tentative, necessarily schematic but not arbitrary explanation might run as follows:

Man sees his existence threatened by powers or factors that he cannot control. His own natural powers do not suffice to avert illness, pain, and death. He therefore resorts to imaginary powers that can offer hope of protection, a reassurance that comes from autosuggestion. He considers the causes of the threats that his own nature cannot control as supernatural, and, moreover, he personifies them. That is, he sets them within a pattern of rational relations that he knows how to manage effectively.

Using the logic of relations between human beings, Man attempts to tame the forces and factors that threaten him. Or else he supposes that there are other contrary forces and factors (always personified) able to overcome and neutralize the threats. He seeks to win them over to his side so that they will protect him.

Powers that are threatening to human beings include many natural phenomena, such as earthquakes, storms, fire, floods, thunderbolts, drought, and famine. They also include the effects of the dysfunctioning or decay of Man's biological being: sickness, aging, disabilities, inherited defects. Man has the instinctive need to attribute these to nonnatural regulators of what appears to be chance: either to inexplicable factors hostile to Man or to friendly, beneficent powers that nevertheless test him or "tempt" him.

Man wants to have good relations with these hypothetical supernatural factors that are favorably or unfavorably disposed toward him. His instinct of self-preservation imposes this upon him as an innate need. He wants to constantly win their sympathy and their good will, or at least not to provoke their opposition and anger. However advanced people may be in intellectual development, critical thought, or scientific knowledge, when faced with mortal danger they resort instinctively to some supernatural protector. (It has rightly been observed that "when a plane enters a zone of violent turbulence, nobody on board is an atheist!")

Referring back to supernatural beings is hypothetical but consistent with human logic. That is, it satisfies Man's need (and it is also natural) to *interpret* the natural word around him, to attribute rationally to the same beings (beings inaccessible to sensory verification) even the *cause* of the reality of all that exists: the creation and preservation of a world that has been brought into being by them, or the direction and preservation of a world that is self-existent.

The unknown frightens Man, especially ignorance of *cause* and *purpose*. Human nature defends itself with knowledge; it uses it to anticipate dangers, and therefore reacts against ignorance, experiencing it as a threat. It cannot bear leaving whatever threatens it shrouded in obscurity. It cannot endure treating the decay and transience of existence as enigmatic. In the face of death, nature generates panic, the mind-reeling effect of confronting the absurd.

By supposing the existence of supernatural beings, even if without the support of intellectual hypotheses, Man consoles himself and assuages the fear provoked by ignorance. If any evil threatening Man has a supernatural cause or agency, then it is reasonable to think that the same supernatural factors that provoke it or permit it also have the power to deflect it.

Consequently, for Man to find ways of mollifying and winning over these factors, he needs some equivalent force that can "control" or "manage" supernatural powers. Man seeks the power and capacity to render these supernatural factors subject to the goal of his own salvation from evil, his own "eternal" happiness.

This power, this capacity, is what is demanded by religious need, and it is this that the institutionalized religions promise.

Religion may be defined as humanity's natural (instinctive) need (1) to suppose that there are factors that generate existence and existent things, together with the *evil* that is intertwined with the fact of existence; and (2) to extrapolate from this rational supposition methods and practices for the "management" of these supernatural factors, so that hopes of humanity's salvation from evil, of humanity's unending happiness, are built up.

Somewhere within these boundaries we may locate the logic of religion, a logic that is biologically determined, which is why the phenomenon of religion has always existed in every human culture. The common marks of the phenomenon, common at all times and in all places, are to be found in the (practical) manifestations that depend on the instinctive needs that give rise to it:

First is Man's need to *know* the factors that determine his existence. We need to possess reliable knowledge, to be reassured by certainties. We need to have at our disposal an effective antidote to the fear that arises from ignorance, to the panic generated by the dark and enigmatic aspects of metaphysical theories.

That is why every religion offers (and presupposes) *dogmas*: *a priori* received teaching, axiomatic definitions, "truths" that do not admit of doubt or of any control for their confirmation or falsification. The religions assure people of that which the needs of human nature demand: guaranteed certainties with regard to metaphysics. Even if they have no support in common experience or reason, they are "truths" that the infallible authority of the representatives of the "sacred" or a supernatural "revelation" turn into certainties.

And for the sacred to be "objectively" pinpointed, it is identified with the formulation of dogmas—precisely in the way the sacred is also objectified in an idol perceptible to the senses (as a statue, a representation, or a fetish). The letter of the formulation is made into an idol, in such a way that fidelity to the letter guarantees the psychological security of possessing the truth and meritorious reverence of faithfulness.

This is the reason why, in every age and indeed in every society, religious people are ready to slaughter each other for chance offenses against the letter of religious dogmas; why they have been ready to tear to pieces, to stone, to burn at the stake the authors of these offenses; why they have been ready to denounce, to devise the most terrible methods of execution (physically and morally) of their "heretical" opponents. The instinctive panic that seizes people when the psychological certainties of their religious "convictions" are shaken appears inexorable, and their aggressiveness toward those who try to shake them seems ferocious.

Second is Man's need to tame, to win over as far as possible, the supernatural powers (always personified) that are assumed to be a threat to his existence or a possible protection for it. This is the need to win their approval and sympathy by the means that Man himself knows: by sacrificing (destroying by fire) the best of the fruits of the earth that he cultivates, or the choicest of the animals he rears, or—perhaps—someone beloved over whom he has authority (son, daughter, wife, or slave). Or he might internalize the sacrifice, expressing it as the privation of desired food (fasting) or of sexual pleasure (chastity).

The logic of sacrifice is a logic of demonstrating a devotion of the senses, of proving in a practical way that God is more precious than the best and dearest that Man has. There is also indirectly discernible a logic of bribery. By the quality of the gift he offers, Man places God under an obligation, just as by giving gifts he places those human beings on whom he depends under an obligation (the king, the tyrant, the master). Man offers something the privation of which is painful to him, in such a way that the specific god should perceive the greatness of his devotion and submission to the *sacred*.

Together with the sacrifice, or instead of the sacrifice, Man may express his devotion and submission by some ceremonial *logos*—by all the capacities for "logical" expression that he possesses: the *logos* of poetry, of music, of dancing, of drama; the *logos* of painting, of architecture, and of sculpture. We call *worship* of the transcendent (a constituent of the identity of religion) the actual referring to it of prayers, supplications, doxologies, and praises, in the various modes of human expression—hymns, dances, and ceremonial rites—and in places and buildings of the greatest possible majesty and beauty.

Third is Man's need to secure the favor of the divine not only by worship but also by disciplining his everyday behavior through regulative principles that he believes reflect the divine will and desire. We call *morality* (another element constituting the identity of religion) the codified commandments (both preceptive and prohibitive) that Man accepts as *law* laid down by God.

Moral law has to be of divine authorship—written by God himself, or dictated by him literally, or (at least) composed under divine inspiration. For it is only thus that it offers the psychological self the strongest possible guarantees of security: if observing the law is obedience to the will of God, then whoever observes the law is undoubtedly judged to be a worthy person, and observing the law constitutes a meritorious individual achievement of *virtue*. On the basis of the law, virtue is a provable certainty; it is certified and measured objectively, offering to the individual the psychological security of being covered with regard to the transcendent.

Perhaps there is something else too. People who obey the commandments of the divine law (the principles of religious morality) often have the certainty (conscious or unconscious) that "the divine" *owes* them some reward for their virtues. They feel that God is bound by the merits of human beings, obliged to guarantee them protection, to help them through life's difficulties, and to prolong their admirable existence everlastingly.

The truths that the clinical experience of modern psychology reveals with regard to the instinctive character of the human need for a moral law with religious support call for a special study on how and why the law determines on the level of the unconscious the relationship between the ego and the superego, on how the superego, "sadistically" internalizing the law, becomes an instrument of judgment or punishment and forces on the ego a "masochistic" withdrawal through feelings of guilt (*Schuldgefühl*), or even a need for self-punishment (*Strafbedürfnis*).[1]

It is not fortuitous that in almost every religion the typically sadomasochistic syndrome arises out of *guilt-redemption-justification*. This is a syndrome whereby the ego unconsciously and masochistically provokes guilt (always with reference to the law), so that by paying the penalty (however painful) that the superego demands for the redemption of the guilt, the ego may win a legally assured justification.

1.2. . . . *Always Centered on the Individual*

Religiosity is fundamentally an innate urge, an instinctive need, and is therefore by definition centered on the individual. Like all our inherent drives, it is an indicative mark of human nature—it characterizes humanity *as a whole*. But the biological intention-

1. Sigmund Freud, *Mourning and Melancholia*, in vol. 14 of the *Standard Edition of the Complete Psychological Works of Sigmund Freud*, ed. James Strachey (London: Hogarth Press and the Institute of Psycho-Analysis, 1953–74); *The Ego and the Id*, chap. 5, in vol. 20 of the *Standard Edition*, trans. Strachey et al.

ality of every drive, even if it serves the species, is expressed as a paramount need of the individual.

As a manifestation of the instinct of self-preservation, religiosity aims at armoring individuals against the insecurity and fears that are bred by ignorance, against the terror and panic of death. Religion armors individuals with metaphysical "convictions," with moral "principles," with certainty regarding the eternal prolongation of their existence. It nourishes the superego, offering self-confidence, pleasurable self-satisfaction, a sanctified narcissism.

The typical religious person operates with his individual self, his ego, as the axis and center of every aspect of his life. This is because religion offers him a legitimate justification of egocentricity, for it sets before him the goal and obligation of *individual salvation*. The juridical character of religious morality imposes an individual notion of salvation as self-evident. Those who are saved are those who keep the law, and keeping the law is an individual achievement. The individual obeys the stipulations of the law in order to have objective (assured, measurable) presuppositions for salvation. An individual who does not observe the law cannot be saved, however many intermediaries intercede for his salvation.

The individualistic character of salvation is strengthened by recourse to the *freedom of the individual*, which is recourse to sound logic when freedom is defined as the power to make individual choices. Only such a version of freedom offers the support of psychological certainty to the religious individual, and consequently this version of freedom always accompanies natural, instinctive religiosity in the form of a typical syndrome.

In the religious perspective the individual chooses his convictions, that is, his "faith." He chooses to keep the moral commandments of his faith; he chooses to remain faithful to his choices. Whoever freely chooses unbelief or agnosticism, disobedience to the divine law, also freely chooses the refusal of his salvation, his eternal condemnation.

This implacable logic, also manifestly a product of the instincts of self-preservation and self-protection, functions as a presupposition for religious faith and juridical virtue to work together to armor-plate the ego. Any form of mental reservation, any doubt about the individualistic, self-chosen character of salvation, opens up enormous chasms of insecurity, uncertainty, and fear in the individual.

If one's freedom of choice proves in practice to be shot through with relativity, if choices are determined not only by the conscious will of the individual but also by the *unconscious* (by inherited dispositions, repressed desires, childhood traumas), if one's family environment, social background, and cultural milieu also play a role, then any individual achievements of the religious person are also relativized. It becomes difficult for such achievements to function as armor plating for the ego.

Augustine took the logic of the freedom of choice to its ultimate conclusion, to the conclusion, for example, that the saved in heaven feel joy at seeing the torments of sinners in hell! In a manner absolutely consistent with the logic of the instincts, natural religiosity is individualistic even to the point of inhumanity and sadism. It allows no room even for natural sympathy or compassion. Even when the religious individual has pity on the poor, when he carries out the acts of altruism and philanthropy laid down by the law, he still has an eye on merit, he still serves his ego—as becomes immediately obvious from the calculated, rationally controlled manner of his offering. He can "give away all that he has," he can "deliver his body to be burned," not because he really loves, but only so that the achievement can be credited to him as an individual.

Instinctive and inexorable, humanity's religious need demands that the individual should have (1) objective certainty that he is assuring his salvation and (2) irrefutable arguments for the correctness and validity of his metaphysical convictions.

Objective proofs of salvation are provided by "good works": the individual's fidelity to the letter of the formulations of religious dogmas, the individual's consistent application of the commandments of the moral law, his observing of the obligations of worship. Without the individual's amassing of such "good works," the psychological security of atomic salvation is not attained. And the more tormenting the fear and insecurity (from a combination of many factors), the more anxious is the effort to achieve visible and measurable "good works."

Fidelity to the letter of dogmatic teaching is a meritorious achievement for the individual, and therefore every dogmatic "orthodoxy" makes this (the certainty of the protection of the individual) its boast. This boast, however—the certainty that it engenders—also demands the support of objective (apodictic) evidence for what has been received. Thus religiosity is very often intertwined with claiming rational validity for metaphysical convictions, with prioritizing intellectualist methods of *proving* this validity.

Faith ceases to be a struggle to establish relations of *trust* and becomes identified with intellectual *convictions*—it becomes the self-evident synonym of ideology. The doctrines are understood as *a priori* (logically necessary) received teachings, uncontrolled axioms, obligatory ideological principles. And as in every ideology, the acceptance of these teachings is a personal choice, with the result that religiosity is understood only in terms of the personal preference of the individual. Preference for, and choice of, religious "faith" is facilitated (sometimes even compelled) by rational arguments to counter objections and reservations, by "proofs" of impeccable rational coherence—chiefly for the existence of God. These "proofs" are classified according to the epistemological field from which they draw their arguments (we have *ontological, cosmological, moral,* and *historical* "proofs" for the existence of God).

Blind and ineluctable, the instinct of self-preservation imposes on the individual a protective armoring of certainties. And the need for metaphysical certainties generates religious convictions, together with the defense of these convictions by syllogistic arguments and the justification of faith by "scientific" *apologetics*—it renders theology a *sacra scientia*. It is not fortuitous that the supreme manifestations of intellectualism in human history are products of religious need.

This same religious need inherently gives rise to schemes and institutions designed to defend convictions and principles and impose them in an active combative manner. It is not fortuitous that the first forms of *totalitarianism* in human history are religious.

The devising of (that is, the need for) an "infallible" leadership, the juridical control of thinking, censorship, the index of prohibited books, the use of torture as a method of interrogation in the trials of heretics—these are all of religious origin. Sometimes the instinctive need to defend religious convictions leads to wars of atrocious cruelty, just as it leads not only to the moral but also to the physical annihilation of those who think differently by a "cleansing" death—the "cleansing" requiring, for example, that they should be burned alive at the stake.

Behind this whole range of manifestations of the natural individualistic need for religious certainties, what predominates is always the priority of rational "objectivity," an absolute trust in the atomic intellect. The religious individual makes an idol of his intellectual capacity; he worships the powers of logical thought. He wants to place the certainty that his own convictions and his own principles are the only correct ones on unshakable foundations. He wants to be absolutely sure that when he defends his own convictions and his own principles, he is upholding the only metaphysical truth and the highest morality.

1.3. *Nonrational Thought and the Emotions*

The natural individualistic need for religious certainties makes an idol of the individual's mental capacity; it worships the powers of the rational method. This same need is very good at nullifying reason; it overturns the rules of every methodical apodictic in order to safeguard even more unassailable certainties.

What makes intellectual arguments vulnerable is the way they are constructed. The apodictic force of a rational proposition is built up by the systematic refutation of possible objections—the objection is presupposed as a methodological principle of the proof. Thus every metaphysical proposition that seeks support from the methodology of the positive sciences is potentially subject to the requirements of the apodictic methodology of testing through possible objections, objections that at any given moment may be new and unexpected.

The likelihood of objections is only circumvented by abandoning the rational control of metaphysical propositions. This relinquishing becomes apparent within the context of religious traditions as a trend, “school,” or tendency opposed to the intellectualism of apodictic proof. More commonly, however, this trend coexists with intellectualism within the same tradition—sometimes even within the work of the same great religious teacher or writer.

The relinquishing of the rational control of metaphysical propositions very often (and seductively) appropriates the name of *faith*—it becomes synonymous with faith. Faith is identified in the popular understanding with individual convictions that lie beyond the reach of any possible application of systematic logic—they have been chosen by the individual as *a priori* and undemonstrable truths that are not subject to rational control. The phrase *credo quia absurdum* (“I believe because it is absurd”) summarizes this version of faith versus reason very well—faith as bereft of reason.

It is difficult, of course, for us to set clear boundaries differentiating the *irrational* from the *suprarational*. There is a logic in the denial of apodictic methods—a logic, for example, of recourse to a transcendent *authority* with a view to verifying or validating a proposition. Instead of resorting to the power of rational proof, we resort to some “factor” that transcends the limitations and the relativity of the human intellect—a factor that guarantees whatever the intellect does not have the capacity to confirm methodically, and moreover excludes any possible objection.

Recourse to such a factor of transcendent authority is necessarily irrational or nonrational, since it denies the common (conventional) methods of verification that render knowledge communicable. It is not unreasonable (or incoherent), however, because it obeys the logic of a subjective mental choice—the logic of the denial that metaphysics should be subject to the rules of perception-understanding-interpretation that govern physics. If this denial is accepted as a rational presupposition for the knowledge of metaphysical reality, then the phrase *credo quia absurdum* also has rational validity.

The epistemological uncertainty of religious opinions lies elsewhere. Both in the case of metaphysical intellectualism and in the case of rationally "blind" faith, we have as a common starting point or presupposition an absolutely subjective choice that is made on a nonempirical level—an individual choice of what is inferred intellectually or is methodologically unprovable. In either case the starting point or presupposition is not the desire to investigate common experience, but the satisfaction of the instinctive need of the natural individual for metaphysical certainties—an individualistic satisfaction within the context of the volitional powers of the individual.

The sufficiency of individual choice is decided on a level prior to that of the intellectual process. The preliminary decision is the result of unconscious psychological operations. Both with regard to methodical (intellectual) inference and with regard to the abandonment of rational methods (for the sake of recourse to the weight of superior authority), this psychological need of the individual for absolute security clads itself with certainties. Sometimes such absolute certainty is sought in rationalism and sometimes in the rejection of rationalism. Sometimes it is sought in "religious feeling" or "mysticism," sometimes in "intuition" or "insight" or "existential experience"—always in some real or hypothetical epistemic capacity of the individual. In every case it is concerned with subjective choice exercised by the individual, that is, within a strict framework of reference of atomic presuppositions and intentionalities.

Recourse to some *authority* responds to the need not only for verification or validation but also for the generation of a religious certainty. The conviction prevalent in religious traditions that the knowledge of metaphysical truth is conveyed directly from God as a "grace" (or charism) to the individual worthy to receive it is characteristic. Individual readiness is a necessary condition for the bestowal of the gift of knowledge, for "faith" (or religious certainty) is understood as a divine response to individual merit.

Of course, every kind of knowledge or cognition of sensible and intelligible reality is always a subjective event (even when it is acquired through the attainment of relation as self-transcendence and self-offering). But for the religious mental outlook, knowledge as "grace" is understood (more or less) as the mechanistic conveyance of a capacity from the unknown transcendent to the individual human being—from an individualized pole of absolute knowledge to a pole of relative and restricted knowledge (rather like the charging of a battery).

There is also the "logic" of religious *mysticism*, a "logic" that covers a broad range of assertions, from the identification of faith with feeling to the certainties deriving from ecstatic states and revelatory visions.

By the word *feeling* (*synaisthēma*), something like knowledge or certainty is affirmed, something that is unrelated to the information conveyed by the senses and the operation of the intellect; such "knowledge" is only with difficulty distinguished from intense desire and emotional autosuggestion. "We know" by our feelings something that draws us, that attracts us, that grants us an enthusiastic psychological sense of well-being and exaltation, without our being concerned with the shared affirmation of the existence or the nonexistence of the object of our knowledge, with whether it is genuine or illusory.

Mysticism appears to be a kind of systematization of the "certainties" that are gained on the emotional level. It broadens the field of the claims of the emotions relating to cognition, borrowing the vocabulary of an explicitly nonrational *esotericism*, that is, of a reference to inward (belonging to the "soul" or the "inner man") capacities of knowledge with discrete boundaries. The kind of phrases that predominate are: "the intuition of interiority," "the deep self," "the limpid operation of the psyche," "inner knowledge," "radical inwardness," "inner vision," "the shudder of inwardness," and so forth—all referring to a hermetically sealed subjectivism.

There is no room in mysticism for the sharing of experience, for the shared verification of individual (esoteric) "knowledge." And yet this unmitigated cognitive individualism is presented as an "experience" of direct knowledge (which has no need of the common lucidity of information deriving from the intellect and the senses), on the basis of the "validity" of an "introspection" that is in theory accessible to everybody. Accordingly, it also operates as an alternative source—clearly superior to intellectualism—of metaphysical "certainties" that strengthen the individualistic character of natural religiosity.

Within the context of the convenient popularization of the main lines of mysticism, wc find a number of self-evidently simplistic schematizations. The following is a typical example: "We arrive at scientific knowledge through the use of reason, at religious knowledge through the emotions." It is regarded as entirely consistent that religious culture (its qualitative/axiological gradations) should be judged as a conglomeration of psychological states—that religiosity should be judged by "what the individual feels," "what he sees within himself." There is no concern for what unconscious factors shape the psychological states of religious euphoria or religious unease.

The more imperative the urge for individual security, the more is religiosity dominated by psychological priorities. What is especially valued is an emotional charge, an enthusiastic "reaching up," an exquisite "exaltation." Prayer, participation in worship and the sacraments, and even good works are evaluated in accordance with the "joy" they guarantee, with the fascination of mystical experience, with the intensity of the majesty that is evoked, with the "feeling" of inward catharsis, and with the individual justification that they procure.

Dostoevsky set out three modes (factors or possibilities) by which we human beings voluntarily give up our freedom, selling it off with pleasure and placing ourselves in an incontrovertibly submissive position: *miracle*, *mystery*, and *authority*—three fundamental marks of the identity of natural religion, three established practices of organized institutional religion.[2]

We call *miracle* a supernatural event, that which manifestly goes against the law of nature and obliges us to submit to the power and authority of the miracle-working agent (whether person or institution). A miracle does not leave us any room for freedom. The supernatural character of the event forces our natural reason and will to accept the validity and power of the person or institution

2. "The Grand Inquisitor," in bk. 5, chap. 5 of *The Brothers Karamazov*, trans. David McDuff (London: Penguin Books, 2003), 335.

working the miracle as self-evident—we submit to any opinion, order, declaration, or claim, the believability of which is guaranteed by the miracle. Thus a miracle nullifies faith, if *faith* means the arduous attainment of *trust*. The thaumaturgic power has to be accepted. You do not have the freedom to endanger your *relationship* with its bearer, which requires you to trust it and believe it. A miracle imposes only certainties, precisely those certainties that are demanded by the urge of self-preservation, the urge that makes the natural individual protect itself.

The function of *mystery* is analogous to this. We call *mystery* a ritual, a sacred rite, an act of worship in which the religious mind believes that the transmission of "grace" is effected from the unknown transcendent to the individual human being. That which is transmitted characteristically is not only the illumination of suprarational knowledge but also the strengthening of the ability to be more consistent in one's moral practice, as well as some kind of pledge of eternal salvation. The mode by which grace is transmitted is identified with the ritual, which acquires a veiled or occult character, cloaking that which is enacted in symbolic meanings and forms of worship that are often intensely emotional. The word *mystery* derives from the Greek word *myō*, which means "I close my eyes"—in the case we are considering here in order to "see" something not in sensory terms but by an "interiorized" vision, by an immediacy of cognition. We thus abandon any possibility of shared knowledge gained through the intellect and the senses. We abandon relations of communion, that is, we abandon the presupposition of freedom. The individualistic character of mystical experience serves the instinctive need for indisputable certainties with a beguiling self-sufficiency.

The *authority* of institutions and persons is the third means by which the principles and normative rules of religion are recognized and imposed. This too responds to the need of the natural individual to find security through submission, to receive assurance by voluntarily laying down his freedom. What is wanted is the glory, real or constructed, of high esteem, of consistency, of effectiveness—the fame of the abilities, of the moral and ascetic achievements of a life of virtue. For that is how institutions and persons acquire the validity that makes the submission of the individual self-evident. Of course, this glory, so difficult to attain, can be supplemented by impressive artificial means that induce psychological submissiveness, such as (everywhere and at all times) vestments, a strictly graded hierarchy, and majestic ceremonial. Often the antiquity alone of the institution is sufficient: its historic titles, its cultural pedigree, and the famous figures who have made it illustrious. All these things are elements of indisputable authority, of which the chiefly religious character of the institution or function magnifies the significance, rendering it an act of hubris to disobey or question anything.

1.4. *The Armored Shell of Authority*

Logically contradictory but affirmed in practice, the greater the uncertainty regarding knowledge, or the insecurity about the relativity of "convictions," the more infrangible the armored shell of authority surrounding institutions that guarantee knowledge and "convictions."

It is logically contradictory but psychologically very obvious: such an institution has been constructed precisely in order to make good, as a sovereign authority (by its cohesiveness, structure, and effectiveness), the lack of certainty regarding the knowledge and security of its convictions. In accordance with this, even religious institutions must have their causal principle in their need to satisfy the religious urges of individuals (in the need to overcome the instinctive fear of ignorance and death), and perhaps also in the equally instinctive human demand for authority, dominion, and power—a demand that reflects the implacable law of "natural selection": the survival of the fittest and strongest individuals and species.

Such a theory seems to explain why the origin of socially powerful religious institutions (powerful priesthoods) is lost in the depths of prehistory—institutionalized religion seems to be inherent in human society. Religious teachings are hermeneutic and regulative propositions that are among those most burdened with uncertainty, most obviously subject to the relativity of linguistic usage. That is why the religious institutions that express them and guarantee them need a special authority. The need for authority easily slips into a quest for the power to dominate. Often in the course of history, religious institutions have exercised a power greater than that of the organs of government belonging to society as a whole.

People submit rather easily to all kinds of institutions that have to do with the exercise of power—in many cases one could speak of the pleasure of submission or of fanatical submission. What explanation may be offered for this situation?

One possible interpretation is that submission relieves the individual of responsibility, risk, and freedom—it relieves him from the fear of growing up, the fear of coming of age. Others—not the same individual—decide, choose, and risk error. The individual simply obeys; he follows. The mother's embrace and care, the father's strength and prerogative, the leaving of responsibility for decisions to this protective affection and authority—all find a desirable substitute in authoritative institutions and persons. It is a pleasurable postponement of weaning, a convenient refusal to grow up. The secret of our willingness to submit to and to obey every form of authority lies rather in our need to find a substitute for paternal and maternal protection; it lies in the fear of freedom.

More than any other kind of authority, religious institutions and priesthoods respond to the natural need of human beings for pleasurable submission. The motives are clear: religious institutions and priesthoods offer deliverance from the fear of not knowing. They offer certainties and convictions (with regard to the inaccessible transcendent) clad in the authority of the sacred or of revelation. They offer the individual guarantees of eternal survival and specific practices for the "objective" securing of this "salvation." They have preserved with astonishing skill (diachronically, or through the ages) the human need for *miracle*, *mystery*, and *authority*; they encourage an extended (without risks or insecurities) childish dependence on authority figures.

The authority that religious institutions acquire (and manifestly exercise) in societies of every age is a consequence of the investing of religiosity with the individual's resolute need for self-protection. That is why any doubting of this authority (of the institutions and the persons that embody it) is experienced as a threat to the individual, a threat to this existential security—those who are opposed to, or reject, the institutions are regarded as enemies, often as mortal foes.

This appears to be the explanation for the fanaticism, sometimes the blind and unhesitating fanaticism, that flourishes in religious environments, or for the fact that religious wars are among the most horrific in history. The same explanation must also hold for the phenomenon of *totalitarianism*, which as a mode of exercising power was born historically from religious institutions and continues as a typical syndrome in almost every form of organized (with effective executive structures) religious life.

By the word *totalitarianism* I mean the claim and (systematically organized) attempt of a governing authority to control the whole of life, both public and private, of those under its authority, with the aim of subordinating every aspect of life (even the convictions, intentions, and judgments of individuals) to the rules that the authority lays down. The fact that such a claim is able to be made, to be put in place as a regime for organizing society as a whole, cannot simply be a result of imposition from above. The compliance of individuals' thinking, judgment, and intentions with the lines laid down by the authority presupposes in the first place a social group that willingly (and perhaps with pleasure) is inclined to make such a submission—it is on this that the general imposition of the claim is based. Without this given critical mass, or the latent (and perhaps unconscious) inclination to submission, no force could impose and maintain a totalitarian regime.

Submission and obedience to orders from above is, in most instances, a result of the fear of coming of age, the fear of freedom—a product of the instinct of self-preservation and self-protection. The exercise of power, however, the ability to make others subordinate to you and lead them, constitutes another kind of pleasure, perhaps superior to any other—a product of the satisfaction of the (similarly blind) instinct to dominate. For someone to have authority over the thinking, the judgment, and the will of his fellow human beings, to exercise a "spiritual" authority over them, to dictate the behavior and practices of their daily life, to dominate their psychological attitudes, and to control their relationship with the transcendent must be tantamount to an intoxicating sense of power and self-assertion.

At the same time, the person who exercises such power is worshiped by those who have taken pleasure in submitting to him. He elicits their respect. They honor him; they admire him. His presence evokes awe, even ecstasy, chiefly when the authority he wields is manifested as the exercise not of secular but of supramundane power, reflecting a metaphysical authority and judging the eternal future of human beings, whether they "perish" or are "saved." The person who exercises such power is regarded thereafter as a being almost beyond the bounds of the natural. He is wrapped in the splendor of the sacred. The imposition of his authority is irresistible.

The irresistible power of religious authority is also inevitably sought by individuals who have little or no chance of winning the respect of their fellow human beings by their own merits and their own efforts. It is difficult for anyone to ascertain when, unfittingly or unworthily for the sake of office, individuals of this kind (in almost all the religious traditions) have assumed the external appearances or objective marks that immediately make the "form" of the functionary stand out and that render respect for him a requirement. *Clerical robes* as everyday dress are one such indication, as is also long hair and a beard—or, alternatively, a tonsured crown and a clean-shaven face. Bows, hand-kissing, and prostrations have also been adopted to show respect for those who exercise sacral power, while (no doubt unconsciously) what is also satisfied in this manner is the need of the many to be confirmed in their submission and the pleasure of the few in being recipients of it.

That which is inexpressible, inconceivable, invisible, and incomprehensible, which is the field in which humanity conducts its metaphysical quest, is very easily substituted by infrangible convictions, sacred dogmas, and holy canons, the management of which demands an authority reinforced by prerogatives, rights, and the undisputed power of imposing them. Nature—the urge for self-preservation, for dominion, for the enjoyment by the individual of security and pleasure—is all-powerful. It triumphs over our human attempts to break out from the asphyxiating bounds of mortality and ignorance.

Chapter 2

The Ecclesial Event

2.1. *The Reversal of Religious Terms*

On its first historical appearance, the ecclesial event possessed distinctive features indicating the reversal of the terms of natural, instinctive religiosity.

I would locate these distinctive features in the texts that record the experience and witness of the first ecclesial communities. I would locate them in the organic structure and functioning of these communities, in the language by which they expressed themselves and in the manner in which those with experience of the ecclesial event understood, interpreted, and ordered its original manifestation.

The Greek word *ekklēsia* (*ecclesia* in its Latinized form) was chosen to express not a new religion but a social event—a *mode* of relations of communion. There had existed earlier the *ekklēsia tou dēmou*, the popular assembly. The citizens of Greek cities used to come together in popular assemblies not only to deliberate, to judge, to make decisions on matters of public concern, but also above all to constitute and manifest the *polis*, the city: a specific *mode* of relations of communion, a mode of human existence and coexistence.

Let us pause to consider the meaning conveyed by these words. *Polis* for the ancient Greeks was not a settlement that had grown to a quantifiable size. It was a *common struggle*, the struggle aimed at attaining life *according to truth*. What it wanted was that social coexistence should have truth as its goal, that it should not simply have a utilitarian purpose. The Greeks regarded as truth that mode of existence and coexistence that knew nothing of alteration, change, decay, or death. Moreover, they located truth in the common *logos*/mode (the given rationality) that always determines the form (*eidos*) or shape (*morphē*) of every existent thing, as it does also the *configuration* (the *dia-morphōsis*) of their coexistence. This is the *logos*/mode of the relations that make the universe a *cosmos*, an ornament of harmony, order, and beauty. Such a mode of existence *according to truth* was what the city, or *polis*, sought to imitate and realize.

With the same semantic content (the same semantic charge of historical experience), the word *ekklēsia* was chosen so as to manifest the identity of the first Christian communities. *Ecclesia* continued to signify a collectivity of people who want to live together within the struggle to attain true existence, to make existence *become true*, as their common goal. By their living together they want to realize that *mode* that knows no limitations of decay and death.

If truth for the Greeks was the (given and uninterpreted) rationality of the relations that constitute the ordered beauty of the universe, for the Christians it was the mode of those relations that liberate existence from the necessities, limitations, and predeterminations of *nature* or *essence*. In both these versions of the fact, or event, of *ecclesia* (the Greek and the Christian), there was a very clear metaphysical axis: the reference to and orientation toward the mode of existence *according to truth*. What was absent was a religious character. The ecclesia of the Greeks assembled in the agora, the ecclesia of the Christians in private homes for meals.

The Christians of the first ecclesial community in Jerusalem fulfilled the religious obligations imposed on them by their Jewish tradition at the Temple of Solomon—"day by day attending the temple together" (Acts 2:46). But they also broke bread in their homes, devoting themselves to the apostles' teaching and fellowship and the prayers (cf. Acts 2:42, 46).

The first Christians (drawn from the Jewish people) constituted the ecclesia, or Church, apart from any religious rituals—outside of any sacred place (or temple). They constituted the ecclesia "in their homes" as a *supper*, a supper of *thanksgiving*. From the first moment of its existence, the Christian ecclesia was precisely that: a gathering for a thanksgiving supper.

For the Christians the historical model for a thanksgiving supper was the *paschal* supper of the Jews. Once a year, at a supper of thanksgiving to God, every Jewish family celebrated the *Pascha*, or Passover, of the people of Israel from Egypt and slavery toward the "promised land" and freedom. In the same way, by the supper of thanksgiving, the Christians too celebrated (every week, but also more frequently when they could) their own paschal passing over to freedom from the limitations of our created human nature (from bondage to place, time, decay, and death).

There was an obvious difference from the model provided by Jewish tradition; the Church's supper referred not to the *anamnēsis*, or "commemoration," of a historical past but to the expectation and imaging (in its potential realization here and now) of an eschatological future: of a *mode* by which human beings could exist in a state of freedom from their nature, from the predeterminations and necessities that this nature imposes.

The difference from any other kind of banquet is also clear. The supper that constituted the Church was the realization of a different *mode* of receiving food. The Christians took bread and wine (the basic forms of food) not simply in obedience to the natural need for individual self-preservation but in order to commune in a real way with life, with existence. They did so in order to commune not on the level of an emotional or psychological sense of exaltation but on the level of the vital function that eating and drinking represent. They wanted to transform the necessity of *nature* into the freedom of *relation*, into love.

The "peaceful and loving" sharing of bread and the drinking of wine in common are a symbol, a symbol that refers to a homogeneous communion of life, that constitutes a participation in the struggle of a common *mode of existence*. And this *mode* is the taking of food/life as a gift of manic love for every human being—the same taking of food/life constitutes *thanksgiving* (*eucharistia*) to the provider of food and existence, the author of the potentiality that life should be shared in as love. Thanksgiving is also a living communion with the Causal Principle of life.

"Christians" was the name given to the disciples of *Christ* (Acts 11:26). Christ (the *kechrismenos*, the "anointed one") was the sobriquet of a historical person, Jesus of Nazareth. The disciples of Jesus Christ were those who *believed* (placed their trust in) his witness, teaching, and life.

Christ did not bear witness to himself. He used to say that it was his works that bore witness to him.[3] He called the works that bore witness to him *signs*, his works indicating who he was, the identity and truth of his existence. He never declared or even hinted that he was the founder of a new religion. In his own person he embodied and outlined for humanity a new *mode of existence*.

The *mode of existence* that Christ embodied and to which he called humanity had no elements or marks that were characteristic of religious demands. It did not lead to atomic convictions; it did not presuppose meritorious atomic virtues; it did not lay down prescriptions about observing the law, about conforming to types of worship. In all these fields Christ's teaching overturned and reversed the rules and presuppositions of religion.

In the language of his place and time, Christ spoke of the *mode* of existence and life "according to truth" as the *kingdom of heaven*. And he preached that those who guide us toward this *mode* are not pious religious people, those who find satisfaction in being virtuous, those who shore up their ego by keeping some kind of law. Those who guide us are people who have lost all confidence in their own selves, people who expect no personal reward whatsoever, and only thirst to be loved even if they do not deserve it—despised sinners: tax collectors, robbers, prostitutes, and prodigals.

Christ declared (and his works testified) that the mode of true existence and life is *love*—love not simply as a quality of behavior but as freedom from the ego, freedom from an individualistic ex-

3. "If I testify about myself, my testimony is not true . . . The very works that I am doing, testify on my behalf" (John 5:31, 36).

istence, freedom from the necessities imposed by nature. Love, in the teaching of Christ and the testimony of his disciples, does not mean doing good, being affectionate toward each other, or showing altruism. It means existential freedom: the active refusal to identify existence with natural atomic onticity and with the predeterminations, limitations, and necessities that govern it. And this active refusal is possible when existence is realized as a *relation* free from the demands of nature, that is, as self-transcendence, self-offering, and love.

From the first moments of its historical existence, the Christian Church has proposed a single and unique definition of true existence and life, which is also the definition of the Causal Principle of all that exists. Within the framework of the semantic possibilities of human language, possibilities that are always relative, it has defined God in terms of love: "God *is* love" (1 John 4:8). It is not that God *has* love, that love is a moral or qualitative attribute of God; not that God first exists, and because he exists he moreover loves. The phrase "God *is* love" reveals the *mode* that makes God what he *is* (that makes him God).

The *mode*, the signifier of Godhead, is not located by Christians (as it is by the religions and philosophies) in the attributes of omnipotence, omniscience, unbegottenness, or immortality. From the first records of the Church's witness, the mode of existence that differentiates God from every existent thing is *freedom*, his absolute existential freedom—not freedom as an unlimited power of choice but primarily freedom from any existential predetermination, limitation, or necessity.

It is to this freedom that the word *love* refers—we always understand love only as deliberate choice, not as necessity. And it is to the same absolute existential freedom that the linguistic signifiers of the Church's witness refer, the signifiers that concern the *triad of hypostases* of the Causeless Cause of existent things.

If there is an element of "revelation" in the testimony of Christ's disciples, it lies in three words: the linguistic signifiers *Father*, *Son*, and *Spirit*. These reveal "another" version of the existential event, "another" mode of existence and life from the given mode of sensible reality. In radical contrast to the religious version of God as "supreme being" or as a totality of "supernatural" (divine) beings, the Church's experience witnesses to three self-conscious and rational (*personal*) hypostases of the Causal Principle of that which exists, hypostases that confirm existence as a freedom of communion of existence, that is, as love.

The signifiers *Father*, *Son*, and *Spirit* do not reveal three individual beings (specific self-complete realizations) of a given common *nature* or *essence* (analogous to the *natures* that we infer as the common *logos*/mode of every uniform class of existent things). These names reveal that the existence (or more correctly, the reality beyond existence) of each hypostasis of the Causeless Cause of all things "is realized" as freedom of loving relation. Each hypostasis exists as self-conscious freedom of love. Each hypostasis *is* love.

Thanks to the name *Father*, we have a linguistic indication of the subjective identity of the causal hypostasis of *being*. What is indicated is that the causal hypostasis of being "exists" in a manner that does not bind the hypostasis to the atomic sense of existence (the sense of onticity, of ontic self-completeness). The name *Father* reveals that the specific hypostasis that is causal of *being* is neither known nor exists by itself and for itself. It exists as the hypostasis that "generates" the Son and causes the "procession" of the Spirit. The "generation" of the Son and the "procession" of the Spirit (nontemporally and lovingly—out of love alone, and only as a result of freedom) is the mode by which the *being* of the Father is hypostasized. He is a hypostasis (a real existence) *because* he rejects atomic, ontic self-completeness and freely realizes *being* as relation, as love.

What the Father *is* is not revealed as *Godhead* (which would have implied being bound to the existential predetermination of a given "divine" nature). It is revealed by his *fatherhood*: his nonpredetermined and uncircumscribed freedom to exist—a freedom that is confirmed (that becomes an existential fact) with the "generation" of the Son and the "procession" of the Spirit.

Thanks to the name *Father*, freedom is signified not as something simply to do with the will (the power of making unrestricted choices) but as the cause of being, of the *hypostasization* of *being*, of *being* being constituted as hypostatic reality. With regard to its causal principle, existence is neither obligatory nor an automatic given but is identified with the hypostatic self-determination of the Cause of all things as Father, that is, as love. He who constitutes the cause of existence exists not because he is God but because he *wills* to be the *Father*, the hypostatic freedom of loving self-transcendence and self-offering.

The same absolute existential freedom is also revealed linguistically by the name *Son*. By *sonship* is signified a hypostasis of *being* that is not predetermined existentially by its "nature" or "essence" but is self-determined as freedom of relation with the Father. The relation is loving: a free response to the love of the Father, a love that is constitutive of the existential event, and it is this that "generates" a hypostasis of personal self-consciousness, of rational otherness. The hypostasis is signified by the name *Son* precisely in order that *relation* should be manifested rather than *nature*, a free will for existence, not a predetermination or necessity.

The name *Son* reveals that the specific hypostasis of the Son is neither known nor exists by itself or for itself. He wills to exist because he loves the Father. His existence is a hypostatic response to the Father's loving will. As an existential event he refers to the Father; he "witnesses to the Father," not to himself.

What the Son *is* is signified by the voluntary *sonship*, not by the essential (belonging to the essence and thus necessary) *Godhead*. He is God because he exists as *Son of the Father*. His existence is not prior to his sonship; it is not bound existentially to predeterminations of atomic (ontic) self-completion. He hypostasizes the freedom of loving self-transcendence and self-offering.

The same is true for the word *Spirit*. It reveals the hypostatic otherness of personal self-consciousness, which is neither known nor exists as ontic atomicity but refers as existence to the *love* of the Father, to the ontopoeic and life-giving truth. He is signified as the *Spirit of the Father* as the counterpart by linguistic logic of the *Son/Logos of the Father:* the Son is "generated" (or "begotten") by the

Father and through his existence manifests the Father, witnesses to him, as the love that is foundational of *being*. The Spirit "proceeds" from the Father and manifests through his existence the "property" (the *idion*, the existential identity) of the Causeless Cause of *being*: the *ek-static* character (the creative, life-bearing, and wisdom-bestowing character) of the Father's love.

The absolute accuracy of the signifiers that the Church's metaphysical testimony employed before the advent of any demands for philosophical analysis or the development of any systematic ontological framework is truly astonishing. I am referring to the descriptive accuracy of *freedom* as the causal principle of the existential event—a *personal* freedom that is not subordinate to the necessities imposed (predetermined) by essence or nature. I mean also the use of signifiers referring to a Triad that is causative of *being*, a Triad of hypostatic differentiation with a single existential identity (with a common mode of existence): *love*.

From the Church's first appearance (at a time when philosophical influences and the demands of systematic thought had not yet emerged), the words *Father*, *Son*, and *Spirit* mark a radical boundary dividing Christian metaphysics from Greek ontology (which then predominated in the cultural paradigm)—and not only from Greek ontology but also from all later philosophical metaphysics up to the present day. This is truly astonishing because the environment (both historical and geographical) was manifestly trapped in the logic and language of the theology of atomic onticities, of essentialist metaphysics, of a religiosity based on naturalism.

The astonishment that the Causeless Cause of *being* should be a *personal* hypostasis (a hypostasis that is self-conscious, self-willing, and self-activating)—a freedom that transcends any delimiting autonomy—has lasted for twenty centuries. So too has the astonishment that this transcendence should be signified as "the reality of love" (as *ontōs erōs*), a Triadic realization of *being* in loving communion and an existential mutual indwelling of personal hypostases.

2.2. *Historical Realism*

The hermeneutic proposal for interpreting the *really existent* that was conveyed by the Church's witness did not have the character of a philosophical innovation, of a theoretical discovery. It was a testimony, or record, of a specific historical experience (and one that was shared): the historical appearance of Jesus of Nazareth. This allowed the first Christians to assert that they did not preach "cleverly devised myths" (2 Pet 1:16) but facts supported by evidence—that "which we have heard, which we have seen with our eyes, which we have looked upon and touched with our hands . . . we testify to it and proclaim to you" (1 John 1:1–2).

The bearers of this testimony had seen and touched a human existence the same as all the others—a natural individual in a specific historical time and social space—some of whose works, however, had the character of particular *signs*: they *signified* the power to transcend the existential boundaries of human nature, to overcome the predeterminations, limitations, necessities, and bonds that govern every human existence. Without any display or deliberate dissemination (on the contrary, often with insistent appeals not to publicize the *signs*), it became evident that this person, Jesus the Christ, although in every respect like all the others, was himself able to be free (and could make some of his fellow humans free) from subjection to natural necessities, to natural laws.

Stories of "wonder-working" men or "gods" who appear in human form and intervene in human affairs are very frequent in many religious traditions. What is different in the Church's witness is the refusal to take Christ's *signs* as "wonders," or to use them as such. That is, the option that the *signs* should be taken as proofs, or should function as such, so as to render submission to the "authority" of Christ, his disciples, or his teaching free from any grounds for refusal (i.e., obligatorily, unfreely) is firmly rejected.[4]

In the Church's experience the *signs* performed by Christ (indications of the abrogation of the limitations and necessities of

4. See the temptation of Christ, Matt 4:1–11.

human nature) do not point to an unexplainable ("supernatural") existential possibility belonging to a specific individual. They reveal a *mode of existence* that is realized by a natural human individual (human in every respect) and that therefore is conceivably attainable (potentially—not without presuppositions) by every human being.

The transfer of what is signified from the exclusivity of the individual to a potentiality for all is not arbitrary, nor does it constitute an interpretation based on ideology. Historical realism is claimed not only by the testimony to the *signs* (which was not disputed by contemporaries) but also by the affirmation of eyewitnesses that Christ deliberately refused to make his *signs* or works depend on his individual capacity or his existential identity.[5] This deliberate detachment of the miraculous works from the one who performed them—for which the testimony is emphatic—this voluntary relinquishment of any individual *personal goal*, even of any claim to existential autonomy, reveals nothing less than a new (revelatory for the facts of human existence), universally proposed *mode of existence*, whose results are the *signs*.

What is this *mode of existence* that Christ teaches through his actions and that frees humanity from the existential predeterminations, limitations, and necessities of its nature?

It is that which we have already analyzed in our study of the linguistic signifier *Son* in the written testimony of the first ecclesial community. Indeed, if the words *Father*, *Son*, and *Spirit* indicate the *mode* of that which truly exists, the freedom of love as the enhypostasized Triadic Causal Principle of *being*, this semantic system simply remains a philosophical notion (a striking one, perhaps, but unrelated to humanity) if the testimony of the eyewitness to Christ's presence among them is ignored.

The written testimony of the disciples asserts that with regard to himself, as a declaration of his identity, Christ used the designation *Son of the Father*. He does not refer his works, which functioned as *signs*, to himself; he does not regard them as his own.

5. Cf. John 14:12: "The one who believes in me will also do the works that I do and, in fact, will do greater works than these."

They are "works of my Father," which he has undertaken simply in order to "accomplish" them, "works of him who sent me."[6] Every action of Christ, everything he carried out, manifests a drawing back from atomic existential self-completeness; every action refers to the will of the Father's love.[7] And in one of the texts of the written testimony of the disciples (in John's Gospel), the expressions used for the existential relationship between Jesus Christ and his Father have an undisguised ontological content; they reveal a mode of existence.[8]

The proclamation of this mode of existence that Christ embodied and to which every human being is called is the Church's *gospel*, or good news: the message of the existential freedom that the ecclesial event sets as its goal. The Church's gospel is summarized in the preaching of *love*. But for the Church love is not an atomic virtue, a quality of the behavior of the individual—it is not simply mutual friendship, compassion, altruism, affection. Before anything else it is a denial of egotistic priorities, a renunciation of self-interest. It is the struggle of human beings to free themselves from subjection to the demands of their atomic nature, to draw existence from the freedom of *relation* and not from the necessities of *nature*, to exist by loving and because they love. Love is the realization of the mode of existence that is "according to truth," the imaging of the Triadic model of real existence and life.

In the historical person of Christ, the Church touches the *mode* of the freedom of existence from the predeterminations and necessities of nature or essence. If the *Son of the Father* is a hypostasis of freedom from any predetermination and necessity of "Godhead" (divine nature or essence), this either remains an abstract philo-

6. John 10:37; 14:10; 9:4.

7. Cf. John 5:30: "I seek to do not my own will but the will of him who sent me"; John 4:34: "My food is to do the will of him who sent me and to complete his work."

8. John 14:10: "I am in the Father and the Father is in me"; 14:7: "If you know me, you will know my Father also. From now on you do know him and have seen him"; 17:21–22: "That they may all [all those who have believed in me through the word] be one. As you, Father, are in me and I am in you . . . so that they may be one as we are one."

sophical notion or is encountered historically in his *incarnation*. Only the incarnation, in a specific historical time and social space, affirms the freedom of the *Son of the Father* to realize existence both in accordance with the terms of divine existence and in accordance with the terms of human existence, without being subject at any time to any natural necessity whatsoever. For that reason, without the encounter with the historical person of Jesus Christ there is no gospel of existential freedom either.

But the incarnation too would have also remained a bare philosophical notion if the historical person of Jesus Christ had submitted in a final and definitive way to the implacable necessity of the death that holds sway over human nature. The gospel of existential freedom and the foundation of the ecclesial event is Christ's *resurrection* from the dead, the historical encounter with the *risen* Christ, the victor over death. If Christ's resurrection was not a historical event, then Christianism (the Christian faith) remains yet another imaginary "-ism," a manifestation (perhaps the most fully developed one) of humanity's natural need for religion.

Nor is Christ's resurrection from the dead put forward by the Church as a "wonder" (the highest or supreme wonder)—the inexplicable "supernatural" fact of the revival of a corpse. The testimonies of Christ's disciples affirm the resurrection too as a *sign*, a sign of *sonship*: the manifestation of the hypostatic identity of the Son/Logos of the Father.

The resurrection *signifies* the Son's freedom to exist both in accordance with the terms (in our relative human language) of "divine" nature and in accordance with the terms of human nature. He is free from the existential prescriptions (limitations and necessities) of any nature whatsoever: he is subject neither to the obligatory eternity of God nor to the inescapable death of Man. He draws his existence and hypostasis only from the freedom of his *relation* with the Father, not from any given nature.

Christ's resurrection as a "wonder" would have pointed to a new religion; resurrection as a *sign* points to a new *mode of existence*. It is this *mode* that the ecclesial social event wishes to realize. Death is the most burdensome and unbearably irrational existential limitation of human nature. And in his historical existence Christ assumes this irrationality, he dies, in order to *signify* that even death may be experienced as freedom of *relationship* with the Father, that is, as life without limitation. He assumes human nature "unto death, even death on a cross" (Phil 2:8), one of the most horrific forms of execution. And he does it so that this most horrific death should become a salvific *sign*.

An individual human being is able to exist without the existential limitations of human nature: this is what is signified by the signs of the resurrection in the person of Christ. Thanks to the leap of *relation* (which is realized through nature's energies/capacities beyond the necessities of nature), nature's hypostasis "draws existence" not from nature but from the *relation*. It is then that the natural necessity of death is also abrogated—the linguistic signifiers of the *stasis*[9] or readiness that abolishes this necessity are preserved in the phrase used by Christ with regard to the Father, as witnessed by his disciples: "Not what I want but what you want" (Matt 26:39).

The will of the Father's love is that Man should be saved: that he should become "whole"[10] (integral), that he should be restored to the fullness of his existential possibilities. And if the fullness of existential possibilities is love as a triumph of freedom, then Man's "salvation" can only be a free choice. Even dissemination of the knowledge of the possibilities of salvation can only be made through *signs* that hint at it—not through any kind of persuasion that would violate freedom of choice. In the incarnation of the Son, in the death and resurrection of Christ, the will of the Father's love is hinted at by the *signs* (the words and deeds) of his incarnate Word.

In these *signs* (which are supported and certified by a coherent historical realism), the Church detects the possibility that death should be conquered. And it communicates this possibility, again with the experiential signifiers that point to what it has

9. [In Greek *stasis* ("standing") is the root of the word for "resurrection," *anastasis*, literally a "standing again." – trans.]

10. [The word *whole* (sōos) is closely related etymologically to the verb *to save* (sōzō). – trans.]

detected. It proclaims that the natural necessity of death is abrogated when Man freely, not simply by making choices but by practical self-denying *asceticism*, liberates his "gnomic" will, that is, when he makes it independent of the ego's imperatives, the individualistic demands and necessities of self-preservation, sovereignty, and pleasure, which make up the urge for existential self-containedness that is a natural given.

The Church proclaims that such a detachment from the ego cannot be an achievement of the ego itself. It is only won through the struggle of a shared self-denial, the struggle of entering into relations of communion in life: it is an attainment of love. The love that frees us from death is signified as an existential reflection of Christ's obedience to the will of the Father: an obedience that is conceived as the exact opposite to a disciplined conformity to legal requirements, as a manifestation of "erotic passion," a mode of existence that generates love.

The Church's reference to a Triadic Causal Principle of that which exists (*Father, Son, Spirit*) has the experience and testimony of the advent of Christ as a starting point, rooted in historical realism. And the end or goal of this etiological reference, rooted in an equally coherent realism, is freedom from the contingencies and necessities of an individualistic self-containedness.

That which is individualistic, egocentric, and self-contained is for the Church a mode of survival for natural mortal onticity—it is *sin* (*hamartia*, an existential failure to hit the mark) and death. That which is self-transcendence, self-denial, a voluntary letting go of the ego, love, and eros is life, a triumph of life over death. "As for knowledge, it will pass away; as for tongues, they will cease; as for prophecies, they will pass away; love never ends" (cf. 1 Cor 13:8).

2.3. *Relativity of Language and Priority of Experience*

The ecclesial event is founded on a coherent historical realism, on the experience of encountering the historical person of Christ and his works or *signs*. The gospel that he conveys is knowledge, and knowledge derives from the experience of relations of personal immediacy.

The transmission of this knowledge to succeeding generations also presupposes an experience of *relation*—the Church's gospel does not function as the communication of information. The relation that conveys knowledge as experience is no longer that of personal historical testimony, of actually having met the historical person of Christ. It is a relation of trust (*faith*) in those who once were eyewitnesses to his presence, in the persons who from generation to generation, in an unbroken chain of the same experiential participation, transmit the testimony of their encounter with the gospel's *signs*.

Nothing in the ecclesial event functions as an "objective" fact of knowledge, as a parcel of information that is passed from one individual to another. There is no "revelation" that adds knowledge about the transcendent, no information that reinforces the epistemic self-sufficiency of the individual, the instinctive quest for metaphysical certainties. The Church's gospel communicates a *mode* of relation and is shared in only as an experience of relation. It is like the relation between two people, one who loves, pouring out his joy at his discovery of faith/trust, and another who responds by similarly loving in order to share in this experiential discovery.

Faith/trust is a constant struggle to maintain a relation, and the knowledge that faith conveys is the coherent articulation of that struggle. The struggle signifies an attempt to attain something without the certainty that one has attained it—however long the struggle lasts, nothing is sure or safe, nothing may be taken as given. The relation of love is gained or lost from moment to moment. At any given moment self-completeness threatens to nullify the relation—the natural urge of self-preservation and of the exercise of dominion lies in wait for us. This urge seeks to make the knowledge conveyed by the relation subject to the armoring of the individual with certainties.

That is why the ecclesial event does not convey objective "truths" capable of constituting the "convictions" of individuals. It does not presuppose "dogmas," axiomatic statements, obligatory "principles," as the religions do. The only "objective" information compatible with the ecclesial event is the invitation "Come and see" (John 1:46), that is, a call for human beings to participate in specific *relations*, relations of communion with life, in a common struggle for each person's individual self-transcendence and self-offering. And the goal is the knowledge that comes about when a person loves.

"This is the ignorance that transcends knowledge."[11] Is the phrase merely wordplay? Clearly not. It refers to the form and mode of knowledge that is acquired by those who have experience of the ecclesial event. "Ignorance" here (often translated as "unknowing") signifies an attainment, the voluntary renunciation of the constructed "knowledge" of psychological certainties. It signifies a stripping away of the instinctual (biological) need for metaphysical certainty, for the armoring of the ego with "infallible" convictions.

This ignorance is an epistemic realism. It is a cleansing from illusions, an attitude incompatible with the inferences of hypothetical syllogisms, with mental idols, with wishful thinking. It is a realistic awareness of our difficulty in acquiring knowledge of what is meta-physical, what lies beyond nature, by the means (the cognitive capacities) that nature provides. Intellection, judgment, imagination, intuition, mystical "insight"—none of these suffices.

Such a renunciation of any atomic (natural) epistemic possibility is experienced as a mind-reeling void, as total despair. It nevertheless proves to be a presupposition if we are to free ourselves from our ego, our nature, and give ourselves up without any reservation to the relation of love, to faith/trust. And it is this self-surrender that renders the fruit of a knowledge transcending any "objective" localized information.

Within the ecclesial event knowledge is a fruit of relation, a consequence of faith/trust. It has the realism of experiential immediacy, as does every attainment of relation. In a religion "faith" may mean the blind acceptance of principles, doctrines, axiomatic statements, the castration of thought and judgment. But in the

11. Isaac the Syrian, *Discourse 32*, in *The Ascetic Writings of Our Holy Father Isaac the Syrian*, ed. Nikephoros Theotokis (Leipzig, 1770), re-edited by Joachim Spetieris (Athens, 1895), 140.

Church *faith* (*pistis*) recovers its original meaning: it is the attainment of trust (in Greek, literally "enfaithment," *empistosynē*), the freedom of self-transcendence—a dynamic realization of relation, with knowledge as its experiential product.

[Individual self-transcendence, or freedom from the ego, does not abolish the *hypostatic* reality and active otherness of the rational subject, which is always one of the terms or factors of a relation. An event of relation is not constituted without real actors, self-conscious terms/factors of the event. Only irrational existences or objects are simply correlated, linked, or associated, losing their individual identity in the resultant mass.

Freedom from individualism (which is the foundation of the ecclesial event: faith as a product of knowledge) is freedom from subjection to the impersonal necessities of nature, not a denial or blunting of subjective identity and self-consciousness. Consequently, it is from within atomic self-transcendence, self-offering, freedom from the ego, that the existential otherness of the subject—his unique, dissimilar, and unrepeatable identity—is most of all realized and manifested.

Subjection to the necessities that govern the natural individual, the psychological ego, signifies conforming to the undifferentiating law of nature (the law that makes all the individuals of a species identical with each other). By contrast, the more steadfast a person is in the struggle for individual self-transcendence and self-offering, in the struggle to attain a relationship of love, the more evident is the existential realization and manifestation of his subjective identity as active otherness, as unrepeatable uniqueness.

In the Greek language we distinguish the concept of the individual (*atomon*) from that of the person (*prosōpon*). By the word *atomon* we mean the undifferentiated unit of a uniform whole that can only be distinguished numerically. By the word *prosōpon* we mean the self-conscious active (creative) otherness that can only be realized and known in the immediacy of relation.]

Even if the knowledge that is gained through relations of experiential immediacy is ultimately never subject to the objectivity of language, it is nevertheless not incommunicable. It is signified by linguistic signifiers, as is any empirical knowledge (as poetry, for example, also expresses realistic experience through words or beyond words). Like every *sign-system*, or *semantics*, of empirical knowledge, the language of ecclesial communion merely *signifies* empirical knowledge. It refers to it; it does not replace it. The understanding of the signifiers does not also entail knowledge of what is signified.

Before it became subject to the corruptions of religionization, the ecclesial event was expressed historically in a language that was absolutely consistent with the epistemological principle of *apophaticism* (a vital element of the identity of the Greek philosophical tradition, of what was once the totality of the Greek paradigm). We call *apophaticism* the denial that we can exhaust knowledge in its formulation. The formulation of a truth (of an empirical attestation) and the understanding of the formulation do not replace the knowledge of the truth/attestation. I may understand a formulation (linguistic, visual, or any other) but be ignorant of the truth (reality) to which the formulation refers. Knowledge of any truth is not the understanding of the signifiers that specify it. What constitutes such knowledge is the immediacy of the relation (or experience of the relation) with the signified reality or with the testimony of the experience that confirms it.

For someone who participates in the ecclesial event, there are no *a priori* truths or intellectually obligatory beliefs. There are no presuppositional principles (likewise imposed intellectually), no codified methods of interpretation, no legally prescribed stipulations of behavior. Every liturgical and declarative (kerygmatic) manifestation of the ecclesial event refers to the experiential immediacy of relations of communion. It testifies to the experience of relations of communion and confirms them. It summons to the experience of participation in the relations of ecclesial communion.

A characteristic indication of the realism of the above statements may be seen in the following historical datum.

The symptoms of the corruption of the truth/reality of the Church (symptoms of the religionization of the ecclesial event) are countered, at least in the first eight centuries, by institutions that ensured (as a primary criterion for distinguishing authenticity from alienation) the witness of the experience of the ecclesial body. These institutions were the office of the *bishop* and the *conciliar* system.

The incidence of any corruption of the ecclesial event was expressed by a council of bishops. Each bishop brought to the council not his personal opinion and viewpoint but the experience of the local church at whose eucharistic assembly he presided and for each of whose members who shared in the life of the body he was the father and generator.

Thus a council of bishops summarized the ecclesial experience of the *whole* (*katholou*) body (the catholic, total, and unified body) of the local eucharistic communities whose presiding bishops constituted the council. This summary of the common experience of all was something radically different both from the *homognōmia*, or being of one mind, of the ancient Greeks and from the much later (indeed formulated only in the modern period) *principle of the majority vote*. A council of bishops did not function by the expressions of opinions, so that those which were approved by the majority would be regarded (by convention) as more correct, whereas the minority (by the same convention) had to conform to the opinion of the majority.

There could be disagreements and differences in the formulation of the common experience. But if the different formulation also pointed to a different experience, an experience that did not coincide with or was incompatible with that which was shared *universally*, then the possibility that the difference could be regarded as compatible was *ipso facto* excluded. It was not excluded because of a clash of fanatical "convictions" but because experiences that were different also constituted relations of sharing in the experience that were different.

It is often said, as an abstract historical inference, that in the early centuries of the Church's life the judge of whether the decisions of a council could operate or not was the ecclesial body as a whole. Yes, but again not as an arithmetical whole or as a voting majority. The wholeness of the body, the manifestation of the *catholic* Church, was (and always is) an event of the preservation of the *whole* (*katholou*) truth/reality of the ecclesial gospel as a visible and living eucharistic community, without any kind of stable and permanent local center.

It sometimes occurred that a bishop offered a testimony at a council that was incompatible with the experience of his local church. As a result, when the bishop returned to his see, the populace demonstrated against him and had him deposed. Sometimes, however, the opposite happened. A bishop might express something new at the council and the populace subsequently might discover in the bishop's innovation a fuller insight into their experiential goals.

In the life of the Church, no representative figure or institution was ever the bearer of "infallibility": neither the bishop, nor the populace as an arithmetical/quantitative factor, nor an ecumenical council—nor, of course, any particular local church. Nowhere could the urge for the natural individual to find security for himself latch on to an objective "authority"; from nowhere could the individual draw "objective" certainties for the defensive armoring of his psychological self.

The truth and authenticity of the ecclesial event was and always is a common quest, never a fixed possession—it is a dynamic, active "Come and see" that cannot be pinned down to specific institutions, a "perfection beyond perfection," a "completion beyond completion."[12] Even the decisions of the ecumenical councils do not transcribe ecclesial truth as codified (ideological) coordinates. They simply *define* (in the etymological sense of setting protective semantic boundaries to) the empirical quest (in the *common struggle*) of the eucharistic community. They are indicative presuppositions for participation in the ecclesial event, a participation that is visibly crowned in the common cup of the Eucharist.

A member of the body of the Church for the most part believes/trusts and to a lesser extent, if at all, finds assurance through pinpointing the truth of the Church. This *relation* of trust is pursued

12. Luke 17:20: "The kingdom of God is not coming with things that can be observed."

with all the natural capacities for relation that we have at our disposal (thought, judgment, rational control, critical testing)—capacities for transcending the temptations of convenience, of blind submission to an individualistic assurance, in order to avoid the risks of responsibility.

The faithful Christian places trust in the knowledge conveyed by relationship with and participation in the eucharistic community, but this relationship is a struggle for self-transcendence, and the struggle will be accomplished through the deliberate activation of the capacities of nature—not through the mechanistic intervention of "supernatural" (magical) *grace*, as is demanded by the objective logic of religion. The faithful Christian realizes the relationship by activating the capacities of nature in order to transcend the necessities of nature—in order that his existential *hypostasis* should draw its existence not from a nature that is subject to necessities but from the freedom of relation according to the model of Christ.

Thus the "common struggle" that constitutes the ecclesial event, the authenticity (not the alienation) of the struggle, is *defined* (*orizetai*) without being *determined definitively* (*kathorizetai*). It is defined by the decisions of the councils, by the writings of the Fathers/teachers of the ecclesial body, by the language of liturgical drama and works of art, without the definition exhausting the event itself of ecclesial truth and authenticity. The visible sign of the specific location of the ecclesial event is the cup of the Eucharist. And the visible criterion of ecclesial truth/authenticity is participation in the common cup, which presupposes remaining *within* the boundaries/definitions of the decisions of the councils.

2.4. *Authority as Service*

The ecclesial event is formed as a communion of persons, an active voluntary collectivity with a specific objective. For an active collectivity to be formed with a specific objective, a functional interconnection is required, some organizing structure—a differentiation of ways of contributing to the dynamic cohesion of the whole. Differentiated ways of contributing entail a distinction and ranking of responsibilities, a hierarchical grading of powers, obligations, and competencies. Thus forms of exercising authority arise. This is an unavoidable presupposition if a collectivity is to be functional and effective.

The (almost self-evident) objective for forming a collectivity is the serving of common needs—the "sharing of needs." In the case of the ecclesial body, the need that is shared is not one of general usefulness. It does not concern matters of practical utility to human life, or psychological benefits, or even the satisfaction of the instinctive need to form a group for protection and security.

The common need in the ecclesial body is that an existential goal should be pursued, a specific *mode of existence*. This pursuit forms a "common struggle," and the common struggle presupposes the functional cohesiveness of the collectivity, an ordered ranking of the participants in the struggle. Some lead, and others are led; some plan, and others are recipients of the plans; some "purify" and "enlighten," others are "purified" and "enlightened."

The goal for which the ecclesial body has been formed is common for all, the difference of functions serving the common pursuit of the same goal. The goal (described schematically) is that human beings should draw existence not from their existentially finite *nature* but from their existentially unlimited *relation*. It is that the collectivity should aim at *love* as the *mode of existence*, according to the model of the Triadic hypostases of the Causeless Cause of that which exists. It is that existence should be shared in as loving self-transcendence and self-offering.

Thus within the Church the differentiated modes of contributing to the "common struggle" (the distinguishing and ranking of responsibilities, the placing on a hierarchical scale of capacities, obligations, competencies) function not in terms of the preeminence and power of some who are "superiors" over others who are "inferiors" (as always happens where authority is exercised). The hierarchical distinctions operate only as functional variations of the same struggle for self-transcendence and self-offering.

Some are leaders and guides because they love in a kenotic, or self-emptying, fashion, and others are led and guided because they entrust themselves in a kenotic, or self-emptying, fashion. Some "purify" and "enlighten" because they have actively renounced any pursuit of any atomic purity and enlightenment attained by their own efforts. Others are "purified" and "enlightened" to the degree in which they commit themselves to an active self-renunciation.

In the first written expression of the Church's experience, we encounter the clearest denial and rejection of the criteria of the way in which power is exercised, the criteria that are applicable, as a rule, in any collectivity. We read, "You know that those who are supposed to rule over the Gentiles lord it over them, and their great men exercise authority over them. But it shall not be so among you; but whoever would be great among you must be your servant, and whoever would be first among you must be slave of all" (Mark 10:42–44) . . . "Rather let the greatest among you become as the youngest, and the leader as one who serves" (Luke 22:25–26).

In the above passage why is the assumption that authority, always and everywhere, is exercised tyrannically regarded as self-evident? Obviously because common experience confirms it. Every form of authority has its causal principle in the need for society in its collective aspect to function properly and be able to make effective decisions. Accordingly, every exercise of authority has in the first place the character of an office; it is respected by everybody as a *ministry*, and whoever is in a position of authority serves the common good, the needs of his or her fellow human beings. Common experience, however, confirms something quite different: the exercise of authority manifests characteristics diametrically opposed to those we suppose to belong to its original purpose.

The exercise of authority brings very great pleasure to people; it is a pleasure perhaps greater than any other. This means that it satisfies some biological need that is more important even than the perpetuation of the species, some instinctive demand so essential for the operation of the law of nature that the fulfillment and realization of this demand are accompanied by an overwhelming abundance of psychosomatic pleasure and enjoyment.

Clinical psychology allows us to recognize in the need for power (a need that can even become a mania) a typical manifestation of the *urge to dominate*. What is expressed most of all in this urge is the biological need for the individual to respond to the demands of *natural selection*, the function that assures extended survival and genetic reproduction to the more resistant or powerful individuals, those at any rate that are more suited to serving the dynamic of the evolution of each species (in contrast to those individuals that are weaker in various ways and more easily captured).

The urge to dominate has ramifications forming a complex of needs that fulfill the ego's demands for pleasure. This complex may be summarized by giving a representative list of signifiers: narcissism (a mirror-like relationship with a constructed image of the self), an inflated superego, an overcompensated sense of inferiority, psychologically driven phobias and insecurities, and unconscious needs for sadistic satisfaction (the pleasure elicited by the humiliation or suffering of another person).

With these as given, one could conclude that the phenomenon of the exercise of power, as a quality of one's existential *mode*, is precisely at the opposite pole to the ecclesial *mode*. That is why the ecclesiastical hierarchy of functions, the different modes of contribution to the formation and active cohesion of the eucharistic body, manifestly presuppose the reversal of the terms under which power is usually exercised—a genuine overturning of them.

Without an overturning of the terms of the power phenomenon, there is no ecclesial event, just as there is no ecclesial event without the eucharistic meal. The comparison is bold but not arbitrary. It arises from the same "logic" that governs ecclesial witness as a whole.

The eucharistic meal dynamically realizes and foreshadows the reversal of the stipulations of the natural need to receive nourishment: the bread and the wine in the Eucharist are *shared in*, not consumed individualistically, and the eating and drinking serve relation, not nature; life, not survival. Sharing in the bread and wine of the Eucharist refers to the transformation not of morals or of conduct but of *mode of existence*. That is why the Eucharist is the *sign* that reveals the Church's identity, the event that realizes and manifests the Church.

The same characteristics may be attributed to the hierarchical ordering of the Church's ministries. The offices of deacon, presbyter, and bishop; the synod; the metropolitan system; the pentarchy of patriarchates—all realize and manifest the reversal of the stipulations of the natural need for the collectivity to maintain an effective cohesiveness. The Church's offices presuppose the officeholder's renunciation (*kenosis*) of the natural supports that sustain the exercise of power, namely, the conventional prerogatives of office, the maintenance of a relentless attitude toward human inadequacies and weaknesses, the demand for discipline and the submission of all to the common goal, the unquestioned assumption that special honor is due to those who are at the top of the hierarchy, the imposition of penalties, the projection of an impressive presence.

The Church's offices are not meant to answer the *need* for collective cohesion; they are meant to promote the *freedom* of relations of communion. They serve the dimension of *relation*, not of *nature*. That is why the hierarchical ordering of responsibilities among the ecclesiastical offices (the mode of ministering to the common struggle for unity) is also a *sign* (as is also the Eucharist). It manifests the Church's identity, a *kenotic renunciation* of any individualistic claim, a loving self-denial. It is not about a difference of ethos or conduct in the exercise of authority but about the manifestation and realization of a different *mode of existence*.

When the ecclesiastical offices do not witness to a *kenotic renunciation* of any (conscious or unconscious) self-interest, then the *sign* of the Church's presence is lacking. The absence of the *sign* is also the absence of the ecclesial event. The institutional shell may remain, along with a splendid external appearance and psychological substitutes, but not the ecclesial event, not the hope of a transformation of the *mode of existence*.

All this does not mean that the Church is ineluctably the historically consummate articulation of its gospel. Such a view would negate the ecclesial event as a realistic struggle that may be accomplished in a dynamic manner. It would transpose it to the level of a romantic illusion or an unattainable ideal.

Because the ecclesial event is a struggle, it also presupposes failure; it contains failure within it as a definitive (and defining) element of the struggle. It contains within it the sin/missing the mark of humankind. The Church defines itself as a field in which wheat grows together with weeds (cf. Matt 13:24–30), as a net that draws good and bad fish out of the sea (cf. Matt 13:47–48).

What is revealed in this statement is the difference between the necessities of *nature* and the freedom of *relation*. In a collectivity that is subject to natural (serviceable) necessities, humanity's sin/missing the mark, with regard to the goals and terms that have been set for the common endeavor, sets the individual *outside*. For the collectivity to be able to function, any fractious individual who undermines it must clearly be marginalized, isolated, and in extreme cases annihilated. It is not by chance that every organized collectivity lays down penalties, for if transgression or undermining remains unpunished, the cohesion of the collectivity collapses.

The disciplinary exclusion of sin is a necessity that accompanies that nature of a collectivity. By contrast, the ecclesial event is constituted by that freedom that is capable of transforming nature into relation, sin into relation, death into relation. The presupposition and measure of participation in the ecclesial event is the awareness of individuals that alone, simply by their natural capacities, they cannot taste the fullness of life. Even the most virtuous, the most talented individual has no chance of gaining life, or freedom from mortality, thanks to his own virtue or talents.

If, then, life is procured only by individual self-transcendence and loving self-offering, the logic of necessities that governs the nature of a collectivity (the legal logic of sin) is overturned. Sin (failure/missing the mark with regard to the goal of the fullness of life) can be insistence on individually possessed virtues, on the delivery of good works. And the charism of freedom from being trapped in the individualism of nature (freedom from death) can be the experience of the inadequacy of the atomic individual through falls and failures, the transference of our trust to love, to self-offering.

When ecclesial experience speaks of the priority of *repentance*, it does not refer to a perhaps wounded narcissism of regret for faults. It refers to an awareness of atomic inadequacy, an awareness that nourishes in a dynamic manner our self-surrender to the relation of love.

In this sense the Church's gospel "endorses" sin: it confirms that in the pursuit of true life the tax collectors, the prostitutes, the robbers—not those "who trusted in themselves that they were righteous" (Luke 18:9)—precede us, show us the way. It confirms that our precursors in freedom from nature are those who have really renounced any trust in nature, trust in their capabilities, the successes in exercising self-control, the psychological satisfactions of the ego. They are those who see their self as so sinful that it does not allow them the slightest margin for placing any trust in it. All that remains for them is to surrender themselves to the relationship, to abandon themselves to love.

Only heresy excludes a person from the ecclesial event. Only someone who chooses to insist on a heretical understanding of, or heretical quest for, life puts himself *outside* the ecclesial event.

Heresy for the Church is not views, convictions, or formulations that are "mistaken" (in comparison with those that are "official"). It is not the transgression of some objective codification of the presuppositions of "orthodoxy." It is affirming the mode of mortality as the path of life; it is imprisoning yourself in the necessity of death.

Heresy is objectifying love, for example, in good works that nourish your narcissism while at the center of your life, like an idol, is only your ego, your authority, your reputation. It is fear of risking relation, fear of opening yourself to love, of being stripped of the exalted "calling" and noble desire to exercise "spiritual" leadership over the "others" whom you are incapable of loving. It is to take as sinfulness a finicky self-reproach for minor faults of behavior that hide from you the true image of your real self: your failure to attain, as an occasion for repentance, a real self-renunciation.

Heretics are not people who sin according to the letter of some dogmatic shorthand but people who cut themselves off from life and from reality. They construct their own imaginary world, their own language, their own self-evident incommunicable truths. In the small, closed universe of heresy, contradictions do not become discernible, false words are reality, and actual (though not deliberately desired) incoherence is nonexistent.

Heresy, moreover, is to pervert the use of signifiers in order to give an illusory sense of power—instead of in order to minister to the illumination of what is signified. It is to alienate the ministry of *fatherhood*, which functions as the "grafting" of people onto the body of the Church, and turn it into the pleasure of exercising authority over consciences. It is to objectify the formulations of ecclesial experience and make them "truths" that have been turned into idols. It is to worship the letter of the formulations, their "correct" understanding on the atomic level, without the slightest inkling about the conditions of participation in the common struggle that the formulations presuppose.

Heresy is the alienation of the ecclesial event into hardened forms of institutional endorsement of the fear of freedom, of the pleasure of exercising power. It is the perversion of ministry into the exercise of authority. It is turning the Church into a religion.

Chapter 3

The Religionization of the Ecclesial Event: The Symptoms

3.1. *Faith as Ideology*

The ecclesial event defines itself as lying at the opposite pole to instinctive religiosity; it constitutes a reversal of the terms of natural religion. The ecclesial event, however, may be *religionized*. It may be alienated into a religiosity determined by natural needs, perhaps even without any of the external visible marks of Christian particularity (in doctrine, worship, and institutional structure) disappearing entirely.

This alienation takes place for the most part "imperceptibly," when unintentionally and unconsciously the demands of instinctive religious need take precedence—when they predominate in the personal life of one or more members of the ecclesial body. The symptoms may be limited to incognizant individual deviations or to a cluster that is difficult to specify: they may constitute a hardly perceptible *heresy*. They may amount to a dominant tendency in one or more local churches and become a fixed mental outlook for a certain time or indefinitely. In any event, these symptoms occur without awareness that they point to the alienation and destruction of the ecclesial event.

A typical mark of religionization is when faith is turned into ideology. By *ideology* I mean a totality of theoretical propositions (ideas, principles, aims, ideals, hermeneutic schemes, deontological approaches) that aim at guiding human conduct, the way we live our lives. The value of an ideology's propositions is judged by their practical effectiveness, by their usefulness to individuals and to organized societies.

The ideological version of faith takes the witness of ecclesial experience precisely as theoretical propositions with consequences of immediate utility for the practical aspects of human life. Faith no longer signifies the trust that is granted to people when they love sincerely; faith does not presuppose the struggle to establish relations of communion for people to be freed from slavery to the ego. The knowledge that is gained as experience of the ecclesial struggle and the linguistic formulations that express this experience are objectified, are taken as ideas, principles, aims, ideals, hermeneutic schemes, and deontological approaches. That is, they are taken as "material" that the individual's intellect can apprehend as personal "convictions."

Thus faith is transformed into an ideological construction that primarily contains "information" about metaphysical reality. The "information" is not controlled by experience, yet the individual's intellect accepts it as certainties because, although it is not controlled by common experience or demonstrated by the rules of correct reasoning, at least it does not contradict correct reasoning. These intellectual inferences for the most part convey certainties because they entail normative rules of behavior that are demonstrably useful for living together in a harmonious society.

As individuals we have an instinctive need to create a protective shell for ourselves through assurances of metaphysical "knowledge," through the certainty of "objectively" ratified convictions. As individuals we cannot bear risking possible (never guaranteed in advance) empirical explorations, the relativity of formulations, the struggle to attain trust.

An ideological version of faith means that intellectual apprehension is reckoned as knowledge, that the formal correctness of an expression is reckoned as truth. Who guarantees the operation of intellectual apprehension? Perhaps the exercise of the atomic (natural) capacity of intellection, perhaps also the established effective aid of a method (of correct thinking). And who guarantees the correctness of the formulation? At this point neither intellection nor method suffices. This instinctive demand for certainty is forced to resort to arbitrary axiomatic pronouncements. "Arbitrary" means empirically and logically undemonstrable but psychologically able to respond to the natural need.

In this way an "objectively" infallible *source* of truth is devised, that is, a source of the validity of the formulations. Validity is objectified in the "source," that is, in a specific idol, in a sacred taboo, as in all primeval religions. A "source" of truth can prove to be a written text: the Bible, the Old and New Testaments. Its validity is regarded as indisputable—it is considered an "infallible" text—because it has been composed under conditions of divine *inspiration*.

Inspiration means that God is the real author, that he inspired the authors to write the texts. Either he dictated them word for word, even down to punctuation marks (the ultimate idolized version), or exercised a supervision that excluded error from the composition of the texts. Validation of this kind from on high clads the individual very fully in protective armor, neutralizes insecurities, and banishes doubts.

Yet even inspired texts need interpretation, analysis, exposition, and commentary. Who will guarantee the correctness also of the hermeneutical approaches to the Bible, so as to avert secondary doubts and insecurities in the comprehension of the sacred texts?

It is to avert such doubts that a secondary *source* of "infallible" guarantees has been idolized, that of *Holy Tradition*. The word *tradition* has been used in the life of the Church to signify the transmission of the experience of the eucharistic body from one person to another and from one generation to another—always with a sharp awareness of the difference between *knowledge* (*gnōsis*), which is conveyed by *participation* in the experience, and the mere *understanding* of the formulations of the experience.

In the Church's tradition the transmission of eucharistic experience is achieved in terms of the struggle to attain a relationship, in terms of trust and love—not in the mode of transmitting "objective" information from one individual to another. Thus the word *tradition* in its ecclesial usage signifies whatever experience is handed on to us that is also the experience to which we surrender ourselves. Something similar takes place in any relationship where experiential knowledge is offered with love and is accepted with trust: in the disinterested relationship between teacher and pupil, between master craftsman and apprentice.

The experience of the *mode* in which we approach the witness of the apostles and the Fathers (our first guides in finding our way toward the life-giving hope) is transmitted within the Church as an achievement of love and trust. This is the experience of the mode in which we "read" and reproduce every symbolic outline of ecclesial experience, that is, the mode in which we paint pictures; build churches; sing; organize the space devoted to worship; celebrate the Eucharist; appoint bishops, presbyters, and deacons; hold councils; pray as an ecclesial body (not as individuals); and fast ecclesially (not as individuals). Tradition is this experience of the *mode* that differentiates the ecclesial event from every religion, the *mode* that we learn experientially, not intellectually as if it were information.

This practical *mode* is not unrelated to "theory," or contemplation (*theōria*), the subtle semantic formulations that refer to metaphysical reality. From the moment "the Word become flesh" (John 1:14), metaphysics has been incarnated in history and its intellectual formulations have *defined* the experience of the historical probing of metaphysics—they are the terms, the boundary markers, of this experience. The philosophical language that the Church has used to express its experience is not necessarily superior in terms of clarity to the language of art, or of asceticism, or of the institutions that express the same experience, the same gospel of hope. The Church's *tradition* is all these rudimentary outlines—the languages and modes of practice—when they operate and are transmitted within the terms of the struggle to arrive at a relation, within the terms of trust and love.

In religionized Christianity "tradition" is something else, something radically different from the transmission of eucharistic experience. It is an additional guarantee cladding the individual in the armor of certainties with regard to metaphysics, infallible certainties shored up by supernatural authority. Tradition is objectified as a second *source* of "infallibility" (alongside Sacred Scripture), again with the blueprints of validity built into it.

The decisions of the ecumenical councils and the unanimous opinion of the Fathers of the Church constitute "tradition." Here, within a religionized perspective, I am referring to written formulations that complete and clarify whatever metaphysical information is offered by the Bible in an elliptical or indirect manner. "Tradition" bolsters the authorized interpretation of the "dogmas"—it refers also to theoretical "principles," as it does too to other manifestations of ecclesial witness. Only that which can be objectified in definitive formulations is included in "tradition," only that which can be possessed as a privately appropriated certainty by the individual.

It is difficult, however, to objectify such criteria as the *ecumenicity* of the councils, or the *unanimity* of the Fathers. There were councils that were convoked to be ecumenical and declared themselves to be ecumenical, but history has nevertheless recorded them as "robber" councils. Many questions also arise about the *unanimity* of the Fathers. Is the validity of their unanimity dependent on arithmetical completeness, a function of quantitative considerations? If not, what criteria (whether qualitative or moral) would guarantee that a doctrine is genuinely "patristic" and would locate the criterion of unanimity only in the "genuine" Fathers of the Church? And is it possible that the same Fathers are infallible when they speak unanimously but are in error when their opinion differs on some matter?

In religionized Christianity such questions are sidestepped, or else answers are sought in legal constructions. It is said and written, for example, that in the councils the bishops do not express themselves as delegates of the faithful but deliver their opinions infallibly *ipso jure*: by the grace that the Holy Spirit assures them in virtue of their office (not in their personal capacity)! However, despite the fact that their decisions are *jure divino* infallible (not through the "consent" of the faithful), an external mark and criterion of ecumenicity is reckoned to be the recognition of conciliar decisions by the whole Church. And another contradiction that clearly remains unresolved is the following: the bishops decide infallibly without the *pleroma* of the Church on the basis of the charism of their office, but a presupposition of the validity of infallibility is the consent of the *pleroma*!

The idolizing demand for "objectification" (in the form of privately held atomic certainties) replaces living experiential tradition with a confused mass of intellectual and legal schematizations. In order to specify what the *consensus Patrum* (the agreement of the Fathers) consists in, we must define with objective criteria which of the bishops and teachers may be considered "Fathers" of the Church and which should be denied such recognition. The most commonly used legal schematization is that we should describe as *Fathers* those ecclesiastical writers whose texts and formulations have been used by the ecumenical councils for the composition of conciliar decisions, or those who have provided "rich material for the construction of a full dogmatic system," even if their contribution was not specifically recognized by a council.

A schematic definition of this kind is unable to include among the *Fathers* of the Church bishops who have not left any writings, even if the ecclesial body has always acknowledged in their persons the palpable realization of its eschatological hope—such as Spyridon of Trimythous, or Nicholas of Myra in Lycia. The problem is "resolved" by the addition of a supplementary criterion for the recognition of "objective" patristic status, the criterion of "holiness," at which point a new cycle of attempts begins in order to define (now with "objectivity") the elements of holiness or the evidence supporting it.

The sequence of legal demands proves to be a vicious circle: needs for assured certainties constantly mount up, schematic constructions for excluding any hint of doubt become ever more complex. Intricate "laws of sacred discipline" (*sacrae disciplinae leges*), like those that nature demands for its self-preservation, undermine the reality of life: the struggle for relations of communion, the adventure of freedom.

When an ideological construct replaces experiential attestation and ascetic investigation, such an alienating substitution immediately finds expression linguistically. Our language is flooded by tautologous phrases, conventional stereotypes, and abstract concepts—signifiers that do not refer to the experience of signified things. These signifiers function by their own power, imposing mere comprehension as "knowledge." Religious ideology is expressed in a language of "intellectual idols,"[13] independent concepts that have been detached from empirical attestation (and this autonomous status excludes any hint of a possible empirical attestation).

Here are a few random examples. Religious language states in summary fashion that "Christ brought the full and final revelation." This statement allows no scope for any concern that such "revelation" might be understood as "supernatural" information that reassures the ego. On the contrary, it is obvious that its aim is to clad the individual with psychological certainty. It wants to persuade us dogmatically as individuals that by following Christ we are making the best choice, that we are securing the best "deal." It obliterates any trace of a form of expression that would constitute a call to empirical verification of what is signified.

"The spiritual world is revealed only to the eyes of the soul." There is no attempt in this formulation to forestall any possible Platonic interpretation (at the opposite pole to the Church's understanding) either of the sense of "spiritual" or of the word "soul." In religious language references to "spirituality," "spiritual life," "spiritual goals," "spiritual world," "spiritual person," and a host of similar expressions are of a kind that very easily lose contact with any ontological realism and slip into a self-referential version of truth, into a "reality" that is in fact conceived only in intellectual terms. The same happens very easily in the case of the word "soul."

"If you do not understand, believe; knowledge is the reward of faith—do not seek to understand in order to believe; believe in order to understand." Again, this is an aphorism that is oblivious to the danger of taking faith simply as a form of psychological autosuggestion, with the consequent emasculation of critical thought, as any instinctive demand always imposes. Both *knowledge* and *faith* function in religious language as attainments of unshared

13. "By making idols within themselves they create intellectual idolatry" (Basil of Caesarea, *On the Prophet Isaiah* 96, PG 30:276C).

atomic self-sufficiency, more or less as grades of completeness of understanding.

"The grace of God is a supernatural gift granted to human beings like an interior illumination so that they should understand what they read in the law and the Church's teaching." A *supernatural gift* that adds the *capacity for understanding* to individuals cannot be something other than or something different from what the linguistic signifiers (and their commonly understood equivalents) declare: some kind of magical force that operates mechanically with measurable efficacy. It is added to the individual; it does not grow like a gift out of the relationship, the loving response to divine love. And grace operates as an *interior illumination*, whereby the adjective "interior" and the noun "illumination" introduce an extremely slippery indeterminacy of subjectivity into the workings of the psyche. In religious language references to "interiority," "interior life," "interior world," "interior vision," and a host of similar expressions very easily become detached from any ontological realism and slip into a "reality" controlled only by subjective psychological experiences.

"Our purpose on earth is to resemble so far as possible the perfect moral character of Christ, to become like Christ's virtue." "We all have a great and eternal interest in acquiring a true and living faith, for only with this will we become eternally happy and blessed." "When Christians love God with all their heart, they love themselves, because they benefit themselves, they love their own progress and perfection, their own eternal happiness and blessedness." "Great benefit is accrued by those people who, coming together in the name of Christ, seek together in common the preparation of their souls and their spiritual perfection. And such people, of course, are benefited when their actions are also in accordance with God's commandments."

These commonplaces of religious language are typical examples of an individualistic and purely secular utilitarianism. They are undisguised symptoms of the instinctive need to armor the ego with self-protection. They do not refer to an experiential and shared probing of the *meaning* of existence, of the world, of history, in the hope of shedding light on the enigma of death.

They are expressed in an ideological language of psychological self-satisfaction and consist of obviously *a priori* statements and axiomatic "certainties."

3.2. *Experience as a Psychological Construct*

I call a *psychological construct* the artificial certainty that arises (and is proclaimed as "truth") when subjective desire unconsciously objectifies its goal, transforming it into the illusion of real experience.

This is a typical psychological defense mechanism that activates the creative capacity of the imagination in order to conceal the painful reality of privation. Fantasies replace the real goals of desire. They become the "place" of unconscious defensive operations that neutralize or idealize the desire and ultimately produce the illusory (but aggressive) certainty of really lived experience.

When desire is the product of unconscious (instinctive) needs, it often has as its starting point vestigial memories of earlier illusory satisfaction (primary or learned and imitated). Desire never ceases to be a search for the real satisfaction of primary need, but very often it is constituted on the basis of a reinvestment in the vestigial memories of illusions.

These vestigial memories refer back to emotional experiences, feelings of elation, sentimental contentment, enthusiasm, compunction, justifying contrition, relief, joy, serene self-sufficiency, and so forth. And their referential dynamic springs from their objectification: the vestigial memories are reinvested in the linguistic signifiers/signs of illusory satisfaction.

Thus the recall of the linguistic signifiers rewords the representations in the memory as confirmation of real experience, transferring the certainty of the real to the level of language (because the illusory satisfaction of desire is now drawn from the linguistic signifiers). The semantics of the signifiers is identified with the subjective certainty of experiential witness, and therefore with the experiential confirmation of the real, thanks to the clarity of the psychological signifiers.

The mode of existence that proclaims and aspires to the ecclesial event (a mode of freedom from the limitations of time, space, decay, and death) is *love*. And love means relinquishing the egotistic protective armor in which atomic nature clads itself; it means existence as participation in relations of communion in existence.

This *relinquishing* and *participating* (the transcendence of natural individualism and the realization of life as loving relation) constitutes both a mode of existence and a mode of knowledge: atomic *understanding* differs from *knowledge* in terms of experience of relation, just as atomic *survival* differs from the erotic fullness of *life*.

As mode of life and mode of knowledge, love (transcendent self-giving) is always a dynamic aim, never a definitive possession—always a "never-ending growth toward perfection." And the ecclesial event, which historically and institutionally defines the communication of this *mode*, is only and always the product of a common struggle to attain a common goal. The language in which it proclaims the ecclesial *mode* of life and knowledge is always *apophatic*: it refers to *relinquishing* the ego and *participating* in life as relation. It does not substitute intellectual certainties for the character of the gospel's signifiers, a character that refers to experience. Nor does it transform the struggle's risk into psychological certainties consisting of illusory satisfactions.

The natural instincts, however, insist on the armoring of the ego with certainties, and the natural insistence imperceptibly alienates the apophatic language, turning it into dogmatic intellectualism, just as it also alienates the reality of the struggle, turning it into a quest for psychological satisfactions. Intellectualism and psychological pressure together religionize the ecclesial event.

Religionized Christianity is not interested in *ontology*: the struggle for the *meaning* of existence, of the world, of history; the struggle for the empirical exploration of the hope for life. What it is interested in is *psychology*: not as a science that investigates the workings of the psyche and the "laws" that may perhaps govern it, but as giving priority to subjective experiences that acquire the value of realities for the subject.

Individuals who practice a religion under the name of Christianity are not bothered (and perhaps have never come across any relevant information) about *relation* as a mode of existence and knowledge, a mode of transcendent self-giving. They are "Christians" not because they participate in the ecclesial event as *members* of a particular eucharistic *body*, but because they "believe" as individuals in the doctrines of "Christianity" and in its moral precepts—"Christian principles" form their convictions as individuals.

Practicing "Christians" try to be faithful as individuals to the duties that their convictions impose. They try to make their conduct conform to the requirements (the normative principles) of "Christian morality." They take part in common worship but in order to pray as individuals and be taught (benefited) as individuals, perhaps unacquainted with and unknown to those around them. Those around them share in the same way of thinking and in the same religion but are only symbolically and in a sentimental fashion "brothers and sisters"—they have no concept of the potentiality (the real possibility) of sharing their existence and their life with them.

They communicate from the common cup and share the common bread of the Eucharist, but for the "forgiveness" of their own individual sins, in order to secure "eternal life" for their own individual selves. They fast for the reward that fasting offers, not in order to share in a common mode of taking food together with the whole Church. They approach the sacrament of repentance and confession in order to be cleansed, again as individuals, from guilt, in order to gain a validly assured "forgiveness"—not in order to bring their failure, their egocentric resistance to self-transcendence and self-offering, to the ecclesial body and share it with that body.

In short, individuals who bear the name of Christian practice their religion in order to gain, by their own efforts and their own merit, their individual salvation, the power enabling their ego to continue to exist for eternity. They live their religiosity as a totality of duties, obligations, and responsibilities that are objective conditions and presuppositions if they are to be rewarded as individuals, if they are to win eternal happiness, purely as individuals, even if the majority of those around them go to perdition or suffer eternal torments.

Religiosity is experienced as a price that has to be paid for individuals to gain eternal happiness. A price means something that has value, that costs—metaphysical security does not come without expenditure, painlessly, and cost-free. Of course, the desired goal of religiosity is also an instinctive desire, an imperative natural need, with the result that any price can be taken as a consolation and be idealized so that the instinct's demand may be satisfied. The unpleasant sense of the cost, however, is never lost, the sense of the restriction of individual choices, of obedience to externally imposed rules, of burdensome obligations, of an anxious vigilance often difficult to bear. The archetypal path of *virtue* is the "narrow way," the difficult path to climb, as opposed to the "broad way" that leads to *perdition*. The imperative character of the instinctive need for the individual's eternal security makes the cost of the "narrow way" tolerable chiefly on account of the psychological compensations of the desired certainty. The human psyche (nature) slips into illusory satisfactions that are strictly individualistic: exalted states of elation, exhilaration, and ecstasy; feelings of enthusiasm; a plethora of powerful emotions and deep compunction.

Every religion offers its believers the strongest possible occasions of such psychological substitutes for the desired assurance of salvation. As a result, religiosity is measured by (and ultimately is identified with) the mainly psychological states experienced by the individual. It is a primary concern of the religions to maximize the different ways of eliciting psychological satisfaction. They use evocative rituals, impressive vestments, stately forms of etiquette, imposing titles and modes of address, carefully planned uses of light and sound. Every kind of art is mobilized, every kind of expression (in its distinct genre) is cultivated, for deliberate psychological effect in each form of art—in music, painting, architecture, sculpture, decoration, and ceremonial. The same psychological priorities are imposed on the manner of speaking, the gestures, the vocabulary, and the practical "pastoral" advice given to individuals.

In consequence of this identification of religiosity with the psychology of the individual, religious people can measure their spiritual progress by the intensity and frequency of their emotional experiences. What is especially valued is a tendency toward mystical states, a saccharine vocabulary and bearing, a theatrical show of rapture or of humility. And what charms is religious addresses of lyrical sensitivity, words full of feeling, rhetorical flights of fervor. A measure or criterion of the piety to be emulated is tears, genuflections, and enthusiasm, together with dramatic self-blame, sentimental outbreaks of joy and of readiness for self-sacrifice.

As a rule (and very clearly at that), all this theatrical behavior has an egocentric and narcissistic character. It operates with the dynamics of satisfying the self, of shoring up the ego—and inevitably it generates self-pleasing, unconscious conceit, and self-admiration. These psychological states do not arise out of participation in relations of communion, out of the struggle for self-transcendence. They lie, rather, at the opposite pole to shared experience. They are individualistic phenomena that insulate one from the dynamics of relation, that imprison one in an egotistic "interiority."

The following typical expressions of religious language convey very clearly the individualistic character (the egotistic "interiority") of psychological experiences.

"May You yourself sweeten me, my faithful sweetness, sweetness who is my joy and security, who recollects me when I am distracted, when I am broken into a thousand pieces and You put them together." "When I call on God, my God and Lord, it means that I first invoke him within myself. I go into myself and despite my weakness see with the eyes of my soul, see beyond my gaze, beyond my spirit, the unchanging light of His truth."

And the following are typical examples of the kind of language that expresses a psychological religiosity:

"I get a very powerful feeling when I pray." "My heart leaps with joy after confession." "My soul takes wing during worship." "This sermon speaks in my heart." "I admire this priest, how he goes into rapture when he is serving the Liturgy."

"Christianity is an existential fullness." "A Christian's existence acquires a profound significance when his or her heart lives in the faith, when it receives the suprasubstantial paradox with deep feeling."

"Let us climb up by the ladder of the virtues to be near to Christ. Let us fly with the wings of prayer to the doing of His will. Let us ascend to His heavenly kingdom through repentance and the divine Eucharist. Let us become princes of the spirit through the study of His word. Let us become signposts to the world by putting His commandments into practice."

"Every Sunday in Church we express feelings of adoration toward God." "The experience of paradise on earth is this: that Christ should govern your heart, that He should guide your steps, inspire your thinking, be your personal savior and redeemer."

These are just a few random examples of the kind of language created by a religionized Christianity. It is a language governed by egotistic introspection (introspection of a psychological character), by how the natural individual feels, by what the natural individual senses. Everything is judged on the basis of the degree of delight that is produced. Religious experience is verified by the psychological enjoyment of the individual.

Religiosity has a need for "objective" supports: it has a need for prayer, for confession, for preaching, for the keeping of commandments. And these are not all just starting points, merely springboards for the principal struggle to attain relation, self-transcendence, and self-offering. They are therefore not experienced as *participation* in the ecclesial event. They are used as objective markers that render the subject's religious efforts measurable, that armor the subject's egotistic self-sufficiency.

The language of a religionized Christianity lacks an ontological backbone. It swings to and fro in the absence of any reality corresponding to it. It refers to psychological substitutes for the real. Its symbolism points to sentimental assumptions. Its images reflect strictly individual emotional sensitivities. The enigma of death is unanswerable in the perspective of an arbitrary and childish extension of the natural ego, an extension that is without an end in time. There is no revelatory dynamic of the ecclesial event whatsoever.

Psychological states become substitutes for the realism of the erotic struggle. Sentimental suggestiveness is reckoned as real experience.

3.3. *Salvation as a Reward for the Individual*

The Greek word for *salvation, sōtēria*, has two possible etymologies, which give rise to two different nuances of meaning.

According to the first etymology, the word comes from the ancient Greek verb *saoō/sōō*, which later became *sōzō*, meaning I make something *sound* (*sōon*), I bring it to its wholeness, its integrity.

The second etymology derives the word from the noun *sōtēr*, which indicates the agent of the verb *sōzein*, whereupon *sōtēria* is the action or the result of this agency, deliverance, or liberation from some threat, from a difficult situation, danger, or disaster.

In the Church's gospel *salvation/sōtēria* reflects the first etymology more than the second. The common struggle of the Church is directed toward making human persons existentially *sound* (*sōoi*) or whole, toward leading them to the integrity of their existential possibilities—to freedom from the limitations of createdness. Its aim and purpose is that human persons should be granted existence as *relation*/self-transcendence/loving self-offering.

The religionized version of Christianity tends toward the second etymology. It identifies salvation with attaining security, with the certain (permanent) preservation of that which already exists (the individual psychological ego), with the deliverance of that which already exists from suffering, danger, the threat of extinction, and death.

In the ecclesial perspective salvation is something that is actively sought, a hoped-for wholeness that is always open to a fuller completion, that is never bounded—"the perfect uncompleted perfection of the perfect."[14] And the wholeness of existential possibilities (freedom from the limitations of createdness) can only be conceived of as a grace, a charism—only as a gift to the created human being from the uncreated and personal Causal Principle of existence and life. It is a gift that humanity's equally personal freedom accepts or rejects, because the causal connection operates existentially as the freedom of interpersonal relation. And the affirmation of the relation (love, eros) is realized dynamically without its fullness ever becoming fixed.

What we are discussing here is the dynamic of hope, the "relation" and "fullness" that the ecclesial struggle aims at "in hope." The only experiential foretaste to which participants in the struggle testify concerns the difference between the hoped-for "complete" and the present "in part"—the difference between the desired fullness of life (life "abundantly," in the words of John 10:10) and the present atomic reality of each of us. "For we know only in part, and we prophesy only in part; but when the complete comes, the partial will come to an end" (1 Cor 13:9–10).

The difference between the "in part" and the "complete" is indicated by an example, the difference in maturity that separates a child from an adult. It is impossible for a child to conceive of (to foresee or imagine beforehand) that which he will *be* and that which he will know as an adult. And it is impossible for an adult to return to a child's level of knowledge: "When I was a child, I reasoned like a child; when I became an adult, I put an end to childish ways" (1 Cor 13:11).

The religious person is not satisfied with goals of dynamic indeterminacy or with standards of qualitative differences. Instinctive religiosity demands psychological certainties with regard to the ego's eternal security, and only in this way (as eternal security) does it understand *salvation*.

By the strict (even if usually mistaken) logic of self-protection, the certainty of salvation cannot exist if salvation is a charism/grace rather than something won by the individual. Certainty is

---

14. John of Sinai, *The Ladder*, Step 29, § 3, ed. the hermit Sophronius (Constantinople, 1883), 165.

strengthened when the individual has objective indications of *entitlement* to salvation, when salvation has been attained by one's own efforts by paying the required price—that is, when salvation is owed as a *reward* for acts worthy of salvation, for the individual's *meritorious* virtues.

Consequently, for the certainty of salvation to function, what is needed in the first place is an objective (legal/juridical) framework that would codify the terms of humanity's relations with God by specific divine requirements/commandments on the one hand and by human obligations/duties on the other. What definitely needs to exist is that demands should be made by God of humanity and that these demands should be expressed in specific commandments, the keeping of which should guarantee humanity's salvation.

A clear legal framework implies that the keeping of the commandments (the presupposition of salvation) should be ascertained and measured with indisputable objectivity. The individual should be left no margin of doubt about the definition of "good" and "evil"; the legal code of the commandments should legislate in detail for every case of conduct (and even of thinking and intending), for every possible dilemma. Only a legal code broadened to become an extensive body of casuistry can offer the individual the assurance of certainty of obedience to God's commandments, the knowledge that salvation is being won as of right.

The law! In the written testimony of the earliest Christian experience, the word refers to a dark threat tormenting humankind. The law is a *curse* (Gal 3:10), the *power of sin* (1 Cor 15:56). This is because it imprisons human beings in the anxious effort to overcome mortality by their own powers, by the capabilities of their mortal nature. People are deceived into thinking that they can overcome death by observing the law, by making their conduct and their intentions subject to their individual mind and their individual will. If *sin* (existential failure/missing the mark) is insisting on an individualistic existence, then the power of sin really is the law, because it is the law that traps people in the illusion that by individually focused efforts they can be saved from atomic self-centeredness.

The realism of those who share in the ecclesial event confirms that "it is not possible for anyone to defeat his own nature."[15] Only the eventuality of *relation*, of loving self-transcendence, and of self-offering can lead to freedom from the necessities of nature—only our renunciation of any reliance on self, our surrender to the grace/charism of God's love. "For where God, who transcends nature, dwells, created things also come to transcend nature."[16]

This indwelling of God is the charismatic and the exceptional, whereas the usual and prevailing situation is reliance (perhaps even unconsciously) on the powers of nature. That is why historically too the religionization of the ecclesial event, its rolling back toward the curse of the law, has predominated.

Already in the Church's earliest years, we find Judaizing Christians in the Palestinian communities. These are Christians who even within the ecclesial event want to attach importance to the natural need for religion. They demand that Christians of Gentile origin (those who had not followed the religious practice of the Jews) should have imposed on them the religious obligation of *circumcision*[17] and the observance of the Mosaic law.[18]

---

15. Ibid., Step 15, § 4, p. 86.

16. Ibid., Step 26, § 3, p. 124.

17. Circumcision (the cutting off of the foreskin or prepuce of the penis) was practiced by numerous peoples, and the Jews must have received it from the ancient tribes of Palestine. They nevertheless made it the "physical sign" of the *covenant* that God made with his people of Israel, a sign that is a testimony for the Jew that he belongs to the "chosen people" of God. "This is my covenant, which you shall keep, between me and you and your offspring after you: Every male among you shall be circumcised. You shall circumcise the flesh of your foreskins, and it shall be a sign of the covenant between me and you" (Gen 17:10–11). Every male Israelite must bear this "sign" on his body from the eighth day of his life, and the blood that is shed by the cutting of the prepuce is called (at least in later Judaism) the "blood of the covenant."

18. The *Mosaic law* (the Torah of the Jews) is the large number of regulative precepts contained in the books of the *Pentateuch*. In the Jewish tradition it is attributed to Moses as prophet, that is, as the communicator of God's will, the "mouth of God." The ordinances of the Mosaic law are intended to regulate the life of the "people of God" in all its aspects. It consists of principles of moral conduct (with the *Decalogue* as its core), rules of worship, and legal precepts that regulate the operation of family, judicial, economic, and social institutions. The keeping of the commandments of the Torah allows every Israelite as an individual to conform to God's will. Chiefly, however, it assures him (as a practical and

In the so-called Apostolic Council,[19] the Church of course rejected this first undisguised attempt at its religionization. It refused to make the hope of the gospel subject to the individualistic security provided by the law and circumcision, and repudiated the insidious notion of objective/juridical presuppositions to salvation. The Apostolic Council, however, did not deny the "necessity" of certain obligations of individual conduct: "signs" of the objective/social distinction of Christians from pagans. It laid down that Christians of Gentile origin should abstain "from what has been sacrificed to idols and from blood and from what is strangled and from fornication" (Acts 15:29).

In the first three centuries, there was no need for any more precise determination of objective boundaries that would safeguard the ecclesial body's visible homogeneity and unity of life. For the Christians there was the common and constant possibility of *martyrdom*, which governed their life and was the measure and criterion of witness to salvation—a practical witness and manifestation of the *mode of existence* that differentiates the "new creation" of Christians from the life of the "world."

In the course of the historical life of the Church, however, after the period of the persecutions and martyrdom, the "necessity" of the obligations that the Apostolic Council had laid down for Christians was increased dramatically. The legal presuppositions for participation in the Church's eucharistic assembly—or for exclusion from it—constantly multiplied and became ever more specific and casuistic.

The increase in legal criteria was perhaps not unconnected with the recognition of the Church (after the end of the persecutions) as the "official religion" of the Roman Empire (the *Religio Imperii*). This recognition must have influenced in some measure both the way the Church functioned as an institution and the mental outlook of Christians—it may perhaps have contributed to the *religionization* of some expressions of the Church's life.

---

visible presupposition) participation in the "chosen people" and in the promises that this people has received from God.

19. Acts 15:6–29. For the Judaizers see also below, pp. 130–35.

In particular, the symptom of the progressive multiplication of the *canons* (legal/canonical stipulations) that were enacted by (originally) local and (later) ecumenical councils raises the question: Does this indicate a dulling of the consciousness that the Church is a "new creation" not a new religion; another *mode of existence*, not simply another (more ethical) mode of behavior?

Even as late as the seventh century, the canons of the ecumenical councils (which have universal validity for the life of the Church) avoid setting limits on the conduct of individuals, or defining and evaluating cases of the sins of individuals that entail *excommunication* (expulsion from the ecclesial body, self-exclusion outside the boundaries of the body). Almost all the canons from the first four ecumenical councils refer to matters of ecclesiastical discipline, the rights of the clergy, the validity of ordinations, behavior toward heretics, and so forth. The very few cases of individual deviant behavior that are mentioned in the canons have consequences for the eucharistic structure and functioning of the Church (see Canon 17 of the First Ecumenical Council, "On clerics charging interest"; Canon 2 of the Fourth Ecumenical Council, "On not ordaining for money"; Canon 16 of the same council, "On virgins and monks not being permitted to engage in marriage"—where the following addition is very characteristic: "If any are found to have done this, let them remain without communion. We have decreed that the local bishop has authority to show clemency toward them"; etc.).

It is only from the end of the seventh century (and specifically with the Quinisext Ecumenical Council, or Council in Trullo, of 692) that a rapid increase begins in the number of canons referring to general cases of sins committed by individuals, to reprehensible instances of social behavior (of clerics and laypeople), to the fixing of penalties for social crimes, and to the coordination of physical life (especially its sexual aspects) with participation in the life of the Church. Thus, although all the canons produced by the first four ecumenical councils together scarcely amount to 68, the Quinisext Council alone formulated 102 canons and moreover ratified (recognized as canons valid for the universal Church) a very high number of the stipulations of earlier local councils and the opinions expressed by various Fathers on general themes and individual cases of personal (moral) conduct.

Canons that serve the requirements of individual self-esteem, narcissistic respectability, egotistic self-sufficiency—canons that have no relation to the Church's gospel but are connected rather with an exaggerated religious puritanism—clad themselves with the authority of an ecumenical council. The exaggerations are striking, for the canons of the Quinisext Council impose *deposition* on clerics and *excommunication* on laypeople if they attend "mimes and theatrical performances" (Canon 51), if they "play dice" (Canon 50), or if they "style their hair" (Canon 96).

From the Quinisext Ecumenical Council onward, the cases (in number and kind) of the sins of individuals that are covered by ecclesiastical canons are really astonishing. The canons seethe with the most incredible perversions, the most inventive forms of licentiousness—various kinds of bestiality, incest, homosexuality, and onanism. They extend over a very broad field of social crimes: usury, perjury, grave robbery, theft. They lay down demands for a blameless social life, especially for clerics. They objectify presuppositions for the validity of the sacraments, especially marriage, turning them into laws. They insist on the detailed regulation of marital relations between spouses.

Even if one approaches such canons in a very positive spirit, one cannot fail to discern the shadow of a new law, in many ways analogous to the Mosaic, that threatens the life of the Church. As if the struggle of the generation of the apostles to reject slavery to the law had not taken place—as if the Church were not the end, the transcendence, and the abolition of the religious version of the law—the canons bring back the distinction between "clean" and "unclean" objects, "clean" and "unclean" human beings. And it is not in the least strange that finally there is a canon "on not making a journey without necessity on a Sunday" (Canon 1 of the Seven Canons of Nicephorus, patriarch of Constantinople),[20] faithfully copying the Jewish law.

---

20. The *Sabbath journey* (the distance a Jew was permitted to walk on the Sabbath; see also Acts 1:12) was reckoned as 2,000 cubits (about 920 meters).

The juridicalization of the Christian outlook is a clear sign of the religionization of the ecclesial event, and religionization brings with it a reserve or a hidden fear especially about sexuality and the natural functioning of motherhood. There are canons that regard a woman who has recently given birth as "unclean" and forbid her from entering her child's bedroom if the infant has already been baptized.[21] Other canons forbid women from partaking of the eucharistic cup on days when they are menstruating; they regard the physiological function that serves the gift of motherhood as "unclean."[22] Others demand abstinence from marital relations both before and after communion.[23] Others deny ordination to anyone who has been sexually violated in childhood.[24] They also deny it to anyone who has had sexual relations outside marriage, even if he has lived a life of repentance that has resulted in a charismatic gift of working miracles, even of raising the dead.[25]

These canons lose sight of the boundaries differentiating the ecclesial perspective from an instinctive religiosity that demonizes the reproductive urge and socially marginalizes and depreciates women (treating them as propitiatory victims of the fear of women). Growing gradually in strength, religionization led to a host of supposedly "Christian" regulations shooting up like weeds, regulations that present a gloomy and inhuman legalism and moralism, a typically pathological fear of erotic love, as an "evangelical" rule of life. These regulations identify Christianity with associations of guilt and fear, with a legalistic stifling of life. They contribute to the elaboration of impressive codes of law, complex and labyrinthine bodies of casuistry—a dark area of narcissistic self-defensiveness and timorous resistance to growing up.

See Leonidas Philippidis, *Historia tēs epochēs tēs Kainēs Diathēkēs* (Athens, 1958), 462, 487. Isaac Bashevis Singer writes on Jewish legalism, "One law in the Torah generated a dozen in the Mishnah and five dozen in the Gemara; in the later commentaries laws were as numerous as the sands of the desert" (*The Slave* [London: Secker and Warburg, 1963], 117).

21. Canon 38 of Nicephorus, patriarch of Constantinople.
22. Canon 2 of Dionysius, archbishop of Alexandria.
23. Canon 5 of Timothy of Alexandria.
24. Canon of John the Faster "On Raving after Men."
25. Canon 36 of Nicephorus of Constantinople.

Instances are many and varied: the *Corpus Juris Canonici* of the Roman Catholics; the police-like moralism of the Calvinists; the pietism of the Lutherans; the puritanism of the Methodists, Baptists, and Quakers; the idolized Manichaeism of the Anabaptists, Old Apostolics, Zwinglians, Congregationalists, and Salvation Army. We find the same neurotic fundamentalism in the "Genuine Orthodox," both in Greece and in the Slavic countries.

Each of these groups and many more represent several generations of people, thousands or millions of human beings, who have lived their one unique life on earth in a hell of imaginary guilt, repressed desires, relentless anxiety, and narcissistic self-torture. Whole generations have been trapped unwittingly in the torment of legalism, in the disabled existence of a loveless life. They identified erotic love with the fear of sin, virtue with repugnance for their own body, and a perceptible expression of affection with disgust at a humiliating concession to the brutish side of human nature.

All this has taken place to serve an instinctive need for the guaranteed certainty of individual salvation, for the eternal safeguarding of the self.

3.4. *The Eucharistic Assembly as a Sacred Rite*

The *definition* of the Church (the realization and manifestation of the ecclesial event) is the eucharistic meal. It is there that the new *mode of existence* that ecclesial experience proclaims is *imaged*, that is, is potentially realized and manifested. Such a mode of existence is a mode of freedom from the limitations of createdness, an exploring of the possibilities of fullness of life and existence, an attaining of likeness to the *mode* of the Triadic Causal Principle of all that exists.

In the Eucharist we receive our food, the basis of our life. We receive it as bread and wine, as food that is representative and inclusive of every kind of nourishment sustaining human life. This receiving, however, is effected only as eucharistic communion. We attempt to experience the basic requirement of our life (the taking of food) not as an individual need but as a demand for communion—not in conformity with the urge of self-preservation but choosing to share the basic requirement of our life: we undertake to transform the natural necessity for preserving our existence into the act of communion or sharing (an event of freedom).

This undertaking, within the context of the eucharistic meal, is not a moral aim, nor is it simply a matter of intellectual resolve. It is an *imaging*, in the biblical sense of the word, where *image* means glory, that is, the *manifestation* of an ontological reality.[26] Our own activity is our coming together for the meal and our desire to share the bread and wine with our fellow human beings, our brothers and sisters—the same piece of bread and the same cup of wine. Up to this point our activity would not go beyond the didactic or sentimental dynamics of a symbolic rite.

For our activity to function as *image* (to realize the desire for partaking of life as a postulate), it must refer as a specific act (not as a concept) to a given (not hypothetical) existential event; it must refer to an ontological reality, to an attainable *mode of existence*. The eucharistic meal refers to the historical event of the *incarnation* of God *in the person of Jesus Christ*. The incarnation cannot be a circumstantial occurrence if it really does constitute a *mode of existence*, an ontological reality. This ontological reality is rendered an actual postulate (an act of *reference*) by the eucharistic meal.

In the Church's experience Christ is "the image of the invisible God" (Col 1:15; cf. 2 Cor 4:4). His being *images* (manifests dynamically) God's freedom from any predeterminations (limitations/necessities) of nature or essence. If Christ is God *in the flesh*, his historical presence confirms God's freedom from any predeterminations of divinity. And if Christ in reality "has risen from the dead," his resurrection reveals that on his incarnation he remained free even from the predeterminations of humanity.

The abstract concept "God" does not adequately manifest Christ's existential freedom from the necessities/predeterminations of divine and human nature. We have seen that this freedom is declared in the linguistic definition Son/Word of God the Father: Christ, as the incarnate *Son/Word* of *God the Father*, reveals the

26. See "Image" in Xavier Léon-Dufour, ed., *Dictionary of Biblical Theology*, 2nd ed. (London: Geoffrey Chapman, 1995), 223–25.

"accord" of the Son's will with the will of the Father's love.[27] The active will refers to the mode of freedom, and the "accord" of the wills is signified as the Son's *obedience* (cf. Phil 2:8), that is, as the freedom of love. Christ, in the language of the Church's experience, is free from the limitations of divinity and of humanity only because he loves the Father and his love, as freedom of *obedience* ("accord" of the wills), is the *mode of his existence*. The historical presence of the incarnate Son/Word is a *revelation* of freedom as love, and of love as unbounded existential freedom. Love is the causal "principle" of the voluntary sonship and the voluntary fatherhood in the incomprehensible mystery of the Triadic Godhead.

The eucharistic meal *images* (realizes in a dynamic fashion, or manifests) the ontological reality of the incarnation of God. What actual factors constitute the *image*? They may be summed up succinctly as the partakers (*oi koinōnountes*) of the meal, the things partaken of (*ta koinōnoumena*), and the goal of participation/communion (*koinōnia*).

The partakers are those who by the act of participating in the meal actively manifest their desire to exist in a state of love and because they love—or desire to renounce any demand for atomic existential self-sufficiency—in the measure of Christ's own *obedience*. The partakers of the food and the drink share in the nourishment/prerequisite of our individual onticity: free wills converge (in a specific act) in the common demand for existence to be shared in as love. And this convergence is an active remembrance (an *anamnēsis*)[28] of Christ's obedience to the ontopoeic and life-giving love of the Father. It is our conforming to this obedience: a *referring back* (*anaphora*) of our mortal life to the Father, in faith/trust/expectation of resurrection.

27. "I can do nothing on my own" (John 5:30); "The Son can do nothing on his own" (5:19); "The works that the Father has given me to complete, the very works that I am doing, testify on my behalf that the Father has sent me" (5:36).

28. "Do this in remembrance of me" (Luke 22:19); "For as often as you eat this bread and drink this cup, you proclaim the Lord's death until he comes" (1 Cor 11:26).

The things partaken of in the meal are bread and wine: basic and inclusive forms of our food that also recapitulate the annual cycle of human life (sowing and harvesting). We refer the prerequisite of our life back to the Father in order to actively manifest our desire to participate in the existential *mode* that Christ's incarnation revealed: a mode of freedom from the necessities and limitations of createdness. Christ revealed this *mode* not by imparting information (teachings or admonitions), but by the "signs"/works that he performed, his death on the cross, and his resurrection. He inaugurated (was the first to realize through establishing the power of its realization) our freedom from our human nature—the real flesh-and-blood existential power of transcending the limitations of createdness. The inauguration of this power is Christ's gift to humanity—that which in the Eucharist is called the grace of the Lord Jesus Christ and the love of God the Father and the fellowship (*koinōnia*) of the Holy Spirit—the Church's gospel.

Flesh and blood constitute each hypostasis of human nature; they are the real terms of real human existence. The flesh and blood of Christ hypostasize human nature that is free from the limitations of createdness; they are the real terms that hypostasize the grace/gift of God's love for humankind. The ecclesial event invites us to appropriate the gift likewise in terms of real existence, terms that are essential to existence, namely, food and drink. What is offered in the Eucharist is the grace/gift of freedom from createdness under the terms of the real incarnation of the gift (the body and blood of Christ). It is offered to us humans as food and drink, that is, as the vital prerequisite of our real existence: shared food, participation/communion (*koinōnia*) in bread and wine.[29]

29. "'I am the bread of life. Your ancestors ate the manna in the wilderness, and they died. This is the bread that comes down from heaven, so that one may eat of it and not die. I am the living bread that came down from heaven. Whoever eats of this bread will live forever; and the bread that I will give for the life of the world is my flesh.' The Jews then disputed among themselves, saying, 'How can this man give us his flesh to eat?' So Jesus said to them, 'Very truly, I tell you, unless you eat the flesh of the Son of Man and drink his blood, you have no life in you. Those who eat my flesh and drink my blood have eternal life, and I will raise them up on the last day; for my flesh is true food and my blood is true drink. Those who eat my flesh and drink my blood abide in me, and I in them. Just as the living Father sent me, and I live because of the Father, so whoever eats me

All these things (broken and distributed but not divided) are what are partaken of in the ecclesial Eucharist. Food (bread and wine) is partaken of as a real reference to the *mode* by which the Son shares existence with the Father. This same *mode* hypostasizes the incarnation of the Son; it is the body and blood of Christ—the existential reality of freedom from the limitations of createdness. In the Eucharist what is shared is the gift of participation in this *mode*, and the sharing of the gift is a reality: from one bread and one cup we receive the prerequisite of life. The gift is received by shared participation, not as something possessed individually, in such a way that the actual reception is also a real offering, with nothing objectified as a support for a privately possessed individual guarantee. "Your own of your own we offer to you."

Nothing is objectified as a definitive given fact in the eucharistic meal, the ecclesial event. The ontological reality of the flesh and blood of Christ, the *mode* of freedom from createdness, cannot be an object that the human individual can possess and have sovereignty over. The bread and wine of the Church's Eucharist can never be a religiously sacralized magic fetish offered for individual consumption so as to guarantee individual salvation.

Nevertheless, the religionization of the ecclesial event has in many situations and historical periods succeeded, progressively and imperceptibly, in making even the eucharistic meal subject to the demands of egocentric priorities. A vital achievement of religionization was to turn the food and drink that is shared into a supernatural object in itself, an interpretation that results in the satisfaction of the instinctive religious need of the natural individual to possess the miracle, the mystery, and the validity, as an object. The miracle, the mystery, and the validity are summarized and objectified in the sensible forms of bread and wine thanks to the idea of their *transubstantiation* in the Eucharist.

The term *transubstantiation* (*transsubstantiatio*, a change of essence or nature) first began to be used in the Roman Catholic

---

will live because of me. This is the bread that came down from heaven, not like that which your ancestors ate, and they died. But the one who eats this bread will live forever'" (John 6:49–58).

Church in about the twelfth century—one century after the definitive extinction of Latin ecclesial Orthodoxy in the West and the predominance of the *parvenu* (in terms of both Christianity and culture) Franks. The term is used to answer the disputed question whether the bread and wine of the Eucharist really are the body and blood of Christ. Objections were first raised by the Frankish theologian Berengar of Tours (ca. 1000–88). In order to refute his views, Hildebert, archbishop of Tours (1055–1133), employed for the first time the term *transsubstantiatio*: what appeared to be bread was in its essence the flesh of Christ, and what appeared to be wine was in its essence the blood of Christ.

The term was officially adopted in the West by the Fourth Lateran Council (1215) and thereafter also penetrated the Greek East. It was translated as *metousiōsis* and was used for the first time by the emperor Michael VIII Palaiologos (1224–82) in a letter addressed to Pope Gregory X. It was later borrowed by Gennadios Scholarios (1398–1472) and subsequently defended in the *Confessions of Faith* of Peter Moghila, metropolitan of Kiev (1638–42), and of Dositheos, patriarch of Jerusalem (1672), both of which have a Roman Catholic coloring, as well as in the "Orthodox" *Dogmatics* of Christos Androutsos (1907) and Panayiotis Trembelas (1961), compositions of a similar Roman Catholic character.

The controversy surrounding the term *transsubstantiatio* runs through medieval and modern European history—from Thomas Aquinas and Albert the Great to Descartes, Hume, and Hegel.[30] The disputes were intensified chiefly when Protestantism aggressively rejected the notion of *transubstantiation*. Luther, for his part, resorted to the intellectual subterfuge that the nature/essence of the bread and the wine of the Eucharist was not transformed but that somehow "in" and "under" the bread and the wine (*in et sub pane et vino*) there is present the body and the blood of Christ, which are transmitted only "in the use" (*in usu*) of the sacrament. Calvin and Zwingli are more forthright. They described the forms of the bread and the wine of the Eucharist as *symbols* only: stimuli for the

30. See Matthias Laarmann, "Transubstantiation," in the *Historisches Wörterbuch der Philosophie*, ed. J. Ritter, K. Gründer, and G. Gabriel, 13 vols. (Basel: Schwabe-Verlag, 1971–2007), 10:1349–58.

remembrance of the sacrifice of Christ on the cross, sensible signs that can transmit some kind of grace and power to us when we receive them as common food and drink.

Both the reception and the refutation of the *transubstantiation* of the bread and wine of the Eucharist appear to be approaches equally enmeshed in the terms of the religionization of the ecclesial event. The first term of religionization (its starting point and causal principle) is in the *individualization* of participation in the Eucharist, which also entails the *objectification* of participation. The reception of the bread and the wine is isolated, separated from participation in the event of sharing in the relations that constitute the Eucharist (the eucharistic body of the Church)—communion becomes an atomic event, unrelated to existential change, to a change in the *mode* of existence.

I define as *atomic* an event that is exhausted within the terms of the needs and aims of the individual, whereupon it is inevitably judged by the standard of the satisfaction of individual demands, of individual usefulness, benefit, and efficacity. Thus even the eucharistic species, from an individualistic perspective, are assessed principally for what they are in themselves—their reality is defined—with a view to judging how far they respond to individual religious need. Are they simply *symbols* and *representations* (*figurae, similitudines*) of the body and blood of Christ, or are we dealing with "a change of essence into another essence that happens instantaneously, with the accidents (of the bread and the wine) remaining unchanged"?[31]

The religious need of individuals is to know, with certainty and assurance, what exactly they are eating and drinking in the eucharistic meal. Are they being offered the incarnate Godhead with the elements being received only under the appearance of bread and wine, or is that which they receive in communion to be identified with what it appears to be, and is it only in an allegorical fashion that the bread and the wine recall the incarnate divinity of Christ (refer to it on an intellectual level)? Instinctive religiosity demands

---

31. K. Dyovouniotis, *Ta mystēria tēs Anatolikēs Orthodoxou Ekklēsias* (Athens, 1912), 101.

an "objective" reply, substantiated knowledge that assures the individual—that understands the existential event only through the guarantee of the individual properties of a specific onticity.

It is impossible for natural religiosity to understand that the bread and the wine of the Eucharist *are* Christ's body and blood because Christ's incarnation too was and is an *ontological* reality, a *mode of existence* of human nature, not an objective change of nature (a transubstantiation) of one human individual, not a supernatural artifice or shamanistic miracle. Christ's incarnation did not violate human nature; it only overcame the conditions of nature, the limitations of createdness. "The conditions of nature are overcome" not by the intervention of some supernatural power but only by the *self-emptying* (*kenosis*) of the Son—by the fact that in the historical person of Christ human nature realizes the relationship that the Son has with the Father.

This ontological reality is constituted on the basis of, and is manifested (*imaged*, with the biblical sense of the *image*) in the fact of, the Eucharist. The bread and the wine are transformed into Christ's body and blood, not because some supernatural power intervenes and violates the laws of nature, "transubstantiating" the bread and the wine, but because the participants in the meal share the presupposition of their life (food and wine) as a repetition of Christ's *self-emptying*. In receiving the bread and the wine, the participants in the meal realize, with the prerequisites of their human nature, the relationship that the Son has with the Father: existence as loving communion, life as renunciation of any demand for self-enclosed existence. And "the conditions of nature are overcome": communion of the bread and wine is a sharing in the flesh and blood of Christ, in the mode of existence that constitutes the Church.

Only the totality of all the factors that make up the unique event of Christ's incarnation can shed light on how a meal can constitute a mode of existence, the Church, and on how the bread and the wine of our daily food are transformed into a sharing or communion of Christ's body and blood. It is not a sanctified (supernatural) fetish that is partaken of but an existential event: created nature free from the conditions of createdness. The whole of creation is partaken of in *the freedom of the glory of the children of God*: past time (the eucharistic *anamnēsis*) and the experiential present (the struggle to love that constitutes the Church) are partaken of together with the eschatological future (the hope and expectation of the nontemporal "kingdom").

Slowly and imperceptibly the religionization of the ecclesial event also brought with it an alienated interpretation of the eucharistic meal: the substitution of the *ontological* reality that is *imaged* in the Eucharist by atomic psychological demands. A religionized outlook interprets the Eucharist not as the realization and manifestation of the Church (of the ecclesial *mode of existence*, a mode of communion with life) but as a sacred rite objectively enacted (by a predetermined officiant), a rite that offers individually to each person "attending" the possibility of receiving as communion a supernatural gift, a "fire" that consumes atomic sins and purifies the atomic mind, the atomic "soul and heart," together with the human body, giving assurance of a guaranteed eternal life.

This alienation of the ecclesial character of the Eucharist (its relations of communion), this predominance of priorities centered on the individual, appears fully formed as early as the thirteenth century (at least in the Orthodox East, as a product of a very obvious alignment with the much earlier religionization of Christianity in the Frankish West). The end result finds characteristic expression in a collection of hymns and prayers belonging to what is still called today the *Office of Holy Communion*.[32]

The aim of the office is to prepare each Christian individually for receiving the bread and the wine of the Eucharist. Both the hymns and the prayers have been composed in the first person singular; they are prayers for the individual that all seek to make the individual worthy and capable of receiving the body and blood of Christ as an individual. There is no mention of participation in a

32. [For the text of the office, see, conveniently, "Akolouthia tēs Theias Metalēpseōs," in *Hiera Synopsis* (Athens: Kampana, n.d.), 279–300; translated into English as "The Service of Preparation for Holy Communion" and "Thanksgiving after Holy Communion," in *A Prayer Book for Orthodox Christians*, trans. Holy Transfiguration Monastery (Brookline, MA: Holy Transfiguration Monastery, 1987), 321–65. – trans.]

gift shared with brothers and sisters; any reference (even an indirect one) to relations of communion, to the formation of the ecclesial body, is missing. The office would have been the same even if the transformation of the bread and wine could have been accomplished without the Eucharist taking place or in the absence of the assembly of brothers and sisters.

The whole focus of the prayers and hymns is on the interest of the petitioner in securing a personal assurance, on the annulment of personal sins, on having one's personal unworthiness overlooked. The concern is that the Christian as an individual should receive the supernatural gifts "without guilt" and "without condemnation." The fact that the ecclesial event, the existence of fellow communicant brothers and sisters, is emphatically ignored is truly astonishing.[33]

The hymns and prayers of the office refer to the species offered for communion with definitions, descriptions, and meanings that clearly presuppose an objectified sense of "transubstantiation." And it is natural that this form of expression should prevail the moment the ecclesial character of communion (relations of *koinōnia*) was bypassed or ignored.

33. In the Church's collections of holy canons, there is included a letter by Basil the Great, *To the Patrician Caesaria on How Often We Should Receive Holy Communion* (see Hamilcar Alivizatos, *Hoi Hieroi Kanones* [Athens, 1949], 398). If the letter is genuine, the information it gives us is astonishing. It testifies to the fact that already in the fourth century it is taken for granted, even by a "great luminary" of the Church like Basil, that the reception of the eucharistic gifts may be detached from communion at the meal and participation in the assembly of the ecclesial *body* or *mode of existence*, and may function according to the terms and practices of a need and use centered on the individual: "All those living as monks in the deserts where there is no priest and they possess communion at home may communicate themselves. In Alexandria and in Egypt, laypeople for the most part have communion in their own homes and when they wish to do so communicate by themselves. For once the priest has completed the sacrifice and given it, he who takes it and communicates from it every day should believe that he is receiving communion from the priest. For in the church too the priest gives a portion in addition and he who receives it keeps it with all authority and thus puts it to his mouth with his own hand. It is therefore possible for him to receive either one portion from the priest, or many portions all together."

Of course the prayers that make up the office are attributed to leading Church Fathers: two prayers to Basil the Great, four to John Chrysostom, two to John Damascene, one to Symeon the New Theologian, and one to Symeon Metaphrastes. No historico-literary study, however, has addressed the question: Within what context of needs and with what aim have these prayers dating from various centuries (fourth, eighth, tenth, and eleventh—if they were really written by the Fathers to whom they are attributed and are not pseudonymous) been composed? And to what extent does their inclusion in the Office of Holy Communion place them in a context that reflects the original intentions of their authors?

Participation in relations of communion undoubtedly presupposes the denial or overcoming of egocentric priorities—which is why participation in the ecclesial event is also defined by Christian experience as an effort (an ascetic struggle) to attain loving self-transcendence. The ascetic struggle—the preparation of the individual, the readiness in practice for communion—is presupposed for participation in the eucharistic meal. The Apostle Paul, in the very earliest years of the Church, speaks of the need for this kind of preparation of the individual believer before the eucharistic meal (1 Cor 11:17–34).

The individual's preparation/asceticism/effort, however, which has participation in relations of communion as its goal, is something radically different from any corresponding effort that aims at individualistic goals, even the most "sacred." The individual pursuit of self-denial, when undertaken for the sake of the fullest possible participation in relations of loving mutual indwelling, belongs to one order of reality, and the aim of individual purification from guilt, of gaining individual merit, and of securing individual salvation belongs to an entirely different order.

The texts (hymns and prayers) that make up the Office of Holy Communion all have aims that can only be described as directed toward securing individual benefits and guarantees. They are texts that serve exclusively egotistic concerns for the remission of faults, atonement, purification, and "sanctification." There is not the slightest suggestion that might allow us to infer that what is requested is not fully satisfied by the justification or armoring of the ego, or that what is requested is needed to enable individuals to transcend themselves, to be freed from the natural instincts of attaining self-security, to participate in the ecclesial *mode of existence*. There is no hint of anything along these lines.

When the central purpose of the eucharistic meal, the reception of bread and wine, is alienated into the pursuit of a security centered on the individual, then inevitably every other element of the Eucharist ceases imperceptibly to function as a starting point and springboard for relations of communion. The Eucharist becomes something good that is offered for individual consumption—a private possession on the sensory, emotional, and didactic levels.

If Greek civilization has left its imprint on the historical flesh of the ecclesial Eucharist (on its ritual, its music, its poetry, its iconography, its architecture—all the elements that go into making up the eucharistic event, that contribute to its celebration), it is precisely because that civilization summed up a long tradition of art that was centered on society as a whole, not on the individual. The tradition (and its high achievements) was the result of an endeavor to make art serve the *city* (the *polis*—the struggle to attain relations of communion), not the benefit or enjoyment of the *private individual*.

It may be said, broadly speaking, that the characteristic identity of Greek art was always defined by its *symbolic* character, its character as a *symbol*. The sensible form does not signify (or manifest) *itself*; it functions as a *sign* referring to the *essence* of what is represented (Classical Greece) or to the *hypostasis* of what is represented (Christian Hellenism). The sensible form "passes over to the prototype,"[34] that is, it refers to the immediacy of the *relation* with that which is really existent (the *ontōs on*), and is the foundation of this relation.

At the same time, with a view to functioning as a *symbol*, the sensible form (the work of art) constitutes (in Greek, *syn-ballei*, "puts together") every atomic relation/approach to experience of the *prototype*: this experience is shared in ("it is participated in

34. Basil the Great of Caesarea, *On the Holy Spirit* 45 (PG 32:149C).

by all and is participated in by all separately")—whether what is shared in is the given *logos*/essence of each existent thing (Classical Greece), or whether it is the hypostasis/person and the action of the person's freedom (Christian Hellenism).

This effort that all the elements of the eucharistic meal should function as an occasion and event for relations of communion (with not only the bread and the wine being shared but also the melody, the poetry, the painting, the ritual, the light, the decoration—nothing being intended for individual consumption), this effort is nullified in all its manifestations when the central aim of the Eucharist is regarded as the "purification" and the salvation of the individual.

We need a special study that would trace the history of the gradual subjection of the various elements of the eucharistic event to purposes that serve religiosity, that are centered on the individual. Such a study would shed light on how and where this alienation developed, under what historical and social conditions it developed, and why it was established so easily, with scarcely any resistance.

In the architectural formation and internal organization of the liturgical space, in the ritual, the singing, the composition of the texts, the painting, the lighting, the style of delivery—in every aspect—didactic aims came to predominate along with emotional prompting, sentimental euphoria, enthusiastic elation, and romantic feeling—all of them priorities centered on the individual. The purpose was that people should be impressed as individuals, that they should be moved psychologically, that their instinctive need for metaphysical security should be satisfied, that they should appropriate the transcendent.

In the modern era, under different cultural conditions when the institution of the empire was nearing collapse, state ceremonial was simplified considerably: attempts to project displays of majesty were curtailed; the ways in which subjects were influenced psychologically changed. Yet even this vital change in practice and outlook on the level of state authority did not influence in the least degree the religious leadership of the so-called Christian world. With ingenious justifications of supposedly liturgical symbolism, ecclesial worship, centered on the eucharistic event, manifests itself as alienated in a ritual deliberately designed to present a religious spectacle. Costly vestments of Byzantine emperors or medieval kings; golden scepters, miters, and tiaras studded with precious stones; gold and enamel *enkolpia* and pectoral crosses; and princely mantles with long trains transform those who serve the Liturgy into exotic images of once mighty rulers, who continue as religious leaders (prelates, pontiffs, primates, bishops) to exercise supreme authority and powers. This is precisely what is demanded by the natural individual's instinctive need for religion.

Most certainly it is not sufficient for the retrieval of the ecclesial event that there should be a rational and programmatic "simplification" of liturgical worship. The criterion of authenticity is not moralistic; it is not the renunciation of vainglory, or of ostentatious luxury, or of autocratic arrogance. The criterion of authenticity is only the retrieval of the *communitarian* character of the Church, the return to the relations of *communion* that constitute and manifest the ecclesial event.

The Protestant confessions successfully carried out a program of "simplifying" the form of worship, but they remained fixed in religious individualism with no inkling of the ecclesial *mode of existence*. That is why the result itself of the "simplification" was only another even more tragic decline to a level of naive didacticism, juvenile hymn singing, and an infantile approach to metaphysical questions. The fact that Protestantism has produced some excellent academic theologians has had no effect on the simplistic and naive character of its worship.

3.5. *Art in the Service of Impressing, Teaching, and Stirring the Emotions*

In speaking of art, we are referring to a variety of "languages": to different *modes* of expressing/sharing experience.

Variety among these languages is created by the differences of the "signifiers"—the "medium," the "material" of expression. In poetry and every kind of literature, the signifiers are words/concepts/

sentences (the material of the common language). In music they are sounds; in painting, shape and color; and in sculpture and architecture, the shaping (the syntax, or putting together) of solid materials.

Syntax is the defining (syntactic) element of the language—in every art artists (makers, creators) are distinguished (and differentiated) by their ability to put together their material, to attain an ever more lucidly articulated expression. The syntax puts together the signifiers in a mode that corresponds either to the way the language/art is *representative* of reality (*images* it), or to the way it *allegorizes* it or *alludes* to it. These two modes of syntax, or putting together, are not formally differentiated. Usually they are contrasted, but sometimes they also interpenetrate each other.

When the relationship between language/art and reality is representational, the syntax tends to serve utilitarian priorities: it informs, describes, narrates, teaches, demonstrates, decorates, gives pleasure. When the relationship is allegorical/allusive, the syntax refers through the signifiers to a signified *meaning* of reality, and the priorities are more "revelatory" and less "representational."

In the second instance, language/art functions as a *sign*: it *signifies* something other than its own syntactic integrity, its own morphological sufficiency, its own thematic vividness—it constitutes an allegory (in the etymological sense of "saying something else"). Language/art in this case calls one (is an invitation) to "pass over to the prototype," to ascend from the modes of *phenomenicity* to the mode of *truth*, the mode of real *existence*.

In the case, for example, of ancient Greek art (whether of the sculpture of the classical period, or of its architecture or drama), the artist, by remaining realistically faithful to sensible reality, seeks to transcend the contingent and circumstantial features of given atomicities (or of a specific physical environment) so that by the abstraction of these features he might lead the viewer who communes with the work to the vision/contemplation of the principle of the *essence* of what is represented: the intellectual principle/mode (incorruptible, immutable, nontemporal, immortal—the *really existent*) that makes the sensible atomicity be that which it *is*.

When wanting to represent Aphrodite, for example, an ancient Greek sculptor did not seek to fashion a copy of a particular beautiful woman (as later an artist of the European Renaissance would do). He sought to abstract all the contingent (atomic) features of every beautiful woman and to express in his work the features that endowed *every* beautiful woman with the beauty of femininity—to express the *essence/idea* of feminine beauty. That is why his work was an *agalma* (the general Greek word for a statue, meaning "a glory" or "a delight"), for it produced the exaltation that the vision of truth produces.

The same was true for an architect in ancient Greece. He sought to express in his building those principles (*logoi*, here "relations") of harmony of architectural members that *allegorized* the given laws of the order and symmetry of the universe. He wanted to decode and manifest in his work the relations of analogy (*ana-logia*), complementarity, and proportionality of masses that make material reality into a *cosmos* (an ordered world, or adornment)—that differentiate existence and life from disorder, disproportionality, and irrationality. An architect wanted to show how formlessness and absence of order can be endowed with rationality and form and made into a cosmos that was *truly good/beautiful* (*ontōs kalon*). He also wanted to show how, conversely, sharing in what is needful (*koinōnia tēs chreias*) can be transformed into true communion (*koinōnia kat' alētheian*), that is, into a *polis*, with the same principles/laws of cosmic harmony: the moral potentialities of life.

In what is wrongly called "Byzantium"—the Hellenized empire of New Rome/Constantinople—art had a similar function. Its function was similar because the aim was the same: that art should mean the call to "pass over" from phenomenicity to truth, to the *true* (the "real," *ontōs*) *mode of existence*.

Naturally, in Christian Hellenism the location of truth was not the same; the "really existent" is no longer the uninterpreted (but subject to given laws) *rationality* that constitutes and governs the cosmos. The fact of existence is no longer predetermined by the common rational principle, nor is it exhausted in the aim of endowing with form. Now the truly existent is the *person* as the primary existential given: an independent hypostasis of self-conscious freedom, freedom that is realized existentially/hypostatically as love, as self-transcendence and self-offering.

Furthermore, the change in the location of the truly existent also changed the syntax of language/art, the morphological expression of the signifiers, their functional use. In the "Byzantine" icon, for example, the syntax remains as abstractive as in the ancient Greek statue. Now, however, the abstraction of the accidents (which would have tied the scene to natural atomicity) invites the viewer to "pass over" not from an intellectual perception of the individual to the universal *essence/idea* but from a viewing/contemplation to relation/communion: to approaching the *prototype* of the icon (the hypostatic otherness to which the icon refers) through the struggle to transcend the self, to attain a relationship of love.

At any rate, both in the case of ancient Greek art and in that of the Hellenizing art of the Church (so-called "Byzantine" art), what is aimed at is the detection and demonstration of the *meaning* of the existent. The objective is that art should function as an invitation to work back to this *meaning*, to participate in the sharing of the *meaning*. Ancient Greek and "Byzantine" art served the struggle of metaphysical inquiry; they did not serve "convictions," "certainties," or "teachings" supporting religious (individual-centered) self-sufficiency.

It could be argued that the syntax that serves the *representational* relationship between language/art and reality corresponds preeminently to the demands of an individualistic (instinctive) religiosity. Religious language/art wants to teach, to inculcate convictions and regulative principles, to move people emotionally as individuals, to put suggestions to them, to offer them a sense of euphoria, of mystical experience. Religious language/art "narrates" supernatural events, represents didactic scenes, decorates the liturgical space in an evocative manner, and constitutes it (shapes it) with the aim of impressing individuals, of affecting them psychologically, of compelling respect for the authenticity of the supernatural, for the authority of the "sacred."

That is why the religionization of the ecclesial event also entails the alienation of the Church's language/art, its falling away from a *revelatory* (allegorical, hinting at the *meaning* of what exists) syntax to one that is merely *representational*.

Where there is religionization, language ceases to serve an apophatic expression and art ceases to function as a metaphysical quest. The *terms* (boundaries) of shared ecclesial experience are transformed into *dogmas* (obligatory individual convictions), and the Image in the painting of portraits comes to represent real atomicities. Language and art become subordinated to the instinctive demands of the natural individual, enabling the signified reality to be objectified so that the individual can control it, can possess it. Metaphysics comes to be presented under the terms and with the presuppositions of physics.

Religious language and religious art are addressed to natural individuals, to the understanding of individuals, to their psychological needs, their moral will. They presuppose individuals as impersonal units of a homogeneous whole, as undifferentiated receivers and users. They seek the greatest possible "objectivity" so that the reception/use of language and art should be uniformly accessible to all the undifferentiated individuals. Thus religious language obeys the rules of a commonly received *rational method* that affirms and absolutizes the capacities of the individual intellect. And religious art obeys a commonly recognizable morphological representation of given natural facts (which we call *naturalism*).

When language and art are coordinated with the instinctive religious need of the natural individual, they lose their social dynamic: a dynamic of invitation to relations of communion, to shared participation in existential otherness. By serving the objectivity of word and image, religious language and art bypass the subjectivity of the recipient. That is, they cooperate in an external and coercive subjection of the subject to the objective (general and undifferentiated) necessities of nature—they undermine existential otherness itself, the subject's potential freedom from nature.

Religionization has followed the ecclesial event from the first moments of its constitution and appearance—in a later chapter I shall offer a brief historical review of the process. But the possibility, the temptation, or the aberrations alone of religionization do not constitute a threat of alienation of the ecclesial event. What constitutes a threat is the institutionalization of the aberration. And we begin to discern an institutionalized religionization of ecclesial language and art in a specific historical period and geographical area: in Central and Western Europe a few centuries after the collapse of the Western Roman Empire (AD 476) and the gradual marginalization there of Latin Orthodoxy. Religionization is institutionalized in the context of the new reality that emerged in the West with the invasion and settlement (from the end of the fourth century and chiefly in the fifth and sixth centuries) of (then) barbarian tribes (Goths, Franks, Huns, Burgundians, Vandals, Lombards, Normans, Angles, and Saxons) that swiftly embraced Christianity.

Responsibility for a superficial conversion to Christianity, and for the alienation and religionization of the ecclesial event, cannot be laid on the peoples who in that period could not possibly have perceived the difference between the Church and a religion. It was impossible for them to follow the then prevailing Greek expression (in language and art) of this difference. This expression derived from and summarized the centuries-old struggle of the Greek world in the fields of philosophy and art, a struggle (a "battle of the giants about essence," that is, about the enigma of existence) assimilated by ecclesial experience and finally able to illuminate the most penetrating and fruitful questions ever posed by human thought.

The new populations in Central and Western Europe rapidly adopted Christianity because Christianity was synonymous with access to civilization. Slowly, by a consistent process of evolution, these peoples began to attain a civilized way of life, so that after many centuries they came to make advances hitherto unknown in human history. They were led to create their own cultural paradigm, at the opposite pole to the Greco-Roman paradigm but with extremely impressive achievements—the first and hitherto only civilization with an incomparable global reach.

The peoples of the West, however, at their first (and, for their historical development, definitive) reception of Christianity did not see in it anything other than, or more than, a fuller satisfaction of their instinctive religious needs. A separate study would be necessary to describe with the necessary evidence and to analyze the historical steps of these peoples from the first beginnings toward the institutionalization of the alienation of the ecclesial event. Here I will limit myself to a few brief comments from the field of art.

In the first centuries after their conversion, the new populations of the West imitated the ecclesiastical art, architecture, and painting either of the Greek and Latin missionaries who transmitted the Church's gospel to them or of the native Christian inhabitants whom they had made subject. The so-called *Romanesque style* in architecture and the *maniera bizantina* in painting flourished from the fifth to about the twelfth century. And in both cases borrowings were combined from both the Latino-Roman and the Greco-Roman traditions.

These seven centuries appear to have been an indispensable period of imitation until such time as the religionization of the Church in the West became discernible naturally and undisguisedly in its art. By the twelfth century the severance of the new European Christianity from the historical Greek flesh of ecclesial experience—its departure from the *terms* (boundaries) that distinguish the ecclesial event from a natural religion—had been formally accomplished. First there had been the so-called *First Schism* of 867—the condemnation, by a great council of the remaining patriarchates meeting at New Rome/Constantinople, of arbitrary theological innovations and claims to universal jurisdiction asserted by a Rome now under Frankish control. This was followed by the second and definitive or *Great Schism* of 1054, which institutionalized the severance and differentiation that by then were well established.

The Frankish West's rupture was not only with the Greek East; it was also with Latin ecclesial Orthodoxy—a severance of what was then a minority in the Christian world from the body of the whole (*catholic* in the sense of *ecumenical*) Church. Of course, from as early as 1014 (when a Frank was elected pope for the first time), the Franks had begun to dishonestly appropriate the Latin tradition in a falsified form—just as later (when the Turks had removed Hellenism from the historical scene) they also appropriated the historical continuity of the Roman Empire (falsifying the thousand-year flowering of the Greco-Roman world centered on New Rome/Constantinople by calling it "Byzantium") and just as they appropriated, without any historical justification, an exclusive right to manage the ancient Greek cultural heritage.

From the twelfth century onward, art in the West begins to express the fully accomplished religionization of the ecclesial event—with a clarity perhaps greater than that of theological language. In so-called "Gothic"[35] architecture (technically, of course, of great brilliance both in conception and execution), a religious/ideological intentionality is clearly dominant: the structure of Gothic buildings is meant to impress, to have a psychological impact on the individual, to suggest a sense of the majesty of the building and of the institution that is to be identified with the building. Human beings are meant to feel small and insignificant, and therefore feel awe and reverence for the power of religious authority.

We are at the opposite pole to ancient Greek and Byzantine architecture. The techniques of Gothic construction are not the product of a struggle to express reverence for the rational possibilities of matter—the possibilities that matter should give flesh to him who is without flesh and should comprehend him who is incomprehensible, that the building should manifest the ecclesial body of the Word. On the contrary, in Gothic architecture the material is forced, is tamed rationally, in order to serve psychological purposes or ideological designs.

---

35. I quote the brief but comprehensive entry in the Eleutheroudaki *Concise Encyclopedic Dictionary* [in Greek] (Athens, 1935): "The Gothic style, chiefly a style of architecture, has nothing to do with the Goths but was named thus—by Raphael (Rafaello Santi or Sanzio, 1483–1520)—as a 'barbarian art' in contrast to the classical. It first began to be developed in the twelfth century in NW Europe and was the dominant style for the rest of the Middle Ages. Its characteristic features are the pointed arch and the emphasis on soaring lines. The oldest and most beautiful monuments of this art are churches and public buildings found in NW Europe (Notre Dame of Paris, the cathedrals of Rheims, Amiens, Antwerp, Dijon, Canterbury, Cologne and Upsala, Westminster Abbey and the town halls of Louvain, Ghent, Mons, etc.)."

An intricate interweaving of piers and columns, majestic proportions, a rationally based static equilibrium—all deliberately tend to present a sensible image of authority, of transcendent power, of an institution of monolithic strength and authoritative management of the revelations and commandments of the Godhead. A Gothic church is not a building that is intended to house and express a eucharistic meal shared by brothers and sisters, an *ecclesia* of communion of persons. It is a brilliant architectural monument to the human ambition that there should be represented on earth the might of the transcendent, the awesome psychological authority "to bind and to loose" that has been entrusted to the institution.[36]

From the thirteenth century the Greek style—the style named much later the *maniera bizantina*—was definitively abandoned in painting too. In the work of Giotto, Lorenzetti, Martini, and Cimabue, there begins to be apparent a *naturalistic* representation of persons, landscapes, and historical events. This of course had been preceded by an even more "realistic" style of sculpture: statues that fill Western churches from as early as the twelfth century—with colored statues as the crowning achievement of an aestheticistic naturalism (e.g., of the cathedrals of Volterra or Naumberg).

The unique *sense* of the existent (the anagogical reference to its true reality) is now for Western art its "natural" character, its "objective" fidelity to individual original models. Art presents reality in such a manner that the latter can be mastered by the senses and intellect of the individual, can be subjected to the potentialities of a positive and effective knowledge that is not subject to doubt. In the fourteenth century, and definitively from the beginning of the fifteenth, it seems that there was no longer any search for truth in the visual arts beyond the dimensional aspects of individuality approached in a naturalistic fashion.

---

36. I have discussed Gothic architecture, its relationship to scholastic theology, and how it compares with ancient Greek and "Byzantine" architecture more fully in my *The Freedom of Morality*, trans. Elizabeth Briere (Crestwood, NY: St. Vladimir's Seminary Press, 1984), chap. 12 (see the third revised edition, *Hē eleutheria tou ēthous* [Athens: Ikaros, 2002], where I give an ample bibliography).

In the work, for example, of Van Eyck, Pisanello, or Van der Weyden, the style (use of colors, composition, figures, background) is wholly subjected to the demands of a cognitive certainty that is provided, as immediacy of experience, only through the senses. The "real" is manifested in the portrayal of the "natural" and "objective"; it is perceived only as a response to the subjective sense of the dimensional, of the ontic.

A realistic visual representation wants to subject atomic optics to psychological intentionalities centered on the individual. It wants to teach, but also to stir the emotions "objectively," to make the impressions that define and exhaust the meaning of what is represented subject to the individual's senses. Hence too the optical illusions, the lines of perspective, the receding background, the *trompe l'oeil* effects, and the play of *chiaroscuro* that become the artist's means of moving the emotions, of stimulating our nervous system, of producing a sense of euphoria in us: a sense of resurrection, of exaltation.

It is the subject matter of works of art (and that alone) that distinguishes the "secular" from the "religious"—the received historical "sanctity" of persons, events, or landscapes determines the religious character of the picture. The same persons and objects portrayed are those of the experience of dimensional space and measurable time—there is no ambition or need on the part of the artist to transcend the fleeting phenomenicity of ontic atomicities.

Consequently, in the West's religious painting any young woman can be the model for a representation of the Virgin Mary, or any young man can lend his form for a representation of Christ or a saint. Any landscape can substitute for the place of the apocalyptic "signs" of the gospels. The bodiless angels are represented like beings endowed with flesh and the density of materiality. Even the Causal Principle of all that exists, who is inaccessible to any definition—the invisible, unimaginable, incomprehensible, inexpressible, unnameable *Father*—is represented as a white-haired old man. And the Paraclete, the life-giving *Spirit* of the Father, is shown as a well-fed pigeon!

Oppressively this-worldly, religious painting functions in a way that is subject to the idolized demands of instinctive religiosity. It knows nothing of any attempt "to pass over to the prototype"—to refer to the reality of personal hypostasis, the principle of personal activities. It represents the world of the senses ideologically sacralized, that is, trapped in predeterminations by the atomic intellect, by atomic psychological need.

This kind of art expressed the religionization of the ecclesial event in the West and still expresses it today—with changes of style reflecting current trends. The same kind of art was also borrowed by the Orthodox East, immediately after the headlong religionization of the ecclesial event began there too.

First it was Russian Christianity that unhesitatingly adopted the naturalistic religious art of the West within the context of the more general Westernization imposed by the reforms of Peter the Great (end of the seventeenth to the beginning of the eighteenth centuries). This was followed from the nineteenth century to the present day by the eager (and therefore radical) Westernization of life and the concomitant religionization of the ecclesial event by the Greeks, Serbs, Romanians, and Bulgarians, who drew in their wake the ancient patriarchates of the East. In all these local churches (and even on the Holy Mountain), there was no resistance to the abandonment of ecclesiastical iconography and to the widespread use of the naturalistic style of religious art.

Far fewer centuries were needed for what had happened earlier in the medieval West to be accomplished in the modern East—without this time the existence in advance of any *schism*, that is, a visible break with some (historically active) authentic remnant of the ecclesial event. Fidelity to the Orthodox formulation of "dogmatic" teaching or to some continuity that has been preserved in forms of worship creates in many people the illusion that a vital difference continues to exist between Eastern and Western Christianity. Art, however, not being controlled by ideological choices, confirms very convincingly that an "unconsciously" accomplished assimilation has taken place, that is, that the religionization of the majority of the Christian world, in both the West and the East, has finally been brought about.

In what are still called "Orthodox churches," there continues to be celebrated every year the *Sunday of Orthodoxy*, a feast celebrating the Restoration of Icons in 843, when the ecclesial language of the icons was saved from the attack of the *iconoclasts*—when the ecclesial consciousness that is expressed in the art of the Church's icons was preserved. Iconoclasm was a typical example of a religious outlook that idolizes intellectual concepts and moral teachings, that refuses to risk attaining relation/communion, to risk "passing over" to the "prototype" of the personal hypostasis of being.

The Restoration of the Icons continues to be celebrated by the "Orthodox," but in churches where ecclesiastical icons no longer exist, where naturalistic religious painting predominates either entirely or for the most part. Representations of sensible and ephemeral reality, making idols of sentimental feelings and of a naive didacticism, are honored and carried in procession in the place of the icons, without any idea that the feast is being celebrated with its terms—terms/signifiers of the Church's gospel—completely overturned.

Art loudly and implacably proclaims the Church's religionization. Conceptual language has artifices for hiding alienation, for disguising the fake—and so does religious piety: it is superb at maintaining the illusion of authenticity. Art, however, is not good at subterfuges. It inevitably reveals the *mode* by which those who practice it and those who choose it see reality and endow it with meaning—art cannot hide the needs that it serves. The Gothic style in the Middle Ages (and, successively, the baroque, the rococo, and the neoclassical forms of architecture) clearly sought to provide a setting for religious rites, not to house the event of the Church's Eucharist. The churches built in the "Orthodox" countries from the nineteenth century to the present day have the same aim: they cry out that they are utterly unrelated to the eucharistic event and the eucharistic ethos—they serve an individualistic psychological religiosity, chiefly when they imitate (with stereotypical forms, that is, with a sham intention) the "Byzantine" model.

Whenever and wherever the ecclesial event is operative, every aspect of this operation, down to the smallest detail, is a practical form of *thanksgiving* (in Greek, *eucharistia*): the receiving of the world as a gift of divine love endowed with reason, and as its common/shared rational offering back to the Cause and Provider of the gift. The use of the world (of stone, wood, colors, sounds, candles, incense, bread, and wine) becomes a relation of loving communion—*nature* becomes *relation*.

Nothing functions as decoration in this operation. That is, nothing is directed toward individuals with a view to impressing them, teaching them, giving them pleasure, moving them, giving them a sense of elation. The ecclesial event means that life becomes an *ek-static* anaphora, a loving self-offering, an experience of freedom from a life centered on the individual and programmed for death.

The building that shelters the realization of the ecclesial event, the eucharistic community, also functions in the *mode* of the Church: it expresses the *relation* of the structure with the materials of its construction—a respect for matter and thus a demonstration of its *rational* potentialities, the potentialities of every kind of material to indicate the principle/*logos* of the ineffable. The purpose and the motive for the construction are not ideological, nor are they independently aesthetic, nor are they psychological. The artist undertakes to manifest by the *mode* of execution the same relation that the participants in the Eucharist realize with the bread and the wine.

Nor is the music simply to delight or to teach when the ecclesial event is functioning—it too serves the communion of persons. *Gregorian* plainsong, like today's so-called *Byzantine* liturgical chant, is a musical technique that aims at what I would call freedom from the ego: leaving behind an individualistic enjoyment/emotion/exaltation with a view to attaining participation in a communion that consists in a *mode* of common (ecclesial) offering/intercession/thanksgiving.

By contrast, polyphonic music (a technique that has resulted in indisputably wonderful achievements) responds chiefly to the religious need and demand: it is addressed to the individual in order to serve the individual, the individual's emotional/psychological sensitivity, the religious satisfactions that the individual seeks to enjoy—impressive majesty, mystical credulity, rapture, and emotional exaltation.

The so-called "Orthodox" churches, however, in Russia, Greece, Serbia, Romania, Bulgaria, or elsewhere have not shown the slightest hesitation in welcoming polyphonic music in their worship, adopting it without reservation, as they have done with naturalistic painting. This obvious reception of an individualistic art at the opposite pole to the ecclesial *mode* is evidence, rather, of a firmly established religionization.

In the last decades of the twentieth century, something like an awakening of awareness of the alienation that had been accomplished has begun to be apparent in the life of the "Orthodox" churches. Two names may be mentioned as representative of the need for liturgical art, especially painting, to rediscover its ecclesial character: Leonid Uspensky and Photis Kontoglou. What also helped was the awakening of appreciation and indeed great admiration in the Western art world for icons of the Russian and Greek traditions.

Something similar may also be observed in the sector of ecclesiastical music, particularly in the Greek context. Here the names of Simon Karras and Lycurgos Angelopoulos may be regarded as representative of the attempt to create a broader interest in this striking musical tradition (in its recording, study, and revival). Nor should we underestimate the contribution of the great precentors of the Patriarchate of Constantinople who came to Greece as refugees.

We have been discussing an awakening that is well documented and acknowledged. It is nevertheless difficult to tell whether this awakening is always about the conscious awareness of an accomplished religionization with a concomitant search for ecclesial authenticity, or whether it primarily concerns the rediscovery of a high art that had been thrust aside and depreciated by products of much inferior quality and interest. The dead, formal imitation of "Byzantine" painting, or the performance of revivals of "Byzantine" music for individual, even if pious, consumption do not necessarily indicate a return to the ecclesial event.

The fact is clear: ecclesial art cannot exist without the functioning of a living cell of the ecclesial body: a eucharistic community/ parish.

3.6. *The Eclipse of the Parish*

The religionization of the Church is a facet of the individualization of faith, ascetic practice, and worship. Faith is alienated into the beliefs of the individual, ascetic practice into the morality of the individual, and worship into the duty of the individual. Correct beliefs, obedience to moral precepts, and adherence to obligations of worship are sufficient to ensure justification and salvation for the individual.

Nothing collective is presupposed in the religious version of piety or of salvation—neither community, which is the body of relations of communion that assembles at the eucharistic meal, nor participation in this assembly, nor the seeking of salvation in a change of *mode of existence*: the passing over from the natural urge of self-preservation/sovereignty to loving self-transcendence and self-offering.

In religionized Christianity every form of collectivity is justifiable only so long as it contributes (as an aid, as a strengthening factor) to the cultivation of an individualistic piety. Worship is a group exercise so that individuals might learn from the example of their fellow worshipers in the same place, so that their fervor might be strengthened for personal prayer. Individuals participate in the eucharistic meal as a reward for their virtue and "purity," as a supplementary confirmation of the remission of sins that has been granted to them in confession for the (enigmatic/"supernatural," quasi-magical) advance assurance of "eternal life."

The remaining sacraments in religionized Christianity are all consistently individualized. Cut off from the eucharistic event of the Church's assembly, they are preserved as rites that refer only to a specific individual (and emotionally to that individual's friends and relations), as "rituals" that provide some kind of indeterminate, supernatural blessing/"grace" that is likewise received in a magical fashion. The sacrament of *marriage*, for example, legalizes the sexual relationship of the couple (a relationship regarded as in itself sinful), gives it social recognition, and accompanies it with moral advice. The sacraments of *baptism* and *chrismation* are celebrated in the absence of the eucharistic community into which, supposedly, the newly baptized is incorporated (as a living body)—they are simply symbolic acts for the acquisition of a Christian identity.

In *confession* and *unction* we also have two rituals that have been completely individualized. Any cleric can perform them for any individual, one individual for another, outside any context of a specific eucharistic community. It is as if there is no awareness that we are dealing with "mysteries"—sacraments—which for the Church means the manifestation and realization of its truth, that is, of the eucharistic mode of existence embodied in a community.

Even *ordination*, the only sacrament that remains embedded in the context of the Eucharist, is performed in the absence of the specific ecclesial body for which the ordained bishop or presbyter will have pastoral responsibility. Even the sacrament of ordination in religionized Christianity is a formal ritual and is therefore carried out in any church by any bishop or bishops, as if it concerned the bestowal of a personal religious rank ("priest" or "archpriest," as in all the religions) with absolutely no participation of the body of the diocese or parish that will experience him as a father.

Even if the Church's sacraments or mysteries (*signs* of the realization and manifestation of the Church) have been completely individualized in religionized Christianity, it is easy for one to deduce what is happening with ascetic practice, *askēsis*—the *modes* of the common struggle to coordinate will and practice with the aim of attaining consistency in love. The meaning of *askēsis*, its ecclesial character, is unknown. Its shared mode and goal, the chasm that separates it from ethics, are likewise unknown. In religionized Christianity the individual fasts, prays, gives alms, and contributes to good works because all these secure a personal reward, are guarantees of salvation on an individual basis.

We are losing the awareness that as Christians we pray, we celebrate the sacraments, we believe in/entrust ourselves to the ecclesial gospel, and we undertake the ascetic struggle only *because* we live embedded in the specific body of a eucharistic community. But it is only by being embedded in this way that we can feel our way toward a realistic hope of change in our mode of existence, a realistic hope of freedom from time and death. Without a specific embedding/participation, all the rest remain on the level of ephemeral psychological experiences or illusions of religiosity, unrelated to the reality of our existence and our life.

Religionization destroys the priority of the eucharistic body that constitutes the Church, without abolishing the outward institutional/organizational forms of the ecclesial collectivity: the *diocese* and the *parish*. The outward forms are preserved, although they are radically alienated. The pivotal principle, cause, and goal of their constitution are no longer the eucharistic meal, the realization and manifestation of the body of a eucharistic community. Diocese and parish are determined by priorities of "practical" utility, by the demands of organizational effectiveness.

In conditions of religionization people understand by the word "church" the organizational and administrative mechanism of a religion—of the Christian religion. This is seen as a mechanism that exists to serve "the religious needs of the people." If Christianity is professed by the majority of the population, modern legislation recognizes it as the "prevailing religion" and grants it certain prerogatives. If not, it comes under the same legal regime as any other faith or religious sect.

Church, then, in conditions of religionization is the administrative expression of the "Christian religion." It has its organizational headquarters (patriarchate or archiepiscopal see) usually in the state capital, and local administrative units (dioceses, metropolitanates) in the outlying regions—like all organizations of common benefit. Each regional unit has subsidiaries ("branches") in every urban center or rural community (parishes) to serve the religious needs of the population. Thus, in the mind of many, a religionized church does not differ from any other organization of common benefit (social insurance offices, employment offices, care centers for the elderly, sports facilities, etc.).

It is not by accident that in conditions of religionization people mean by the word *church* only buildings, offices, and administrative personnel. And just as they identify every public organization with its higher management, so they also identify the *church* with the bishops alone, or more broadly with the clergy.

This identification, however, clearly flatters the bishops, who treat it as self-evident. They say "The Church has decided," "The Church judges," "The Church thinks," and they mean themselves as individuals or the administrative institution of the synod of bishops, with unwitting (and astonishing) self-satisfaction. They seem to be unaware that the bishop does not exist without the lay body of the bishopric, nor does the Church exist without the laity for whom the bishop has been established as father and servant.

When the parish ceases to be identified with the eucharistic community, a body of relations of communion, when it is obviously considered to be an "annex" or "branch office" of a centrally administered religious institution, then it is not subject to numerical control: the number of parishioners is determined not by the goal of creating a community but by the goal of satisfying the "religious needs" of individuals. And the parish, in the great urban centers, has proved to be able to satisfy the "religious needs" of thousands if not tens of thousands of people.

Naturally, for these tens of thousands of "parishioners" to be served, a single presbyter is not sufficient. Therefore in the same parish a second and third presbyter are added—a whole team of presbyters. Thus the goal of assembling the eucharistic body with one father and shepherd is wholly lost, for the presbyter serving each celebration of the Liturgy is not always the same one. The Roman Catholic Church, which was the first to lose the sense and reality of the parish, established multiple successive celebrations of the Eucharist on the same day in the same church building. And with the growth of urban centers, the so-called Orthodox churches hastened to imitate them. Thus the identification of the Eucharist with the assembly of the parish community was also excluded liturgically—the parish became fixed in the popular consciousness as an "annex" or "branch" of a religious institution that offers services quantitatively sufficient to satisfy the psychological needs of individuals who are strangers to each other.

In the "parishes" of modern conurbations that number tens of thousands of "parishioners," people participate in the Eucharist in conditions of complete anonymity and isolation from each other. Each "churchgoer" is an unknown person among other unknown persons, more alone than in the auditorium of a cinema, theater, or concert hall, or on the terraces of a football ground. Each prays alone, feels compunction alone, is taught alone, and exults or mourns alone, without communicating anything with those standing in close proximity. And all patiently await their turn to "communicate" of the bread and wine, assured intellectually and psychologically that they are receiving the body and blood of Christ from the hands of a celebrant with whom they do not have even a formal personal acquaintance—just as they have not exchanged even a perfunctory greeting with those who "communicate" before or after them from the common cup.

It is revealing that language, when its semantic function is not controlled by reason, returns with religionization to the vocabulary of a natural religion. Greek-speaking Christians no longer refer, either privately or officially, to *presbyters* and *bishops*; they speak of *priests* and *high priests*, as in any religion. And this change in language reflects a change in the reality of what is signified.

In reality the bishop, under conditions of religionization, is only or chiefly a high priest. He is an official of a religious institution, the bearer of "sacred" authority, the governor and judge of priests absolutely dependent upon his decisions, the monarchic head of services and offices of the organizational machine that constitutes his diocese, and the administrator of often a large amount of capital deriving from the income of parishes and monasteries, gifts, and subventions. There are hardly any institutional possibilities for him to be the father and pastor of a body of relations of communion. Fatherhood and pastoral responsibility are construed as an obligation to hand out pious advice, proffer encouragement, and utter moralizing platitudes—the cross-bearing service of a bishop has been distorted to become a monomania for preaching. The bishop is "obliged" to be a propagandist for ideological convictions and regulative principles of conduct, and also a provider of works of public benefit: philanthropic foundations, welfare institutes, and altruistic initiatives.

The episcopal model in conditions of religionization is clearly Vatican-inspired. The high priest/pontifex controls the fidelity of the clergy to the official religious ideology and their adequacy to the task of serving the religious needs of the people. Chiefly, however, he takes care of his image as "Christ's representative on earth" (*vicarius Christi*)—what is of primary importance is the theatrical grandeur of his liturgical appearance: provocatively ostentatious, opulent, and detached from reality. Everything is justified as symbolic (in a highly intellectualistic sense), whereas its historical provenance confirms the shrewd adaptation of certain personal privileges that emperors granted to specific patriarchs.[37]

The distinguishing mark of the bishop was the *pallium* (*ōmophorion*) worn over the presbyter's *chasuble* (*phelonion*)—as the Fathers of the Church are represented in the iconographical tradition. Today, even in the smallest and most humble diocese the "high priest" (*archiereus*) and "master" (*despotēs*) mounts a throne while dressed literally as a person not belonging to this world among his peasant or working-class flock. He is vested in the tunic (*sakkos*) of a Roman emperor (or a mantle with a long train), a crown (*mitra*), and a scepter (*pateritsa*)—and he is acclaimed incessantly by choirs of cantors (with the imperial acclamation *Eis polla etē despota*, "May you live many years, master") and incensed by the deacons like a pagan statue.

The "high priests" defend this now "traditional" ceremonial, explaining that they need to be clothed in this mythical majesty to symbolize Christ, who assumed human nature in order to glorify

37. See Robert Taft, "The Pontifical Liturgy of the Great Church according to a Twelfth-Century Diataxis in Codex *British Museum Add. 34060*," pt. 1, *Orientalia Christiana Periodica* 45 (1979): 279–397; and pt. 2, *Orientalia Christiana Periodica* 46 (1980): 82–124.

it with a royal glory. They do not explain why they must symbolize only the royal glory of Christ's human nature and never the model he laid down for his disciples: "You also ought to wash one another's feet. For I have set you an example, that you also should do as I have done to you" (John 13:14–15); "And whoever wishes to be first among you must be your slave" (Matt 20:27).

These are words whose meaning has been enervated by the instinctual need of religionization. It is a matter of genuine perplexity how people who receive such honors sacralizing their persons manage to preserve some kind of psychological (and intellectual) balance—especially when they have ascended to such magnificence from relatively low social and cultural origins (as is often the case in modern conditions), and moreover when all this self-evident, programmatic, and institutionalized flattery of their narcissistic instincts is accompanied by sexual privation. Such privation (often or as a rule) has not been chosen because of any inclination toward the monastic and ascetical life, or because of a desire to participate in a common effort to attain communion within the context of a cenobitic monastic community. Sexual privation has been accepted programmatically as a career requirement, as the path to religious offices carrying authority.

At any rate, the most painful consequence of the "high priestly" alienation of the bishop's function is largely the obscuring of the goal (the hope for all humanity) that the ecclesial event serves. The bishop's "high priestly" behavior distorts the eucharistic reality of the ecclesial event, making it a religious spectacle, a satisfaction for individuals to be consumed emotionally without any relation to a change in *mode* of existence. (The priority of the spectacle is so imperative that frequently in "Orthodox" Liturgies the "high priest" postpones participation of the faithful in the eucharistic cup until the end of the service, so as not to interrupt the "theatrical flow" of the ritual. Communion is postponed as if it is a secondary element of a private character.)

The eucharistic event transformed into a spectacle becomes an exclusive matter of the priests and high priests serving it; the laity simply follow it passively as consumers. In religionized worship the laity are not needed for the performance of the rites. The objective of the rites is not so that the Church, the body of a neighborhood, should be assembled and manifested. That is why the Roman Catholics have abolished even the nominal presence of a eucharistic body as a requirement for the celebration of the Eucharist. The priest (or bishop) is permitted to celebrate the Eucharist alone in his room, communicating himself from that which is unshared in communion.

The "Orthodox" have not yet been so consistent as to adopt this position.

3.7. *The Idolization of Tradition*

Tradition in our linguistic usage means that which is handed down to us from our predecessors, the experience that we have inherited from the recent and more remote past. Such experience is expressed in the way we lead our lives in the practices and common customs we follow, in the craftsmanship we need to produce things. It is also expressed in our mode of speech, in our scientific, literary, and artistic achievements, in the perceptions that give meaning to life and to death, in the quotidianity of human existence.

Tradition preserves and transmits to those who come after the achievements, assumptions, and habits of each generation—that which has survived temporally, that is, which has continued to interest successive generations, to correspond effectively to their needs. What survives and is handed on is what has been selected and valued by the commercial judgment of the many—not of course by a conscious (intellectually developed) analysis. Tradition is defined by criteria of evaluation imposed by need, by the practical business of living.

If tradition, then, is of value in itself, its value is to be located in the critical testing by which that which is finally handed on is selected; its value lies in the control (the selection) exercised by common experience on the things passed on from one generation to another. It is not so much antiquity (the remoteness in the past of its origin) that gives value to tradition as the collective critical work of evaluating the things that tradition transmits. And the criterion is correspondence to human needs—that alone.

Ecclesial experience has always seen tradition as an accumulation of wealth, the wealth, to be precise, of the experience of previous generations: the empirical critical testing of the Christian gospel from one generation to another. In tradition the participants in the ecclesial event discern whether the gospel, the good news of their hopes, has any realistic capital in terms of existential *meaning* and perspective, or whether it consists of "cleverly devised myths" (2 Pet 1:16), ideological programs, and religious pseudo-consolations.

For the Church the tradition that was inherited from the first ecclesial community and was recorded in the texts of the New Testament has always had a special value. This tradition concerns the experience and personal testimony of those who were eyewitnesses of the historical presence of Jesus of Nazareth—we are handing on, they declare, "what we have heard, what we have seen with our eyes, what we have looked at and touched with our hands" (1 John 1:1). God's intervention in history, his incarnation and resurrection, is the foundation and starting point of the ecclesial event. That is why the testimony of eyewitnesses of this intervention has been identified in people's consciousness with the foundational truth of the Church.

It is not, however, any intention of offering apodictic proof or any motives of emotional priority that endow the witness of the New Testament's texts with a special value for the Church. The "objective" evidence furnished by the "signs" that accompanied the revelatory presence of Jesus Christ is only of marginal interest, for the knowledge of what is signified by these signs is not exhausted in historical information—many who deny the gospel have subjected the information supplied by the texts of the New Testament to intense scrutiny without their denial being affected in the least.

Knowledge of the witness of the Gospels is an event and experience of *relation*. That is why the texts of the earliest Christian community are transmitted through the practice of worship; they are approached through the experience of relation/participation in the assembly of the ecclesial body. Naturally, individual/private reading is not precluded, but with a consciousness of the difference that is entailed in terms of the power to attain knowledge of the gospel witness. Private reading differs, *mutatis mutandis*, from reading the New Testament "in church" as much as the private study of a musical score differs from following the same score when it is accompanied by participation in the symphonic performance of the work. Only the experience of participation in the things signified (and not simply information about the events) saves the ecclesial event from its alienation into a product of ideology. Only this adequately guarantees a proper understanding, not a misinterpretation, of the texts.

For the Church the witness of the New Testament is *tradition* with a special value and meaning, manifestly because it transmits to succeeding generations, with the clarity of experiential immediacy, the historical facts that are the foundation of the ecclesial event. But there is also a second reason. The Church's witness is *tradition* because it constitutes the supreme legacy that changes in a radical way the *mode* of the metaphysical quest. It presupposes (and defines) knowledge not as intellectual information, theoretical hypothesis, or psychological conviction, but as erotic reciprocity, active *faith*/trust—self-surrender to relations of loving communion of life and hope.

In the legacy of the New Testament, an approach to metaphysics is preserved that is not through thinking but through *relation*. The Church's God is "the God of our fathers," a Personal Otherness who is confirmed through the historical experience of personal relations with him in successive generations. He is not the God of the intellectual conception of the First Cause, the "Dieu des philosophes et des savants."[38] God is known only as *Father*, the love and eros who is causal of every existent thing. He is know through his entry into history "in the person of Jesus Christ," to whom witness is borne as Son and Word of the Father "in the Spirit," in the ecclesial event.

38. "The God of philosophers and scientists" (Blaise Pascal, *Pensées*, in the introductory "Le memorial").

The Church does not claim to be an infallible religion, a combative ideology more effective than others, or a "higher" ethics. It conveys a proposal to participate empirically in an effort to find *meaning* in existence—in a hope. "Come and see." It speaks of a struggle for *faith*, that is, for the erotic self-transcendence that constitutes knowledge. Faith is won by renouncing the demands of the ego, the demands for self-sufficiency. It is won by renouncing assurances, certainty, the protective shell of security—faith has no deontology or support other than erotic reciprocity. That is why it always carries an implicit risk, like any erotic love.

The risk is that the difference between the Church and a religion might be lost: the difference between the freedom of erotic self-transcendence and the pleasurable illusion of self-transcendence that is really a convenient obedience to religious authority. What I call *religionization* is above all this difficult-to-distinguish alienation of the erotic achievement into an egotistic attainment of security for the self—the alienation of trust into submission, of the priority of experience into conformity with given certainties, axiomatic principles, and regulative stipulations.

These distinctions are clear from a semantic point of view but are difficult to distinguish in practice. Indeed, they are scarcely accessible to conscious control because the real facts disguise themselves and morph into psychologically desired illusory appearances. We entrust ourselves to tradition often with the illusion of self-transcendence and faith, while in reality what we are hunting for through our faith/trust is security for our egos. We think we are experiencing fidelity to tradition as a leap of freedom from the laws of nature, from the priority of our self-centered will, from the self-sufficiency of our atomic understanding and judgment. Yet we find ourselves trapped unawares in the defensive armor of the ego once again, though now with our meritorious trust in the "authority" of tradition.

The human psyche slips imperceptibly and very easily into the renunciation of freedom with a view to securing objectively a guarantee of atomic "justification" and "salvation." It uses tradition as a bulwark of security, proclaiming the past to be the supreme guarantee of truth, authenticity, and validity. Truth is detached from the reality of life and is identified with the letter of the historical prototype of a doctrine, with the precise wording of the first formulations, with canons rooted in custom—the idolization of the past defines the only "correct system of belief," that is, *ortho-doxy*. The "Genuine Orthodox" are meritorious "defenders," "guardians," "champions" of tradition. Thus the more the ecclesial event is gradually religionized, the greater the insistence on tradition as the *source* of Christian truth and faith. Christian truth is no longer experience of participation in a new *mode of existence*; it is not a struggle, an adventure of freedom, that is only relatively (*apophatically*) signified in language, in art, or in the form of worship. Truth is the objective givens that are defined as tradition: formulations, canons, customary forms—that which the individual can possess as an object, can appropriate as the defensive armor of religious security.

For a significant portion of the Christian world, the *Protestant*, *Reformed*, or *Evangelical*, such a *source* of Christian truth is only to be found in written texts belonging to the past, sacred texts of divine "revelation": *Holy Scripture*, both the *Old* and the *New Testaments*. For *Roman Catholic* and for *Orthodox* Christianity, the "sources" are two: *Holy Scripture* and *Holy Tradition*. The latter includes memorials of Christian truth and faith also in writing—the *definitions* ("dogmas") and the *canons* of ecumenical councils—as a primary and obligatory deposit. It also includes the writings of ecclesiastical authors (*Fathers* of the Church), the forms and texts of liturgical worship, and the organizational structures and customary practices of the ascetic life as a supplementary source of truth of relative validity.

In all the above cases, tradition is objectified as a given truth: it contains the presuppositions that, if obeyed by individuals, afford them guaranteed possession of the truth—they can be certain they hold correct beliefs and behave in a meritorious way. Consequently, they possess the assurance of atomic justification, of atomic salvation. Fidelity to tradition and a consistent adherence to it guarantees precisely that which humanity's instinctive religious need demands.

To put it more accurately, such fidelity satisfies every form of instinctive need for atomic psychological security, self-confirmation, and armoring of the ego. For turning the value of tradition into an absolute is a phenomenon not exhausted in religiosity. As a rule, it accompanies every social and political ideology with a longish history, every long-lived institutional structure, and even scientific theories that have likewise survived the passage of time. Marxist ideology and Freudian theory are classic examples of fields in which hardened traditionalist tendencies have developed.

We call *fundamentalism* the hardened and combative manifestations of insistence on tradition, usually on some religious tradition. The English word *fundamental* (from the Latin *fundamentum*, which means "foundation") signifies that which belongs to the foundations, the original form, and therefore the authentic and genuine version, of a teaching, a theory, or a worldview. Already from the nineteenth century, groups of Protestants in the United States were proud to bear the name of fundamentalists. Fundamentalism signified an insistence, in an absolutely consistent manner, on the fundamental and basic principles of the Christian gospel.

This ambition and boast took the form of a social movement or current opposed to tendencies "modernizing" (or secularizing) Christianity, especially the Christianity of the heirs of America's Puritan community. It is well known that American society was originally constituted chiefly by Puritan refugees from England who were unwilling to compromise their faith. These were the first to leave Europe as an organized group with the dream of turning America into a new "promised land," of becoming themselves the "new Israel of God," of realizing there the "kingdom of God."

Such ambitions were regarded as being undermined by "modernism," that is, new scientific methods and worldviews, historico-literary criticism of Holy Scripture, and liberal social and political theories. And in reaction to modernism came an enthusiastic "return to fundamentals," a fanatical adherence to the teachings and commandments of Holy Scripture, of the *Bible*. The basic belief of fundamentalists is in the "divine inspiration" of the Bible: the Bible was dictated to its writers by God word for word, and is inspired in the letter even down to the punctuation.

Thus, relying on the Bible, fundamentalists possess the "objective" absolute truth, the infallible formulation of the truth. And the truth is not abstract theory. It consists of very specific commandments, codes of moral conduct, a most precise identification of "good" and "evil," and a standard enabling people to measure the certainty of their individual salvation. Thanks to this idolization of the Bible, fundamentalists have the unshakeable psychological certainty that they possess truth, virtue, and eternal salvation. They take pleasure in legal definitions of "pious" narcissism, a specialized casuistry of grades of imaginary guilt or virtue.

In a fundamentalist environment psychological mechanisms develop that dress up as "sacrifice" and "self-denial" the hell of relentless anxiety about repressed desires, the fear of coming of age, of the responsibility of freedom. They identify religion "heroically" with the fear of "evil," with the terror of sin. And they identify virtue with repugnance for their own body. One wonders how it is that such a primitive religious attitude can coexist with advanced social achievements in science and technology, or how and why "developed" societies can swallow so easily such naive dogmatic clichés, such unsupported "evidence" for their convictions, such misuse of logic and critical thought.

As an instinctive need, religiosity proves stronger than any cultivation of rational thought and scientific criteria, more powerful even than the implacable urge of self-perpetuation (seeing that sexuality is so often nullified by religious need). It is the priority of the instinct for self-preservation that sweeps away the demands of logic, of critical judgment—and even of sexual desire. It requires unshakeable certainties, metaphysically valid beliefs safeguarded by the authority of "divinely inspired" revelation objectified in Scripture or in Scripture and tradition.

Fundamentalism is not symptomatic only of Protestantism. Fundamentalist movements, organizations, tendencies, brotherhoods, or isolated instances flourish in both Roman Catholic and Orthodox Christianity. And they almost always arise as a reaction to modern trends, trends of liberalism, secularization, and relativism, and also as a reaction to syncretistic attempts to bring together different Christian "confessions" and religious traditions.

A typical symptom of fundamentalism in the Orthodox churches may be seen in the *Old Calendarist schism*. This schism refers to groups of Christians who refused to accept the removal of the Church's cycle of feasts from the old (and astronomically inadequate) Julian calendar and its adaptation to the new (and somewhat more correct) *Gregorian* calendar. Simply on the grounds of the repositioning in the calendar of the immoveable feasts (the Easter festal cycle remains for all Orthodox dependent on the Julian calendar), the "Old Calendarists" refused to participate in the same eucharistic body with the "New Calendarists." They formed their own dioceses and parishes of the "Genuine Orthodox" and their own synods—they set up a separate "Church." Naturally, within a few decades all the typical symptoms of a sect appeared: a host of splinter groups, social marginalization, and a pathologically fanatical obsession with minute details of "traditions."

Old Calendarists, however, are absolutely convinced that the gospel's salvation and "eternal life" will be accorded exclusively to the very few "Genuine Orthodox" of their own sect; all the rest—all the billions of people of the past, present, and future—were created by God to be tormented in everlasting hell. This is a characteristic mark of fundamentalism, a sign of the invincible power of the religious instinct: logic, judgment, and seriousness are all sacrificed in order to satisfy the need of individuals for the certainty that they possess salvation, their need for something to counter the fear of death. Salvation depends exclusively and solely on the thirteen days that separate the Old Calendarist from the New Calendarist celebration of the same immoveable feasts.

In every form of fundamentalism, we meet the same (ultimately pathological, either neurotic or psychotic) "absolutization of the relative, which is an inevitable consequence of the relativization of the absolute."[39] Secondary elements and insignificant

39. The expression is that of Igor Caruso, *Psychoanalyse und Synthese der Existenz* (Freiburg: Herder-Verlag, 1952), 59: "Die Häresie ist eine Überwertung von Teilwahrheiten und zieht zwangsmässig die Relativierung des Absolutes mit sich."

details acquire an immense importance for individuals. They become the center of their interest, the pivot of their lives. They assume an absolute priority, dominating them to the point of clouding logical thought and judgment. The true Christian, for the fundamentalist, is not someone with experience of the ecclesial event, someone who participates in the struggle to attain communion with existence and with life. It is someone who clings blindly to forms and expressions that have an absolute value because they have been inherited from the past and constitute "tradition." The religious instinct demands objectified idols of certainties, and the easiest satisfaction of this demand is offered by the idolization of tradition.

The religionization of the ecclesial event brings with it a plethora of symptoms of the idolization of tradition. I am referring to idolization in a literal sense: the worship of idols, the fossilization of the past in forms, expressions, and residual customs whose significance and value are absolutized and raised to the status of a prerequisite of Christian identity.

In particular in the churches that today are called Orthodox, the temptation to idolize tradition appears to have increased, perhaps because "orthodoxy" is understood chiefly in terms of historical authenticity, of fidelity to the apostolic and patristic past. In such a perspective the Christian meaning of orthodoxy does not differ from any secular use of the word—for example, from Freudian, Marxist, or Hegelian orthodoxy. The kind of idols changes, but people's instinctive need to worship idols, with the aim of shoring up the ego with certainties, does not change.[40]

Much space could be devoted to analyzing the idolization of essential elements of ecclesiastical tradition. These elements would include, for example, the theological testimony that is codified in "dogmatic and symbolic documents" of the Church, the canons of the councils (and not only those) that are arranged as "systems of

40. See A. Reckermann, "Idol, Ido(lo)latrie," in the *Historisches Wörterbuch der Philosophie,* 4:188–92, where there is an interesting bibliography, mainly concerning the idoloclastic combativeness of liberal thinkers of the Enlightenment such as Bacon, Locke, Berkeley, Shaftesbury, Hume, Kant, Herder, etc.

canon law" and function as a legal prop supporting transcendent authority, the patristic texts that are sanctified collectively as an authoritative (according to the letter) body of material certifying the "truth," the institutional structures of ecclesiastical organization (the pentarchy of patriarchs), or the forms of worship that are fossilized in repetitions of the acclamations of Byzantine emperors, in petitions for the granting "by heaven" of military triumphs, for "victory over the barbarians," and for the "support of the Orthodox empire."

Instead, the reality of idolization is revealed more clearly in insignificant details transformed into criteria of "orthodoxy" and prerequisites for salvation—precisely like adhering to the Old Calendar. The turning of the significance of such details into absolutes very often torments the clergy and the laity in "Orthodox" environments: the details function as a regulative demand for "authenticity," a point of departure for the exercise of control or even terror over the many by certain Savonarola-like guardians of "tradition."

The Orthodox ethos and "spirituality" of bishops and presbyters are judged, for example, very often by the length of their hair and beard. It may be that an untouched natural growth of hair is sacralized only by a very few, but it is imposed universally as a self-evident requirement of "tradition." A beard in its natural state and not cutting the hair after ordination are considered a sign of godliness and fidelity to Orthodoxy.

This symptom is encountered in many religions and must be attributed to an archetypal symbolism of "dedication" (the sanctification of elements of the tribe). But the symbolism, even by the most favorable interpretation, manifestly no longer functions. Insistence on the maintenance of a dead typology must therefore hide other needs, needs that are psychological and instinctive, perhaps the need for people to idolize the "priest," the controller of access to the transcendent—in order to differentiate him emphatically from ordinary mortals. And the differentiation/distancing is intensified (is signaled more clearly) by the special dress that accompanies the unshorn hair, a dress belonging to a different era and a different society, so that its preservation is justified as adherence once again to tradition.

The Persian *entari*, the wide-sleeved Turkish *cüppe*, and the Italian *kalymmafchi* (the former head covering of legal officials) remain to this day, in European countries with a predominantly Orthodox tradition, the everyday dress of clerics, both married and celibate. Borrowed items of clothing that have been adopted to preserve a distinctively priestly appearance, they function as a uniform of someone exercising authority—the bishop and the presbyter of the eucharistic body clearly conform to what is required of the external appearance of religious functionaries. They return to what the words of the gospel condemned in relation to the Pharisees and scribes: "Do not do as they do . . . for they make their phylacteries broad and their fringes long. They love to have the place of honor at banquets and the best seats in the synagogues, and to be greeted with respect in the marketplaces, and to have people call them rabbi. But you are not to be called rabbi" (Matt 23:3–8; cf. Luke 22:26).

The address *rabbi*, however, is most decorous in comparison with the extremely flattering modes of address for clerics that have long been in use in "Orthodox" environments, preserving an idolized "Byzantine" tradition. A celibate presbyter, for example, is addressed as *panosiologiōtatos* ("all holy and most learned"). His status lavishes on him the most complete holiness and the deepest learning. A married priest is absolutely to be revered: *aidesimōtatos* ("most reverend") or *aidesimologiōtatos* ("reverend and most learned"). A bishop is supremely beloved of God (*theophilestatos*); a metropolitan is supremely venerable (*sebasmiōtatos*); an archbishop is supremely blessed (*makariōtatos*). A patriarch, especially the patriarch of Constantinople, concentrates in his person the full range of holiness: he is *panagiōtatos*, allowing no further margin linguistically for addressing God. The patriarch of Alexandria, in the acclamations sung to him, is addressed as "father of fathers, shepherd of shepherds, thirteenth apostle"!

Every society devises customary expressions of polite address to honor and flatter its distinguished members—in so-called Byzantium such forms of address were cultivated playfully with exceptional skill. But the preservation of the same forms of address many centuries later, in societies accustomed now to modern conditions of mass democracy and the leveling effect of individual rights, provokes much bewilderment—if not malevolent mirth. Yet this (hardly serious, or rather clearly comic) manifestation of instinctive narcissism is also hidden under the decorous appearance of "tradition." No one refuses to accept for himself the established forms of address nor does he dare to question the seriousness of such forms. That which is regarded as incompatible and unthinkable when the ecclesial event is operative is sanctified without objection and imposed as self-evident within the context of religionization.

The elements of tradition that are idolized are not necessarily the oldest, those going back to the apostolic and patristic periods. Rather, they are those, deriving even from the relatively recent past, that respond to the needs of "biological" religiosity—to the psychological demands of individuals (of both the laity and the clergy). The elaborate forms of address and the exotic dress of the clergy satisfy people's need to sacralize, both visibly and in the distinctions bestowed on them, those who control access to the transcendent. At the same time this objectified sacralization flatters, unconsciously but strikingly, the narcissism of the controllers—perhaps producing a supreme pleasure not comparable with any other.

If this interpretation lacks validity, many instances of the idolization of tradition remain without explanation, although these astonish us by their extreme naivety, their undisguised childish character, and above all by the obvious contradiction they present to the Church's gospel.

One thing that would remain inexplicable, for example, as mentioned earlier, is the rapid dissemination (beyond national, linguistic, and customary boundaries) of the use of vestments and insignia (symbols of power) belonging to the Roman emperor as the liturgical dress of a bishop. The privilege of this use was accorded gradually (one element at a time) by specific emperors to specific patriarchs of Constantinople. And it spread without any check so that today even so-called "assistant bishops," simply bishops in a titular sense without diocese or flock (like mayors without a borough), serve the Liturgy in the imperial *sakkos* or *mandyas*, bearing the scepter (*pateritsa*) and wearing the crown (*mitra*) of a Roman sovereign.

We have the idolization of forms, of types, of symbols, of iconographical and musical models, of forms of administration, of hagiographical and patristic authenticity, of confessional texts, and inevitably of liturgical gestures. In the practice of worship nowadays, we encounter formalized movements that function without any meaning, any explanation. They end up being used as magical gestures, but it is certain that any omission of them or suggestion that they should be abolished would be condemned as disrespect for tradition.

Take, for example, the movements that the president of the Eucharist makes at the beginning of the anaphora holding the aer (*aeras*). The aer is a light, embroidered piece of material that covered the offered (*anapheromena*) gifts, the bread and wine. The aer is taken away and ceases to cover the chalice containing the wine and the paten with the bread at the time when the reader is reciting the Creed, the Symbol of Faith. But although its rational use is removed, the aer remains in irrational use. It is moved backward and forward above the gifts all through the Creed; then it is folded and the celebrant weaves his fingers into the fabric and moves it without any rational purpose around and above the gifts. These are unintelligible, literally magical, gestures.

Historical studies of ecclesial worship tell us that the aer had the necessary liturgical role of protecting the offered gifts, especially in hot regions, from the many insects found there—either by covering the chalice and the paten or by being used by the celebrant as a *fan* to keep the insects away. The necessary functional purpose became somewhat redundant, but the gestures that accompanied it came to be idolized as an element of "tradition" and are preserved without purpose or reason, as if magical.

One could list a fairly large number of such movements and gestures, or magical versions of liturgical forms and customary details. They are elements of the idolization of tradition that the human psyche has need of as comforting illusions of transcendent signs and symbols.

What we have here is a historical paradox: the ecclesial event appeared in history having as a chief characteristic a militant distinction from and contrast to the traditionalism that dominated Jewish religious life—that oppressed the Jewish people with "heavy burdens difficult to bear." And imperceptibly, in the course of centuries, the ecclesial event arrived at the same, or even at a more burdensome, hardening of grim traditionalism. Perhaps the paradox points to the ever-invincible power of the instincts of our human nature, to humanity's primeval need for religion—that is, to the existential prerequisite of personal freedom that is so vertiginous to rational thought, seeing that the freedom of the created can only be conceived and realized as release from the autonomous existential demands of createdness (of nature).

3.8. *The Demonization of Sexuality*

The religionization of the ecclesial event also brings with it a fear of sexuality. Such fear manifests itself as reserve, aversion, or contempt with regard to humanity's sexual functioning. In religionized Christianity sexuality constitutes a threat: it is uncleanness, pollution, the supreme sin.

Why is it that natural, instinctive religiosity is usually (or rather, as a rule) hostile to sexuality? Here too there is need for a serious study with the aid of clinical psychology.[41] Such a study would investigate and demonstrate the real motives, the anthropological

41. For a useful outline I would commend to the reader the chapter "Sexualité et Morale" in Denis Vasse, *Le temps du desir* (Paris: Seuil, 1969), 123ff. See also Philip Sherrard, *Christianity and Eros* (London: SPCK, 1976); Antoine Vergote, *Guilt and Desire* (New Haven, CT: Yale University Press, 1988), 73–75, 131–32; Stanton L. Jones and Heather R. Hostler, "The Role of Sexuality in Personhood," in *Judeo-Christian Perspectives on Psychology*, ed. William R. Miller and Harold D. Delaney (Washington, DC: American Psychological Association, 2005), 115–32; Celia Harding, "Introduction: Making sense of sexuality," in *Sexuality: Psychoanalytic Perspectives*, ed. Celia Harding (New York: Brunner-Routledge, 2001), 1–17; B. Z. Goldberg, *The Sacred Fire: The Story of Sex in Religion* (New York: Grove Press, 1962); Edward P. Shafranske, ed., *Religion and the Clinical Practice of Psychology* (Washington, DC: American Psychological Association, 1996).

roots, of the phenomenon. At any rate, in the case of Christianity, it is historically fairly obvious that elements of various aspects of a fearful hostility to sexuality were inherited originally from the Jewish religious tradition and social practice.

Christianity is an ecclesial event always with the historical flesh, both social and cultural, of a specific lay body—it is not an ideology, dogma, or ethics of a theoretical character independent of real historical situations. The first ecclesial communities consisted of Palestinian Jews, not by chance, because the incarnation of the Word was realized "from the Jews" and was prepared for by the *covenant* God had made with his people of Israel. The first readings and hymns used at the eucharistic assemblies of Christians were messianic texts of the Hebrew Bible (psalms, prophecies, allegorized narratives). These same texts continued to nourish the Church's poetry, hymnology, and worship, and for the most part the language of preaching, the language of the Christian gospel.

In the Old Testament the Church recognized the foreshadowing of the revelation of God that was realized in Christ, without ignoring the fact that this same testament was simultaneously a record of the history of the Jewish people, that is, a record of their vicissitudes (both collective and individual), their crimes, fanatical passions, corruption, and ferocity in battle—as well as a collection of legal precepts designed to tame humanity's ungovernable nature. The Old Testament tells the story of God's relationship with his chosen people, but this relationship did not always imply a positive response on their part to the special calling they had accepted. It also implied frequent disobedience, disloyalty, hardness of heart, lapses into idolatry, and susceptibility to influences coming from the religions of neighboring peoples.

Many such influences intrude into the Bible of the Jews. They create a language, inevitably, of a religious nature—it is not a requirement of every historical book that it should also introduce a new linguistic code. Perhaps that is why the religious proclivities (or exigencies) of the ancient peoples of Mesopotamia infiltrate the texts of the Old Testament: elements of a primeval feeling of repugnance toward sexuality, a fear of its "pollution" and "unclean" character.[42] Yet parallel to this, concubinage is fully endorsed and prostitution is taken for granted—at least in the period of the so-called *wisdom* books.

The legacy of the primeval fear of sexuality passed into Christianity after some considerable delay—it is specified for the first time in canons of the seventh century. The canons appear to reflect an excessive respect for the Old Testament, although the Church had taken the Old Testament only as a foreshadowing and preparation for the historical advent of Christ. This excessive respect is perhaps the most likely explanation for how elements of the Jewish tradition came to survive in the practice of ecclesial life, elements such as regarding the loving union of a man with a woman as a pollution, of considering a woman as unclean after she has given birth or during the days of her monthly period, and similarly with regard to men if they have had even an involuntary ejaculation.[43]

---

42. See Friedrich Hauck, "*Akathartos, akatharsia*," in the *Theological Dictionary of the New Testament*, ed. Gerhard Kittel, trans. Geoffrey W. Bromiley (Grand Rapids, MI: Eerdmans, 1966–76), 3:427–31; Friedrich Hauck and Siegfried Schulz, "*Pornē, pornos, porneia, porneuō, ekporneuo*," etc., in Kittel, ed., *Theological Dictionary of the New Testament*, 6:579–95. On the sexual urge, see the entry for marriage in Léon-Dufour, ed., *Dictionary of Biblical Theology*, 294–96. In his work *The Slave*, the contemporary Jewish novelist Isaac Bashevis Singer (Nobel Prize for Literature, 1978) describes the laws of the Torah on women during the days of their monthly periods as follows: "He [Jacob, the main hero of the novel] had warned her [Sarah, his Gentile wife] many times about the unclean days, reminding her that when she was menstruating she could not sit on the same bench with him, take any object from his hand, nor even eat at the same table unless there was a screen between her plate and his. He was not allowed to sit on her bed, nor she on his; not even the headboards of their beds ought to touch at this time" (Bashevis Singer, *The Slave*, 158).

43. Obligatory abstention from the conjugal act on Saturdays and Sundays: Canon 13 of Timothy of Alexandria. Obligatory abstention from the conjugal act for at least three days before Holy Communion: Canon 5 of Timothy of Alexandria. A menstruating woman shall not receive Holy Communion but shall pray on her own in the church's narthex: Canon 2 of Dionysius of Alexandria and Canon 7 of Timothy of Alexandria. A menstruating woman shall not receive Holy Communion and her husband shall not have marital relations with her, but if she ignores this rule and approaches to receive Holy Communion the penalty imposed on her is not to receive Holy Communion for forty days; on a woman who has given birth not entering the bedroom while her baptized infant is lying there: Canon 38 of Nicephorus the Confessor. He who has been polluted during sleep by the passion of secretion is excluded from communion for one day; if he

The attitude of the New Testament to sexuality also calls for careful hermeneutical attention. Here we are dealing with texts—not with theoretical ideological declarations but with testimonies to the experience of a particular (historically and culturally) ecclesial community. This was a community necessarily embedded in the language and outlook of the broader social environment, a specific historical time and geographical place.

In spite of all this, in the texts of the Gospels there is not the slightest hint giving us grounds for supposing a fear or depreciation of sexuality or repugnance toward it. Even when the disciples remarked that perhaps it is better not to marry in view of the difficulties of remaining faithful to a monogamous relationship, Christ's reply was clearly cautious. He speaks of those who are deprived by nature of the power to enter into sexual relations and distinguishes them from those whose privation is imposed socially (through an external cause). And he distinguishes both of these cases from the possibility of achieving ascetical freedom, the release from natural necessity, with the sole aim of attaining the fullness of loving self-transcendence and self-offering—"in the image" of the Triadic Model that the Church always keeps before it (cf. Matt 19:2–12).

The material in the writings of the Apostle Paul is more extensive. There we encounter both a very clear perspective on the new *mode of existence* that the Church proclaims and also some reiteration of the prevailing language (and consequently on the perceptions) of the natural religion of his age—chiefly when he dictates principles of sexual behavior to his Christian contemporaries.

Paul's perspective on the new *mode of existence*, in relation to sexuality, is very clear when he proclaims the transcendence of the difference between the sexes in Christ Jesus: "There is no longer male and female" (Gal 3:28). It is also very clear when he seeks an absolute equality between men and women scarcely conceivable in the social and cultural environment of his time: "The husband should give to his wife her conjugal rights, and likewise the wife to her husband. For the wife does not have authority over her own

sings the fiftieth psalm and makes forty-nine prostrations, it is believed that this cleanses the pollution: Canon 6 of John the Faster.

body, but the husband does; likewise the husband does not have authority over his own body, but the wife does" (1 Cor 7:3–4). And it is very clear when he advises married couples not to deprive each other of the joy and pleasure of sex. And this is not so that they might remain subject to the natural necessity of reproduction but only for the sake of their own relationship—except when the two of them agree on a temporary period of abstinence for the purpose of practicing asceticism, a trial of freedom from natural necessity (cf. 1 Cor 7:5).

And the ecclesial perspective on relations between men and women reaches its climax in Paul with the famous passage in his Epistle to the Ephesians where he sees in the loving union of a man and a woman and in the "sharing of the whole of life" the image of Christ's relation with the Church, an image that is not metaphorical or intellectually allegorized but is an image/manifestation of the power of human beings to realize the incarnate Son's vital relationship with humanity (vital in that it is the provider of unlimited life) as an existential event through their psychosomatic created nature. This is a power that defines that which the Church calls a *mystery*—that which sharply distinguishes ecclesial marriage from the natural/social/legal institution of marriage (cf. Eph 5:21–33).

Within the context of the mutually self-transcendent relationship of husband and wife, Paul requires of the wife that she should actively cultivate respect for her husband, should be subject to her husband "in everything," as the Church is to Christ. He asks correspondingly from husbands that they should love their wives "as they do their own bodies" and much more so, "just as Christ loved the church and gave himself up for her." These demands do not constitute regulative principles of social behavior; they are the terms of the transformation of the natural institution into an ecclesial *mystery*, into a struggle to renounce the egotistic will, a struggle of realistic self-transcendence and self-offering. It is only in terms of *mystery* (the ecclesial *mode of existence*) that these demands can be judged, not according to the standards of "the rights of the individual," the standards of modern mass democratic individualism.

We encounter elements of the Apostle Paul's being tied to the language and attitudes belonging to his own era (and determined for the most part by natural religiosity) when he is dealing with social matters then taken for granted, along with the rules regulating life that these entailed. He instructs the Greek Christians of Corinth, for example: "As in all the churches of the saints, women should be silent in the churches. For they are not permitted to speak, but should be subordinate, as the law also says" (1 Cor 14:34). Paul, who describes the law as a "curse" (Gal 3:10, 13–14), and fights against it as the supreme opponent of the Church's gospel, now invokes it as a rule of conduct for Christians at their eucharistic assemblies.

A similar attitude is reflected in his insistence that "any woman who prays or prophesies with her head unveiled disgraces her head" (1 Cor 11:5). He justifies his demand by arguments that draw on assumptions that at that time were taken for granted by everyone. What we should infer is that, for Paul, his role (and that of the Church) was not to demand social changes aimed at securing the equality of the sexes but to show that the (then) established social practice, outlook, and anthropological perspective could serve the passage from *nature* to *relation* that constitutes the Church. (It is, however, very doubtful if the same inference could usefully be made with regard to the equality of the sexes in the modern individualistic culture prevailing today.)

There is also Paul's clearly expressed preference for the celibate life,[44] which can be interpreted in various ways: as a sense of reserve, depreciation, and contempt with regard to sexuality, or as a search for the fullest possible liberation from the natural laws that govern human nature. Paul himself does not clarify his preference analytically, but neither can there be discerned in what he says any disposition or hint of a depreciation of the female sex—there is nothing in them that would allow us to attribute to Paul a demonization of women and of sexuality. Certainly (and indisputably) he speaks the language of the patriarchal society of his own time and of a religious tradition, the Jewish, formed through centuries of

44. 1 Cor 7:1–2, 7: "It is well for a man not to touch a woman. But because of cases of sexual immorality, each man should have his own wife and each woman her own husband . . . I wish that all were as I myself am."

male dominance. Despite all this, he attempts to graft onto such a language and outlook an elementary ontological realism.[45]

His remarks about prostitutes and prostitution also appear to be socially determined. In the Gospels this prejudgment is more circumspect and indirect.[46] In Paul it manifests itself with greater clarity: "Do you not know that your bodies are members of Christ? Should I therefore take the members of Christ and make them members of a prostitute? Never!" (1 Cor 6:15). Evidently, a prostitute is regarded as polluted and polluting, to be identified with sin. Thus fornication and the Lord are placed at opposite poles, in absolute contrast and distinction.[47] Paul does not explain why "the fornicator sins against the body itself" (1 Cor 6:18); he does not demonstrate that fornication signifies subjection to nature's individualism, to the natural need for pleasure, that fornication excludes *relation*. He regards the sinful and dangerous nature of fornication as socially obvious and self-explanatory, and makes no attempt to connect what he writes to the Corinthians about fornication with what he writes to the Romans about living "according to the flesh" (Rom 8:12).

In the end Paul arrives at justifying the natural institution of marriage (not the ecclesial perspective of male-female relations) only on the grounds of avoiding fornication.[48] Parallel to this, however, one may discern two indirect suggestions that the natural sexual instinct can cooperate with the goal of human *salvation* (the goal that human beings may be *saved*, may become *sound* or *whole*, with their existential powers fully integrated). The first hint concerns the man who is helped by the natural institution of marriage to "leave his father and mother" (Eph 5:31), to break away from the ego-boosting assurance of their protection, so as to dare to take the risk of attaining adulthood. And he does this by being "joined to his

45. 1 Cor 11:11–12: "Nevertheless, in the Lord woman is not independent of man or man independent of woman. For just as woman came from man, so man comes through woman; but all things come from God."

46. Cf. "When this son of yours came back, who has devoured your property with prostitutes" (Luke 15:30); "He would have known who and what kind of woman this is who is touching him" (Luke 7:39).

47. "The body is not meant for fornication but for the Lord" (1 Cor 6:13).

48. 1 Cor 7:1–2; see also n. 44.

wife" (Eph 5:31), sharing his body with her, his physical individuality that is identified with his biological ego.

The second hint concerns the woman who "will be saved through childbearing" (1 Tim 2:15). The natural function of motherhood helps the woman too to share her being, her own body, to communicate her bodily individuality, through the self-denial and self-offering that motherhood entails. Both of the hints we find in Paul refer to *potentialities* that are characteristic of the generative function, not to regulative precepts that Paul's "ethics" wants to impose on nature. It is precisely this misunderstanding that has caused (and still causes) much inhumanity—has tormented (and still torments) generations of human beings over many centuries.

I have dwelt on the texts of the Apostle Paul because, when the ecclesial event is religionized, it is these texts that are idolized and proclaimed (not only by Protestants) to be divinely inspired down to the letter. Even their circumstantial, historically conditioned elements are treated as obligatory regulative principles for Christians of every era.

Whenever and wherever Christianity has been religionized, it has seen in Paul's texts an approval of the fear, the depreciation, the repulsiveness of sexuality. And it has built on to such inspired "approval" the demonization of sexuality as a self-evident element of Christian identity (and authenticity). Thus, at least in communities that share in modernity's values, it seems to be taken for granted that Christians identify sexuality with sin, "evil," uncleanness, pollution—and often with the "fall"—that they demonize sexuality with a (literally) neurotic obsession, that they are constantly preoccupied with it as an alarming threat of pollution.

Everyday experience tends to confirm this widely held conviction. The demonization of sexuality manifests itself as a universal fact, an obligatory concomitant of the Christian conscience in every tradition and "confession." Certainly, it becomes particularly evident in fundamentalist circles—in zealous groups (or sects) of puritans and pietists in the Protestant world, in the small number of conservative Roman Catholics still obedient to the Vatican line, and in the various manifestations of the "Genuine Orthodox." In each of these cases, and also in the broader "confessional" tradition, there is abundant material for a study of the psychopathology defined by the symptoms of the demonization of sexuality that has so tormented humanity.

A telling example is provided by the occurrence of such symptoms in the area of so-called "Orthodox" ecclesial life. These symptoms illustrate the dynamics of religionization very powerfully, considering that Orthodox ecclesial life was clearly the field in which resistance to the alienation of the primitive Christian tradition was at its strongest.

There must be a very large number of married Orthodox Christians who willingly endeavor to live according to the *mode* of ecclesial struggle, and yet are tormented sadistically and inhumanely by "pastoral" confessors governed by the demonization of sexuality. Christians have been excluded for decades on end from participation in the eucharistic body of the Church, and this exclusion has been imposed on them as an implacable penalty. They have been burdened with frightening guilt, with panic about the dread judgment that comes after death, and with accusations of betrayal of the faith and contempt for the "law of God."

And all this is not because these specific married Christians have neglected, or have refused, to love the other in the marital joint struggle "as their own body," not because they forget the aim that their love should be an image of the relationship between Christ and the Church—not because of anything like that. They are excluded for decades from the Eucharist only because they have avoided subjecting themselves to nature's blind and autonomous need for self-perpetuation. The first question the confessor puts to married people concerns how many years have they been married and how many children they have. If the figures are disproportionate, if they betray conjugal acts that did not result in conception, the "guilty" parties are excluded from eucharistic participation in the ecclesial body.

What we have here is an understanding of the Christian life with the conditions of the Church's gospel entirely reversed. The Church proclaims that "the conditions of nature have been conquered," that the subjection of being to the necessities of nature, necessities that pursue their own independent goal, has come to an end. Now being is defined not by nature but by relation, by the infinite freedom of love. The "Orthodox" confessor, however, has another gospel: marriage is not a *mystery*, a gift and struggle to realize the ecclesial *mode of existence* of a kind that is not subject to linguistic determinations; it is not an imaging by the husband and wife of the relation between Christ and the Church. Marriage is a religious legitimization of sexual relations, and because this accursed pleasure is legitimized, there is a price that has to be paid for it (a price demanded by an instinctive, zealous psychological sadism). And the price is that the pleasure must be curbed by childbearing—or, to be thoroughly consistent, that the pleasure deriving from sexual relations should be erased and that such relations should be restricted programmatically to a pleasureless mechanistic fertilization of the female by the male.

"Orthodox" confessors have actually boasted of "spiritual children" with impressively large families but who have nevertheless never seen each other naked or allowed themselves to offer their "erotic" companion any caress or occasion of physical pleasure. Even the most fanatical naturalist would have found it near impossible to idolize the impersonal reproductive instinct more fully, to obliterate personal relations, the bodily expression of loving reciprocity, more thoroughly for the sake of a biological goal.

For a "pastoral" outlook and practice of this kind, only the aim of conception justifies the sexual act between spouses. The sexual act in itself never in any circumstances ceases to be dishonorable, unclean, polluting, and demonic. That is why, as already mentioned, participation in the cup of the Eucharist is canonically forbidden if the sexual union of the spouses has occurred the previous night. There are, of course, ecclesiastical canons that excommunicate, cut off from the body of the Church, those who "regard marriage as loathsome," or those who refuse to accept the bread and wine of the Eucharist "from the hands of a married presbyter." At the same time, however, there are prayers "for forty days after childbirth" that are read over the new mother by the president of the Orthodox ecclesial assembly and that wound, insult, and denigrate the woman in a crude manner as "polluted" and "unclean" only because her body has served the function of motherhood.

That the function of motherhood constitutes *uncleanness* is confirmed not only by the prayers that are read over a mother after childbirth, not only by exclusion of women from participation in the Eucharist (or even entering the Church) when they are menstruating, but also by the constant repetition in the Church's hymnology that the Virgin Mother of God "remained a virgin even after giving birth," that she is ever-virgin, that "her giving birth did not destroy the Virgin's keys," did not dissolve her physical (anatomical) virginity.

Psychologically healthy Christians understand that the incarnation/birth of the Son and Word of God the Father from a virgin mother manifests victory over or freedom from the conditions of nature ("The conditions of nature have been overcome in you, O spotless Virgin"). They understand the Son's assumption of human nature as an event of absolute freedom from the necessities/preprogramming of createdness. But they do not understand what precisely can be added to this wonder: a created woman gives birth to the uncreated—"he who is uncontainable by anything" is contained "in a womb," "he who is in the bosom of the Father" becomes an infant "in the arms of a mother"; they do not understand what more sublime truth is secured by the preservation of the anatomical virginity of the Theotokos even after giving birth.[49]

49. How else should we interpret the phrase in the Church's hymnology *ho mētran oikēsas aeiparthenon* than "who dwelt in a womb unpolluted by motherhood"? Fr. Georges Florovsky writes, "She [the Virgin Mother] was not just a 'channel' through which the Heavenly Lord has come, but truly the mother of whom he took his humanity . . . Motherhood, in general, is by no means exhausted by the mere fact of a physical procreation . . . In fact, procreation itself establishes an intimate spiritual relation between the mother and the child. This relation is unique and reciprocal, and its essence is affection or love . . . nor could Jesus fail to be truly human in his filial response to the motherly affection of the one of whom he was born . . . The title of Ever-Virgin means surely much more than merely a 'physiological' statement. It does not imply only an exclusion of any later marital intercourse . . . It excludes first of all any 'erotic' involvement, any sensual and selfish desires or passions, any dissipation of the heart and mind . . . The main point is precisely the purity of the heart, that indispensable condition of 'seeing God'" (Georges Florovsky, *Creation and Redemption*, vol. 3 of The Collected Works of Georges Florovsky [Belmont, MA: Nordland, 1976], 175, 176, 179, 184).

Rather, we should suppose that a religionized piety is not interested in celebrating a woman who has been found worthy to become the mother of God. It is not affected by doxologies about the wonder of supernatural motherhood. It wants to worship virginity, that alone, the exclusion of sexuality from life. In the end the religious person wants unconsciously to idolize his own neurotic eunuchism, his repressed but agonizing sexual privation.

Another striking example of the demonization of sexuality within the "Orthodox" churches is the prohibition of a second marriage for clergy who have become widowers after their ordination. They had chosen the married life and had not thought to follow the path of monasticism. But it so happened that death deprived them of their life companion. Any member of the Church in such a situation can proceed to a second marriage, but not a cleric. Priests and deacons who become widowers are obliged to live the rest of their lives in an involuntary celibacy that they have not chosen and do not want.

That this prohibition springs from a depreciatory view of marriage is fairly obvious: "it is permitted" that there should be marriage before ordination, but when the "office" of "priesthood" has been conferred, the approval of a second marriage would contradict the "concession" that sexual activity could coexist with the "angelic" priestly function. The marriage of an already ordained man would acknowledge sexuality not as a secondary element at the margins of the priestly life. It would give it a primary significance in life and in the struggle for erotic self-denial.

Moreover, it appears to be not at all fortuitous that in the current practice of the "Orthodox" churches a married presbyter can be ordained a bishop after some years of widowerhood. This implies that avoidance of the distraction of family responsibilities was not the motive for establishing the obligatory celibacy of bishops. The motive was a depreciatory reserve, a predisposition to regard sexuality as "uncleanness." That is why some years of "purification" from an active sexual life are required before the "polluted" married priest can be acceptable for episcopal office.

Chapter 4

The Religionization of the Ecclesial Event: Historical Overview

4.1. *The Judaizers*

The demand that the ecclesial event should be brought into line with humanity's instinctive need for religion is already apparent in the very first days of the Church's historical life.

In the Acts of the Apostles, we read about the first test of the cohesion and unity of the newly constituted ecclesial community of Jerusalem. It began with objections made against the Apostle Peter's "permissiveness" in associating with "uncircumcised men" and eating with them (Acts 11:3)—an act that the Jewish law explicitly prohibited. These objections came to a head when the number of *Gentiles* (former pagans) who joined the Church increased very noticeably without their being required also to obey the rules of the Jewish religion.

The objectors were Christians of Jewish descent, particularly those who came from the conservative religious group of the Pharisees. They were teaching Christians of Gentile origin that there was no salvation for them solely through participation in the Church. They needed at least to submit to the *circumcision* that the Jewish religion required and to observe the *Mosaic law* (Acts 15:1, 5).

These Christians were labeled *Judaizers*, and it is clear that they understood the ecclesial event as a repristination or creative transformation of the Jewish religion. They saw that the ecclesial event on its own did not have the formal marks of a religion and did not even aim at acquiring them. The Judaizing Christians themselves, however, needed a religion—they needed a law and visible marks to distinguish them, such as circumcision. It was therefore impossible for them to accept a Christianity free from the rules of the Jewish religion; they were not interested in the Church if it was an event of a different order from that of natural religiosity.

This first demand for the religionization of the Church also functioned in an archetypical fashion: it served as a model for, or encapsulated, all the later demands of a similar kind, whether manifest or hidden, successful or unsuccessful.

All the demands of a similar kind, from the Judaizers to the present day, have the same motivation: the absolute priority they give to individual salvation. It is fairly evident that they understand salvation as a guarantee to the individual (valid in this world and the next). They construct the idea of salvation from objective terms whose fulfillment can be measured, certified, and evaluated without any margin for doubt, namely, the obedience of the individual to a law of absolute validity, to the codified precepts that objectify this law, to specific ritual practices, to objectified forms of religiosity. And they take participation in the ecclesial event to be an additional token of, or help toward, the gaining of personal merit, supplementing all that a consistent religiosity guarantees to the individual.

For the primitive Church this was a challenge that necessitated a response, for it touched on its very identity, on what precisely was distinctive about its gospel.

Accordingly, a *council* was called for the first time, a council that was later called *apostolic*. The Acts of the Apostles says that "the apostles and the elders met together to consider this matter" (15:6). And "after there had been much debate" (15:7)—without the arguments that were presented on either side or the objectives that were clarified having come down to us—a decision was reached unanimously and expressed confidently with complete assurance with regard to its correctness: "It has seemed good to the Holy Spirit and to us" (15:28). This "to us" included the *whole of the Church*: apostles, presbyters, and brethren. That is why it was held to be certain that the council manifested God's Holy Spirit, the Church's Paraclete, for when the ecclesial body is of one mind it manifests its unity as its truth, as a *mode of existence*, that is, as a *grace*/gift of the Paraclete.

The decision freed Christians from the obligation of accepting circumcision and observing the Mosaic law. It required them only to "abstain from what has been sacrificed to idols and from blood and from what is strangled and from fornication" (Acts 15:29), with a view to making the difference between Christians and pagans socially discernible. Thus from the very first days of the Church's life, the ecclesial event's independence from the Jewish religious tradition, its difference from natural religion, was marked off by the decision of the Apostolic Council.

The difference was marked, off but the demand for religionization was not erased. Until the end of his life, Paul continued to fight against the persistent view that insisted on laying claim to atomic salvation through observation of the law and obedience to commandments. He attempted to prove that even in the Jewish tradition the law was not a means of salvation but a means of instruction, a practical way for the Jew to demonstrate his will and desire to belong to the people chosen by God—the people chosen to be an image of the relationship of God with the whole of humanity. Even for Paul, the Jews still had a historical relationship with God, not a natural religion. They had a *covenant* (an agreement/contract) with him that was founded on Abraham's faith/trust in God and was confirmed by the recording of rules/requirements governing the Jews' practical fidelity to the covenant by Moses on Mount Sinai.[50]

But even the most consistent practical fidelity to the terms of the covenant has no existential consequences for humanity. It simply prefigures and prepares in advance that which the Church proclaims as a "new creation" with Christ. By the incarnation of

50. Rom 9:4–8; Gal 3:6–22.

the Son of God and Word of the Father, humanity's created and mortal nature (our mode of existence) is taken up into the *mode* by which the uncreated and immortal God exists: human nature is freed from the existential limitations of createdness.[51]

No fidelity to any law can substitute for the existential transformation that was accomplished for humanity by the incarnation of the Word. Only *faith*, which is trust and loving self-surrender (as a mode of existence that constitutes the ecclesial event), is proclaimed by Paul as having the necessary and sufficient power to enable us to participate in such freedom from necessity and confinement.[52]

The Judaizers were not simply a temporary hiccup at the beginning of the Church's historical life. "Judaizing" was and has always remained the constant temptation of religionization that lies in wait at every moment and in every aspect of ecclesial life. The historical facts force us to accept that the demands for religionization are interwoven inextricably with the ecclesial event, just as the "wheat" and the "weeds" "grow together" in the same field. Even Christ's words confirm that any effort to pull out the weeds from the field is unprofitable, for the attempt to distinguish them is pointless and risky: "For in gathering the weeds you would uproot the wheat along with them" (Matt 13:29).

The real separation of the ecclesial event from its religionization emerges from these words of Christ only as an eschatological expectation: "Let both of them grow together until the harvest; and at harvest time I will tell the reapers, 'Collect the weeds first and bind them in bundles to be burned, but gather the wheat into my barn'" (Matt 13:30).

Eschatological expectation, however, does not erase or diminish the need for Christians to be vigilant about distinguishing (so far as possible) the Church from a natural religion. This is not so as to preserve some kind of ideological orthodoxy and objective (idol-

51. Rom 8:12–21; Gal 5:1–6.
52. Rom 5:1–11; Gal 3:16–22.

ized) "authenticity" but only so as to insist on the realism of the *hope* of the gospel—a universally human hope.

Religionization appears to be interwoven, very often in a manner difficult to distinguish, with ecclesial thinking, even in the works of the Fathers and teachers of the Church, in hymnology and more widely in worship generally, in the way the administrative institutions function, in ascetical practice, and in popular piety. And as a rule it perpetuates the characteristic marks of the demands first projected on to the ecclesial life by the Judaizers: the need for law (i.e., codified rules, degrees of guilt, and the laying down of penalties for the "redeeming" of individual "righteousness"), the need for external forms that can objectify in a perceptible way (like circumcision) the fact that the individual *belongs* to the Christian collectivity, and the need for reining in sexual pleasure, a need expressed aggressively by circumcision.

The interweaving of religionization with ecclesial thinking becomes clearly discernible chiefly from the end of the seventh century, when, as already mentioned, the Quinisext Ecumenical Council formalized the universal imposition of "canons" regulating the personal life of Christians.

The problem does not rest with the absurdly grim moralism of some canons—in accordance with what these canons lay down, stipulations that have naturally remained in force to the present day, almost all Christians on earth are subject to excommunication. The more serious problem is the confusion created around the concept of sin. Sin, as assumed by those canons governed by a religious outlook, has no relation to the *failure* of human beings to graft themselves onto the eucharistic ethos of the Church, their existential *missing the mark*. Sin is not an opportunity to surrender oneself to grace, an occasion for the triumph of God's love, for the manifestation of the Church as the mystery of the cross and resurrection. Sin is the transgression of a law, an objective infringement. It comes under a precept that anticipates it in precise detail and punishes it with a predetermined penalty.

The very term *canon law* (a systematically arranged body of regulative legal precepts covering in a detailed fashion the broadest range of transgressive behavior) reveals how the presuppositions of the ecclesial event have been turned on their head. The canons referring to the life of individual believers and their systematic arrangement confirm the fact that religionization has accompanied ecclesial life from the time of the Judaizers mentioned in the New Testament to the present day. *Law* and *circumcision* were what the Judaizers demanded. A legal system of regulative precepts and, through the canons, an aggressive reining in of sexual pleasure are what the institutionalized religionization of their successors offers.

The alienation of both the eucharistic ethos and the ascetical struggle into a moralism centered on the individual along codified lines appears to be a symptom that is not accidental or coincidental. It is the permanent temptation to make the ecclesial event subject to the religious instincts of human nature. This began in apostolic times and has endured now for twenty centuries.

4.2. *Religio Imperii*

The religionization of the ecclesial event must also be due, to a large extent, to the geographical spread of the Christian presence in the Roman world and the increase in the Christian population. When the majority of the population had been converted to Christianity, the political realism of the imperial administration naturally led to the recognition of Christianity as the *official religion* (*religio imperii*) of the Roman Empire.

With the assumptions prevailing today about the modern "nation state," it is difficult for us to understand the role of religion in the way the Roman *imperium* functioned on the political level. The Roman Empire was one of the first polities in history consisting of an agglomeration of many nationalities and races with a variety of languages and religions. It managed to achieve administrative cohesion and political unity and maintain it for many centuries (from about the third century BC to the fifteenth century AD) thanks to certain fundamental constants of its political and administrative system.

These constants promoting unity sprang from a kind of programmatic transcendence of ambitions centered exclusively on the extension of power or world dominance. The Roman Empire always aimed at being something other than an authoritarian form of dominion over peoples. It wanted to constitute an *order of things* (an *ordo rerum*) on an international level, to play a leading role in ensuring the harmonious coexistence of peoples, to establish peace between them (the *pax Romana*).

The constants that served this aim were: (1) the prestige of imperial authority allied with a consistent administrative decentralization; (2) (the common) Roman law allied with the independence of local courts; and (3) the imperial religion (*religio imperii*), which was common to all peoples and was added to the religious beliefs, traditions, and practices existing among each of them.

The Roman government was not interested, positively or negatively, in the religions of the different peoples making up the empire. It only demanded, as a sign of law-abiding respect for authority, the rendering of additional worship to the gods of Rome, and naturally to the emperor. By this common worship the government ensured a powerful bond binding all its subjects together, the cohesion of the various different communities, and consequently the political unity of the empire.

In the person of the emperor, the Romans projected the master and guarantor of global order and peace, the deliverer of the subject peoples from wars among themselves, from penury and misery. They projected in the emperor the incarnate image of the "ancestral Zeus" and the "new Helios"—a kind of the indwelling of divinity in a mortal human being (a kind of "anthropotheistic theanthropism," as the students of comparative religion call it), an amalgam of Hellenistic and Zoroastrian influences.

Religion in the Roman Empire, thanks to obvious influences from Ancient Greece, appears to have functioned chiefly symbolically and iconologically as a hermeneutic key to understanding the world and human history. In these circumstances religion, precisely as an assimilated (in social practice and outlook) attribution of *meaning* to individual and collective life, becomes the foundation of *culture*, or (in the language of the Romans) of the *order of things*: the way in which life, and consequently the political system, is organized.

Accordingly, a refusal to conform to the *religio imperii*, the denial of worship of the emperor, was regarded not as ideological deviance but as a political crime. It was equivalent to denying the validity of the state, to undermining its cohesion, to revolting against it. That is why it incurred the death penalty. Only thus can we explain the persecution of Christians, the vast numbers of martyrs, in the early centuries.[53]

When Christianity came to be prevalent in the large centers of population of the Roman Empire (when the Church's gospel was accepted freely and without compulsion by major sections of society in spite of violent opposition from the state), the Roman government found itself confronted by new facts that could not be ignored. There was now *de facto* a common majority religion that could spontaneously and easily ensure the cultural unity of the empire beyond the differences of nations, races, and local traditions.

The political dynamic of this new factor, with its potential for ensuring social cohesion, was astutely perceived by Constantine the Great in his military confrontation with Maxentius (in 312). Appealing on that occasion to a supernatural vision, he adopted Christian symbols as emblems for his army, filling his Christian soldiers with enthusiasm and leading them to victory.

A year later, by the *Edict of Milan*, the imposition of an obligatory imperial religion was abolished and a judicious religious tolerance was proclaimed. The ecclesial event was now in a pivotal position for giving meaning to life for a large part of the empire's population. The *pax Romana* had begun to be understood as a *pax Christiana*.

To be sure, the first *heresies* that began to threaten the unity of the Church were also taken by Constantine as a threat to the cohesion of the state—in practice the emperor was already treating

53. See Kurt Pfister, *Der Untergang der antiken Welt* (Leipzig, 1941), 48; G. Grupp, *Kulturgeschichte der römischen Kaiserzeit* (Regensburg, 1921), 110ff.; Theodor Birt, *Das Römische Weltreich* (Berlin, 1941), 83ff.

Christianity as a *religio imperii*. He immediately summoned a council of all the bishops of the empire (the bishops of the "oecumene," of the *imperium*) and although not yet formally a Christian himself presided over it, the First Ecumenical Council (in 325 at Nicea in Bithynia).

Moreover, Constantine assisted the Church actively, granting privileges to the clergy and supplying funds for the building of churches. Finally, his deathbed baptism, his Christian funeral, and his interment in the Church of the Holy Apostles at Constantinople were perhaps his most important gift to the Church. They became the occasion for the shaping of a new metaphysical understanding of politics that did not constitute a break with the past but was rather was a fertile leap in continuity with the Greek tradition of the *polis* and the common struggle for its realization. In the person of the Christian emperor, the mind of the Church saw the servant of political unity as a reflection or image of the ecclesial communion of persons—it saw in the ancient Greek identification of "being in communion with" (*koinōnein*) and "being true" (*alētheuein*) the prefiguring of the eucharistic "kingdom."

The formal establishment of Christianity as the "official religion" of the Roman Empire was brought about, forty-three years after the death of Constantine the Great, by the Emperor Theodosius, who was likewise surnamed "the Great." In between these two dates there had occurred the failure, on the political and social level, of Julian's attempt to restore paganism by instituting a peculiar amalgam of the Twelve Gods of the ancient Greek world with elements drawn from Mithraism and Neoplatonic beliefs. There had also occurred the painful experience of the political consequences that the Christian heresies had for the empire.

Theodosius appeared determined to ensure the unity and cohesion of the empire by returning to the practice of the *religio imperii*, a practice tried and tested over the centuries. By an edict promulgated at Thessalonica on February 27, 380, he established the catholic, apostolic Church as the official religion of the empire. By a law issued on November 8, 392, he proscribed the Greco-Roman religion and forbade access to the temples. In 393 he abolished the Olympic Games, and in 396 the Eleusinian Mysteries. The Christian calendar was established as the basis for determining holidays and days of rest in Roman public life, and conversion to the "official religion" became an essential prerequisite for anyone who aspired to office throughout the empire.

If one takes into account both humanity's "internal" instinctive need for religion and the "external" (for reasons of collective utility) imposition of Christianity as an obligatory religion, one can perhaps imagine the extent of the consequences of the alienation of early Christian authenticity after Theodosius the Great.

This alienation may be studied in every minute aspect of the ecclesial event. It is difficult to date all the alienating changes precisely. That is because an essential factor (productive of alienation) is the objectively indeterminable alteration of mental outlook that in the long term results in institutional changes. Naturally, we lack a primary study of the dating of such mental shifts, for in principle the acceptance of a *fait accompli* alienation is not at all easy psychologically—even today, so many centuries later.

We are discussing an alienation that has as its specific character the *religionization* of the ecclesial event. Consequently, the main lines of investigation are clear: we need to establish whether or not the marks of natural religiosity have intruded into the ecclesial event. And the primary mark is the assigning of priority to demands centered on the individual.

Perhaps even before Theodosius's decree, the great increase in the number of Christians had alienated in many minds the consciousness of the Church as a eucharistic community. Perhaps the awareness that the Church is *existence-as-participation* in a body of relations of communion and that participation defines the struggle for self-transcendence, for love, had already weakened.

The large number must imperceptibly have changed the priorities: no longer participating in the coming together of a parish but "attending" public worship as an individual; not a change in *mode of existence* but an assembly for common prayer, for an impressive didactic spectacle designed to produce compunction; not a struggle to transcend the self for the joy of love but an attempt to secure individual merit.

Religionization means individualization, and the individualization of access to the Eucharist must have been the first unconscious step toward the abandoning of the ecclesial *mode* of participation. Individualized access means that the gospel's "salvation" ceases to refer to the drawing of being from relations of loving communion and becomes identified with the individual reception of the gifts of the Eucharist. Thus both terms of reception (the receiver and what is received) are objectified: the bread and the wine transmit (a supernatural, almost magical) "grace" independently of participation in the eucharistic event. And the individual who receives the bread and the wine is obliged to conform to codified requirements of worthiness for such reception.

The critical step, then, must have been the huge growth of the parish, the weakening or complete loss of awareness that the Church is embodied (and is experienced only as participation) in the eucharistic community. When this awareness is weakened or lost, the road is wide open to all the different forms of the demand for religionization: to understanding the Church's dogmatic teaching in terms of infallible supernatural formulations that offer the individual the assurance of guaranteed metaphysical convictions, to understanding ascetical practice in terms of ethics codified as law (and as "canon law") that armors the individual with certainties of measurable merit, to understanding worship in terms of common prayer and teaching that guarantee the individual an audited "spiritual" benefit.

When these changes have also become embedded, their further consequences emerge without hindrance: the Church imposes itself on people's consciences as an institution of social utility that improves morals, ameliorates behavior, and strengthens social cohesion. Such a useful institution clothes itself in the goodwill of the secular authority and adapts itself to the methods and tactics of social control. Operating with the logic of common utility, the institution inevitably also becomes coordinated with the logic of the exercise of power: the logic of effectiveness, of the demands for objective authority, of the external symbols of power (dress, formal etiquette, a wooden official language), of strict hierarchical organization and codified discipline.

Within the perspective of such an evolutionary trajectory, one ceases to be amazed by any extremism. It is not at all by chance that the bishop of Rome at an early stage came to assume the title of the pagan chief priest, *pontifex maximus*, which had once been borne only by the emperor, and that some centuries later[54] he had no hesitation in organizing the Roman church as a secular state (*Civitas Vaticana*), transforming the ecclesial event into an institutional form of political organization and subjecting the things of God to Caesar.

Both the so-called "Orthodox" churches and the later Protestant confessions condemned "with loathing" the unholy transformation of a local church (the Roman) into a secular state. Yet they were clearly attracted by the enterprise. The Protestant confessions sought to establish a similarly effective exercise of power through cultivating a version of faith as the prevailing ideology in secular/civic life. (Characteristic examples are the turning of Geneva into a police state by Calvin, the intertwining of Lutheranism with state ideology in the Scandinavian countries, the braiding together of church and state in England, or the phenomenon of civil religion in the United States.) The Orthodox churches, for their part, perhaps turning the *catholicity* of every local church into an absolute, let themselves slide into the affirmation in practice of ethnophyletism, making the ecclesial event subject to the ethnic (historical and cultural) self-consciousness of states set up in the modern age, and reconciling themselves to the role of a state religion.

Thus the political privileges of the *religio imperii*, together with the outlook and alienation that went with them, also survived in the Christian churches outside the Vatican version of Roman Catholicism, either in the form of a constitutionally protected "established religion" or with the political strength of a nationalist ideology. At any rate, the splendid *conciliar system*, which was formed to ensure

54. In the time of Stephen II, 754–56.

the unity of the *catholic Church throughout the oecumene*, proved incapable of functioning after the collapse of the Roman Empire, that is, without the support of the power structures of a "Supreme Authority" on the international level.

Roman Catholicism "solved" the problem of the Church's unity *throughout the oecumene* by alienating ecclesial *catholicity* (which has an existential character) into an ideological globalism obedient to the authority of the infallible *cathedra* of the Roman pontiff (and the structures by which his authority is exercised), creating for the first time in human history a fearsome *totalitarianism*. Protestantism withdrew from the problem of catholicity, but also from the consciousness of the Church as a body. It remained content with the convictions of believers as individuals and with the rational validity of such convictions, as well as with the practical utility of a codified system of ethics—breaking up into over three hundred confessions, offshoots, and sects.

As far as Orthodoxism is concerned, it boasts that it maintains the conciliar system and preserves a unity *throughout the oecumene*. Yet it too is content with verbal formulations of an ideological character produced by (rarely convoked) multinational councils, and with the formal *commemoration* in the Eucharist of the presiding hierarchs (all of them by each of them) of the national churches. Just like the Protestants, the Orthodox endure the drama of fragmentation, not into ideological offshoots but into many "autocephalous" national churches—with chaotic consequences for the Orthodox "diaspora" in the multiethnic societies of the modern West.

The appointment of the Church as the *religio imperii* in the context of the Roman Empire seems to have left it the legacy of a strong temptation to exercise effective power (or simply to enjoy the pleasure of power) in the centuries that followed—up to the present day.

4.3. *Augustine*

In the religionization of the ecclesial event, the work of Augustine, bishop of Hippo (354–430), plays a decisive role, even though it belongs to an earlier era. Some centuries after his death, Augustine was the point of departure or cornerstone for a particular version of Christianity, which became the occasion for the breakup of the Church's unity "throughout the oecumene." And this rupture, the *schism* (the so-called First Schism in 867 and the definitive one of 1054) had dramatic consequences for the alienation of the Church's gospel.

As a learned bishop with an exceptional authorial gift, Augustine should have gone down in history as an attractive figure but of marginal importance on account of his serious deviations from the "catholic" witness of ecclesial experience. Later historical developments and political ambitions, however, brought his work to the epicenter of the evolution of Western Europe. They made him the source and guarantor of a particular understanding of Christianity that took hold in Western Europe from the ninth century—and which is today the prevailing version in the whole of the Christian world.

We should recall again very briefly the far-reaching changes that had taken place in the territories of the Western Roman Empire from the end of the fourth to the sixth centuries AD. We usually call the influx of barbarian tribes and nations into the empire and their settlement there "the great migration of peoples." Of a lower cultural level than the native inhabitants they displaced, they brought about in 475 the collapse of Roman rule.

Franks, Goths, Huns, Burgundians, Vandals, and Lombards, they came to constitute the predominant element in the population of Western Europe. And by the late eighth/early ninth century, the military and political power of Charles, king of the Franks, surnamed the Great (Carolus Magnus, or Charlemagne, 742–814), enabled him to subject all the other tribes to his rule and form a vast state stretching from the North Sea to the Pyrenees and from the Atlantic to the Elbe.

The barbarian hordes that dissolved the Roman "order of things" in the West had hastened to adopt the Christian faith because conversion to Christianity at that time was the path to civilization. The question naturally arises: What can "conversion to Christianity" mean in the case of large masses of people who could not possibly have understood what until then had been the Greek expression of (or witness to) ecclesial experience—the Greek philosophical wording of the conciliar "definitions" and the teaching of the Fathers, the incomparable language of Greek art?

At any rate, the Christianized multiethnic kingdom of Charlemagne came to aspire to imperial status, thanks to its geographical extent and military power, on the model of the (unique until that time) Roman Empire. But it was taken for granted by everyone that the empire was an international "order of things": more a common culture than a form of state. It was also taken for granted that Christianity (the *pax Christiana*) was the only basis for a common culture in the international world of that time. Consequently, there was no real room or logical possibility for a second Christian empire so long as the Christian *Imperium Romanum* remained on the historical stage with its center in New Rome/Constantinople.

Charlemagne saw clearly that his ambition to establish an empire presupposed a cultural basis for political unity that was necessarily different from that of the Roman *oecumene*. The new basis had to be founded on the Christian faith. It therefore had to come up with a different version of this faith on both the theoretical and the practical levels, a version that was more correct and more genuine than that of the Greeks, clearly differentiated and, above all, with a distinctive Western identity. Only with such a new starting point for a civilized collective life could a new Christian "order of things" be justified internationally with its center now in the Frankish West.

It would appear to be for these reasons that there arose at that time a polemical literature condemning the "errors" of the Greeks—at least ten works dating from the ninth to the thirteenth centuries bear the title *Contra Errores Graecorum*. At the same time Augustine was retrieved from the historical margins to become the vital ideological discovery and weapon of the Franks.

Augustine was presented as an ideal basis for an exclusively Western version of Christianity that was clearly differentiated from the Greek tradition: a native Westerner himself with a thoroughly Latin education and a rich body of writings without Greek influences—because he did not speak Greek and admitted to reading it with difficulty if at all.[55] At the same time he was recognized throughout Christendom as a brilliant example of someone who had repented of a dissolute life, embraced a life of ecclesial ascetic discipline, and attained episcopal office. He understood the ecclesial gospel in terms of a natural religion: in terms of intellectual individualism, moralistic legalism, and emotional "interiority."

As a Christian writer Augustine clearly forged his own path, given that he lacked familiarity either with the Greek texts occasioned by the theological ferment of the first Christian centuries, or the Greek philosophical controversies that generated this ferment. He adapted Christian teaching to the structures of his legalistic thought in order to make the gospel accessible to the needs of a simplified religious understanding. He did this through clumsy misunderstandings of the fundamental presuppositions of ecclesial experience and particularity.

The main lines of Augustine's distortion and religionization of the Church's gospel may be summarized as follows:

First is a typically religious (consistent with natural instinctive religiosity) *individualism*—an individualized version of faith, morality, and experience. In Augustine's work there is not the slightest awareness or hint of the most important revelation of the gospel: the Triadic God, that is, the *mode* of real existence and life, of existence that is not predetermined by a given *nature* but constitutes the freedom of loving *relation*—that hypostasizes love as personal otherness. There is no awareness or hint that the Church is realized by reference to this *mode* of existential freedom (freedom from

55. See *Confessions* 1.13.20 and 1.14.23: "I hated Greek literature when I was being taught it as a small boy . . . I did not know any of the words, and violent pressure on me to learn them was imposed by means of fearful and cruel punishments" (Henry Chadwick, trans., *Saint Augustine: Confessions* [Oxford: Oxford University Press, 1991], 15, 17). See also *De Trinitate*, preface to book 3, where he confesses his inability to read the Greek Fathers of the Church in the original.

death), that it is the product of a struggle to express communion in existence and in life, a dynamic denial of the individualistic mode of created and mortal human nature, or a participation in existence as a relation of love, self-transcendence, and self-offering. The ecclesial event as an existential goal is entirely absent from Augustine's work. The Church is only a religious institution serving the individual's faith, virtue, and salvation.

Salvation for Augustine means a "supernatural" response of the Transcendent to the desire/demand of human beings for their atomic egos to exist for all eternity, to live forever in absolute happiness. The ego is discreetly disguised under the Platonic invention of the (ontologically indeterminate) "soul," and this is identified with the old term the *inner man*. The soul, or inner man, wins salvation as deliverance from the limitations of *matter*, or the *outer man*. The Christian's "spiritual struggle" is to fight against matter, the demands of the body, on the level of his natural atomic being.

Augustine's religious individualism affirms the equally instinctive need for intellectualist metaphysical certainties. Religious individuals want to possess sure knowledge of the hereafter. They want to be able to control this knowledge by their intellectual capacity, to exorcise by intellectual certainty their natural fear of death.

Augustine's affirmation of intellectualism presupposes, and therefore also maintains, a philosophical *essentialism*[56] (also of Platonic origin), the sense of existence as individual onticity defined by its given (in the Divine Mind—*in mente divina*) *essence*. The human mind, a miniature ("in the image") of the Divine Mind, can know all things through the individual's intellectual conception of the universal ideas/essences. All things are verified in the coincidence of the sensory image of every being with the intellectual conception of its essence. Thus the individual mind defines and verifies knowledge—the mind, not the experiential immediacy of the *relation*. The feeling of the absolute and self-evident priority

56. We should not forget that Augustine had access chiefly to Plato's main works in Latin translation. He came into contact with "Christian Platonism" through his studies with Ambrose of Milan.

(a kind of omnipotence) of the individual based in the individual's intellectual capacities (in the *facultas rationis*) signposts the historical journey of the new peoples of Western Europe. Individualism and intellectualism were to become elements of the identity of European man, and their very obvious starting point and source lie chiefly in Augustine.

An absolute confidence in the individual's intellectual capacity is combined in Augustine with an equally absolute affirmation of emotional urges, forming a closed self-referential dynamic within the limits of which Augustine's anthropology and metaphysics are fully exhausted. Human beings are defined as their "interiority." They are determined by whatever happens "within" them, the interior amalgam of intellectual certainty and emotional well-being. But at the same time they also meet God "within" themselves. They meet him precisely in terms of their individual intellectual certainty and individual emotional well-being. The encounter is a private one, the product of turning their attention inward.[57]

This nonrelational (beyond any possible *relation*) individualistic perspective of Augustine's was to form a characteristic mark of the West's mentality, a determining element of the historical habits of thought that have guided metaphysical inquiry in Europe. God is "within" the atomic individual, within the individual's "inwardness," and this private possession of God is validated either by the emotions (strictly self-referential subjective experience, "mystical" feeling, psychological "blissfulness," joy, and security) or by intellectualist apodictic analysis—more often the two together. Among those who continued Augustine's work, the leading figures were also supreme exponents of intellectualism, apodictic positivism, and the rational method. At the same time they were enthusiastic proponents of the "hidden God" (*Deus absconditus*), of faith as exceeding reason (*Fides excedit rationem*)—Anselm, Thomas Aquinas, Albert the Great, and John Duns Scotus.

57. See the excellent discussion of this topic titled "The correlation between God and interiority" in Ilias Papagiannopoulos, *Exodos theatrou: Dokimio ontologias me ploēgo ton "Moby Dick" tou H. Melville* (Athens: Indiktos, 2000), 81ff.

Augustine transcribed the witness/teaching of the Church into the language and structures of thought of his legal training and juridical experience. This schematic legal approach helped him achieve an impressive simplification and popularization of Christian witness so as to make it accessible to people of low cultural attainment or none at all. However, the legalism (in accordance, to a large extent, with the mentality that accompanied an instinctive religiosity) trapped Augustine's simplifying adaptations in what was actually a religious denial of the ecclesial event and gospel.

Both the Apostle Paul and Christian writers who preceded Augustine had used schematic forms, examples, and images drawn from the language of the law and from juridical experience in order to interpret the relationship between humanity and God. But these modes of expression continued the allusive (rather than literal) style of the imagery of the Gospels, the allegorical relativity of the formulations. Only with Augustine do legal and juridical forms of thinking claim the validity of a *pragmatist* interpretation, obviously satisfying the demands for schematization that accompany an instinctive religiosity. And gradually they became established in people's minds as the only possible version.

Augustine's position on two vital topics of Christian theological speculation, his interpretation of humanity's so-called "original sin" and his account of the reason for Christ's death on the cross, actually functioned as a catalyst for a radical change of mental outlook in the Christian world. The Christian God ceased to be the Bridegroom, the passionate lover of humankind, and was understood as a grim avenger, an implacable inflictor of punishment on the human race as a whole, on account of the first human couple, who had used their freedom in a way that was displeasing to God.

In consequence, the same God was identified with the image of a "sadistic father" because he did not hesitate to inflict a horrific death on his Son simply so that his righteousness could exact a satisfaction equal to the offense that had been given to him. It is abundantly clear that the origins of this appalling distortion are to be found in Augustine's own theological constructions. And if God, who in all other respects is "all-good," satisfies his righteousness with the death of Christ on the cross, why should Augustine not go on to infer that the righteous in heaven, for their part, enjoy the sight of sinners being tortured in hell?

Thus the gospel of the victory over hell has been transformed into a religion of the fear of hell. To this fear is also added the panic of a programmatic uncertainty: the uncertainty of who are "predestined" by God for salvation and who will be damned, programmed without reason or cause to be lost however much they try to please God. The God of Augustinian legalism is not only vengeful and sadistic but is also irrationally unjust, all for the sake of maintaining a rationalist explanation of his omniscience. The teaching on the double predestination of humanity was to set an agonizing stamp on both the religious and the social life of the West;[58] generation upon generation, millions of people were to live their unique life in a state of tormenting anxiety or hopeless rebellion. To this brief sketch should be added Augustine's philosophically embellished Manichaeism: his insistence on the antithesis between matter and spirit, body and soul, moral life and physical pleasure—a depreciation, loathing, and fear of sexuality.

Ignorant of the distinction between *essence* and *energies* with which the Cappadocian Fathers interpreted matter ontologically as the *logos*/manifestation of the personal otherness of the divine hypostases (the result of which is the matter of divine energy, which is not identified either with the essence or with the hypostases of the

58. See Max Weber's classic study, *The Protestant Ethic and the Spirit of Capitalism* (London and New York: Routledge, 2001), first published as *Die protestantischer Ethik und der Geist des Kapitalismus* in 1905, which connects the phenomenon of the "amassing of capital" and the origin of capitalism with the Protestant world's appropriation of Augustine's teaching on absolute predestination. See also Jürgen Moltmann, *Praedestination und Perseveranz* (Neukirchen: Kreis Moers, 1961); Gotthard Nygren, *Das Prädestinationsproblem in der Theologie Augustins* (Lund: printed dissertation, 1956); Rune Söderlund, *Ex praevisa fidei: Zum Versfändnis der Prädestinationslehre in der lutheranischen Orthodoxie* (Hanover: Lutherisches Verlagshaus, 1983); and Olivier Clément, *Hē theologia meta ton "thanato tou Theou,"* vol. 7 of the Synoro series (Athens: Dōdōnē, 1973), where we read on p. 42, "The personal God is presented as a celestial policeman, whose glance petrifies us to the depths of our being and our future, like an absolute Subject who objectifies us and whose omniscience and omnipotence transform history into a puppet theater. Thus humankind is nothing and God becomes responsible for all the evils of the world."

Godhead[59]), Augustine found himself in a hermeneutic impasse. He was attracted by the Platonic invention of the *Ideas*, which predetermine the form/mode and the end/goal of the existence of sensible things, but he was unable to accept their ontological autonomy and transposed the Platonic world of the Ideas into the divine intellect identified with the divine essence. The ideas/forms exist outside of sensible beings and independently of them. They have in themselves a given and complete *essential* perfection because they are contained within the essence of God.

Such a theory, however, leaves the matter of the world ontologically without explanation and attributes to *each particular existent* the character of iconic/virtual (unreal) existence. Augustine knows that if we refer the ontological *principle* of matter to God, we end up in pantheism. If we transpose the ontological *principle* of matter to matter itself, we have to accept, with Plato, the self-existence and eternity of matter. Augustine has no solution to the problem. He resorts to an easy escape: he pronounces matter a reality that in its essence is nothingness, a *penitus nihil*.[60] Thus the residue of his period of attachment to the Manichees settled and developed to establish in the West the interrelated polarizations that would identify Christianity in the popular mind with a religion of guilt, remorse, and anxiety about the corruptibility of humanity and the materiality of the world.

It is not at all accidental that Augustine is universally recognized—independently of the ideological principles or methodological presuppositions with which one approaches historical study—as the cornerstone or begetter of the culture that was born in the post-Roman West. As the foundation of the Vatican version of Christianity, of Scholasticism, and also of the Protestant Reformation; as the theoretical source of religious, ideological, and political totalitarianism and simultaneously of individualism; as a precursor of Descartes' *cogito* and of Kant's critique and autonomous ethics; and as

59. See my *Person and Eros* (Brookline, MA: Holy Cross Orthodox Press, 2007), §§ 19–23.

60. See my *Philosophie sans rupture*, trans. André Borrély (Geneva: Labor et Fides, 1986), § 28.

an inspiration to the chief proponents of intellectualism and also to the outstanding teachers of mysticism and pietism, Augustine summarizes in a single source and root the many-branched and often mutually hostile ramifications of Western European civilization. This civilization has given the greatest possible religionization of the ecclesial event a global dimension. It has also led to a militant rejection of metaphysics, whose identification with a repulsive and oppressive Christianity is everywhere taken for granted.

4.4. *Ideological Catholicity*

Two separate bodies emerged from Christendom's schism in 1054. One defined itself as the *Roman Catholic Church*, the other as the *Orthodox Catholic Church*. These titles clearly revealed two different versions of *catholicity*: one Roman, the other Orthodox. The pivotal difference between these two portions of the Christian world (whether conscious or unconscious) was their understanding of catholicity.

It should be mentioned that until the time of the schism the term *Catholic Church* defined the genuineness and authenticity of the ecclesial event in contradistinction with *heresy*. Heresy (from the Greek verb *hairoumai*, "I prefer," "I choose") indicated the result of an elected version of the presuppositions of the ecclesial event, a choice that led to a distinctively private approach (*idiazein*), to a peculiar understanding and experience of the gospel—peculiar and disjunctive with regard to the whole (the *katholou*) of the ecclesial body. The criterion of the distinction between an ecclesial community (parish or diocese) and a heretical group was not the difference of "convictions," or any codified formulations of experience. It was catholicity. The ecclesial community realized and manifested the whole (the *katholou*) of the ecclesial event, the totality of the gospel's hope. And this catholicity was attributed to it by all the other local churches through the liturgical communion that was ensured by the *conciliar system*.

Even after the schism the Greek East continued to maintain the understanding of catholicity that had been held in common until that time. Of course, for the conciliar system, which ensured the distinction of the Church from heresy, to be able to function, the East depended on the effectiveness of the institutions of the Empire of New Rome/Constantinople, institutions that maintained the political and social cohesion of its Christian peoples. By contrast, the elder Rome had to deal with a European West fragmented politically and socially into a number of barbarian kingdoms, principalities, duchies, and counties where each ruler claimed to decide for himself the correct faith of his subjects.

In these circumstances it was almost impossible for the Church of Rome, the church "presiding" in the West, to guarantee and preserve simply by its ecclesiastical authority the catholicity (genuineness, wholeness, and authenticity) of the local churches to be found there. It was thus led to the solution of itself assuming the role of political leadership so as to be in a position to impose orthodox thinking by employing means effective in the secular sphere. The Roman Church succeeded in winning from the Frankish king Pepin the Short (715–68), Charlemagne's father, recognition as an autonomous state (in 754) with a specific territorial sovereignty and with institutions and functions that enabled it to intervene authoritatively in international relations.

This evolution, a result rather of an inexorable historical necessity (but also of the indisputable struggle for primacy of "jurisdiction" between the patriarchates of Rome and New Rome), produced in the West a new version and understanding of catholicity that was purely geographical and quantitative. Catholicity now meant not the wholeness and fullness of a *mode of existence*, but the international (or even global) character of objective marks of the ecclesial event, such as *faith* as official "doctrine" and conforming to a codified *ethics*.

Faith ceases to be a struggle to attain trust, to attain relations of loving communion. It ceases to be the fruit of self-transcendence. It is identified with convictions possessed by the individual, with the individual's intellectual assent to "official" axiomatic declarations and principles. Faith is transformed into an ideology, and its authenticity is confirmed now not by the dynamic of a shared experiential verification (the conciliar function) but by an institution of infallible authority: the episcopal cathedra or see (supposedly) of the Apostle Peter and of each successive bishop of Rome. The same see also determines the regulative principles of conduct, the morality of those who are believers in this ideological sense, through a juridical system of codified canons and also by means of a constant series of declarations on topical moral problems.

It is easy to understand how and why the quantitative/geographical version of catholicity was an effective solution to the problem of the unity of the Christian world in the West and at the same time the matrix for the generation (for the first time in human history) of the phenomenon we call *totalitarianism*. Humanity had known various forms of absolutist rule, tyranny, and arbitrary despotism. But it had not known a form of authority that controlled not only public conduct but also the convictions of individuals, their ideas and views, their private life. It had not known institutions such as the Holy Inquisition that punished thoughtcrimes, nor the Index of Prohibited Books, the systematic indoctrination of the masses established by the *Congregatio de Propaganda Fidei*, the principle of infallible leadership enshrined in the papal *infallible magisterium*, the use of torture as a method of examination (authorized by a bull of Innocent IV in 1252).

The Roman version of catholicity became identical with the alienation of the ecclesial event in a centrally controlled ideology and codified moralism: its radical religionization. All the elements and marks of a natural religion are manifest in the Roman Catholic tradition as institutionalized responses to humanity's biological, instinctive need for religion. They are manifest in an intellectualist safeguarding of metaphysical certainties; in a moralistic legalism, or fear of freedom; in submission to an "infallible" authority, or fear of growing up; and in the idolization of "dogma," or fear of risking ascetical access to experiential knowledge.

As in any religion, salvation was understood as an event centered on the individual and proclaimed as such—a narcissistic, neurotic goal. Matter was depreciated, the human body became a source of anguished guilt, and erotic love was identified with the terror of a punishable "impurity." At the same time the Church's service to humanity of freeing us from slavery to the egocentrism of guilt was alienated into an authority "to bind and to loose," an all-powerful authority from the moment the full weight of pangs of guilt that are so intolerable for humanity began to be felt. The expression "plenitude of power" (*plenitudo potestatis*) literally means that the bishop of Rome claimed (and for long periods succeeded in enforcing) that he alone (thanks to the absolute power on earth granted to him by God) "invests" the secular rulers, kings, and sovereigns with the insignia of their office, and consequently that it was also he who deposed them when he judged their actions not to conform to true piety. And if kings and sovereigns were directly or indirectly subject to the pope, how much more completely were the laity subject to the "Church," that is, to the clergy.

Those who exercised the authority "to bind and to loose," the clergy as a whole, were charged, moreover, with the authority that came from the obligatory renunciation of sexuality: the priesthood was linked without exception to celibacy. With full awareness of the powerful prerogatives and high merit that went with their sexual privation, the clergy in the medieval West constituted a distinct social class that enjoyed a standard of living incomparably higher than that of the ordinary laity and often even higher than that of the nobility.

The Roman version of catholicity succeeded in solving the problem of the unity of the particular local churches in an impressively effective manner. But there is no doubt that it radically changed the character of ecclesial unity, transforming it into an ideologically disciplined uniformity and a homogenous legal moralism. (The Roman Catholic totalitarian model of unity was reproduced some centuries later by Marxism, in its imposition of a single and once again "infallible" cathedra—Moscow—and an inflexible system of obedience of the "faithful" to the party ideology and morality.[61]) By the criteria of the Church's gospel, the Roman version of catholicity was a dramatic historical failure, even if by the criteria of secular efficiency it may be reckoned a success.

61. See also my essay "Vatikano kai Diamartyrēsē ston Marxismo" in my *Hē neoellēnikē tautotēta* (Athens: Grigori, 1978), 23–31.

Sadly, the historical outcome of the Orthodox version was no better. Ecclesial catholicity as a wholeness of the existential achievement, as a mode of communion and coexistence, remained a theoretical boast of the Orthodox but in practice proved to be a goal that was unattainable and unrealizable. Two basic factors contributed to the alienation of ecclesial catholicity in the case of the Orthodox churches as well. The first was (and still is) the unconscious (and perhaps even conscious) imitation of the Vatican model. The second, of course, was nationalism.

On the collapse of the empire of New Rome/Constantinople, and the subsequent subjection of the cradle of Hellenism to harsh Turkish rule for as long as four centuries, the patriarchate of Constantinople was recognized by the sultan as the sole authority (the sole spiritual—and indirectly political—leadership) representing Orthodox Christians subject to the Turks. The other ancient patriarchates (Alexandria, Antioch, and Jerusalem) could only approach the Turkish government in connection with any needs or requests through the patriarchate of Constantinople. This exclusive prerogative must have encouraged the development of something analogous to a Vatican mentality in Constantinople.

Of course, from as early as the time of the Fourth Ecumenical Council (451), ecclesial experience in its institutionalized form acknowledged a vitally important prerogative in the patriarchate of Constantinople, the prerogative of convoking ecumenical councils of bishops and presiding at them. This prerogative was (and still is) a guarantee of unity of the one catholic Church "throughout the oecumene"—a responsibility of *diakonia*, or service, to ecumenical unity, a prerogative grounded in a responsibility and guarantee founded on the function of *conciliarity* as presuppositional for the ecclesial event. Conciliarity extends the existential unity of the eucharistic body in the totality of its local manifestations.

The extremely difficult conditions of ecclesial life in the centuries of the *Tourkokratia* also limited the way conciliarity could function—it was not easy, and often impossible, for bishops to travel. Thus the councils that had to be convoked to deal with pressing problems (to set the boundaries of ecclesial experience as against heretical deviations[62]) were held with a small number of bishops selected on grounds that are difficult to determine. It remains historically obscure whether the selection of bishops was the result of the difficult conditions of the times or the result of a diminished sense of the Church's nature, a limited awareness of the role of conciliarity in establishing the authenticity of the ecclesial event.

We also find evidence of a mistaken understanding of conciliarity in the institutionalization, dating from the seventeenth century, of the "resident" (as it was called) patriarchal synod—a synod constituted by the bishops "residing" in the patriarchal see. Such a synod no longer referred to bishops summoned to a council with a view to witnessing the experience of the eucharistic body over which each "presided." It referred to clerics who had been promoted to episcopal rank but who for various reasons (chiefly reasons connected with the unfavorable conditions created by the Turkish occupation) had been forced to abandon their dioceses. They resided at the seat of the patriarchate assuming administrative and advisory responsibilities, that is, the role of senior officials of an institutional class of administrators.

This more or less unconscious alienation both of the institution of a council and of the function of a bishop indicated in reality the adoption of a Roman Catholic ecclesiology by the Orthodox East. For the Roman Catholics a local eucharistic community constitutes an ecclesial event only because it is legally recognized as such (by objectified ideological and institutional criteria) by the papal see of Rome—the bishop simply administers or serves it; he does not constitute the presupposition for its constitution as its *head* and *father*. A community in the West can be ecclesial without its own bishop, and a cleric can be a bishop without presiding over an ecclesial community.

This understanding lies at the opposite pole to Orthodox ecclesiology. It amounts to a negation of the Church's gospel, of the *mode of existence* that defines the ecclesial event. The bishop's *diakonia*, or service, as *father* and *head* of a specific ecclesial body ("as a type and in the place of Christ") is for all Orthodox an indispensable

62. Such as the councils of 1638, 1642, 1672, and 1691 held at Constantinople.

predisposition for the realization and manifestation of the Catholic Church: of the whole and integral imaging by the Church of Triadic *true existence.*

From the middle of the seventeenth century, the Orthodox patriarchates began, without any reservation or hesitation, to adopt the Vatican practice of ordaining *titular* bishops, that is, bishops "with the bare title of a diocese." These are granted the title of bishop (of *father* and *head*) of a nonexistent local church "once eminent in antiquity"; in reality they are bishops without a diocese (like mayors without a borough). Their episcopal function is only that of an administrative office within the context of the responsibilities and needs of the patriarchate.

The evolution of this distortion is irreversible. The nineteenth century even saw the rise of a hierarchy of different grades among the titular bishops. The institution of the titular "metropolitan" was created, and the even higher rank of the "active metropolitan" (titular, of course, without a metropolitanate), the *mētropolitēs en energeia*! *Episcopi titulares* were thus established in the Orthodox world, in absolute fidelity to Vatican ecclesiology and in accordance with presuppositions precisely as laid down by papal canon law: *qui peculiari munere sibi ab Apostolica Sede . . . demandato in territorio funguntur.*[63]

In an obvious but uncontested manner, Orthodox patriarchs, even to the present day, are surrounded by permanent synods of (as a rule) titular metropolitans, archbishops, and bishops, organized as "committees" or "departments" with special administrative responsibilities in faithful imitation of the Roman Curia. This now institutionalized bureaucracy replaces the conciliar system of apostolic and patristic tradition and excludes the active pastors of the ecclesial body scattered throughout the territory falling within the boundaries of the patriarchate from participation in central synodical responsibilities. In other words, it excludes the witness of the ecclesial body from patriarchal decisions.

63. Latin: "who perform in the territory the special function entrusted to them by the Holy See."

Another decisive factor that contributed toward the historical failure of the Orthodox version of ecclesial catholicity was nationalism. It could be argued that the Orthodox version of the unity of the Catholic Church "throughout the oecumene" functioned satisfactorily so long as "ecumenical" was identified with the administrative, political, and cultural unity of the Roman Empire. The institution of the so-called *pentarchy* of the senior patriarchates (Rome, New Rome, Alexandria, Antioch, and Jerusalem) was pivotal for the operation of the conciliar system, which ensured unity "throughout the oecumene" on the basis of the cultural homogeneity of all these Hellenized communities. Hellenism functioned as a catalyst (or servant) of the ecumenical homogenization and uniform cohesion of the discrete local churches.

The Franks were the first to aspire to independence from Greco-Roman "ecumenicity." They were the first to set up an empire beyond the boundaries of the Greco-Roman world, a Germanic "oecumene" with its own institution for ensuring ecclesiastical unity, a patriarchate defined along nationalist lines. The resistance of Latin Orthodoxy from the ninth to the eleventh centuries delayed the complete realization of this ambition. When a Frank was for the first time appointed bishop of Rome (1014), the road lay open for a Germanic "oecumene"—and its autonomy was aggressively defined by the *schism* of 1054.

The Frankish example was followed by the Bulgars, initially without success. At the beginning of the tenth century, King Symeon conquered the entire area from the Black Sea to the Adriatic and from the Danube to Mount Olympus. He then hastened to unite his conquests ecclesiastically as well under the archbishopric of Ochrid, which he declared independent with a purely national character.

Symeon's state collapsed, but not the Bulgars' ambitions of national ecclesiastical autonomy. In 1235 the purely Bulgarian provinces in the Balkans were united ecclesiastically under the independent archbishopric of Trnovo, whereupon the archbishop assumed the title of "patriarch." A century later (1355) Patriarch Kallistos of Constantinople declared that "he is called patriarch of Bulgaria but is not to be numbered with the other most holy patriarchs and therefore is not to be commemorated in the sacred diptychs."[64]

The next attempt was made by the Serbs. They too wanted to set up an empire and in consequence to found at the same time a national patriarchate. In the mid-fourteenth century, under their ruler Stephen Dušan (1308–55), the Serbs reached the limits of their conquests. Dušan then proclaimed the Serbian archbishop of Peć "patriarch" with the intention of being crowned "emperor of the Serbs and Greeks" by him. But this achievement was short-lived.

After the Frankish *schism*, the second great and definitive achievement of nationalism on the ecclesiastical level was the successful claim to the title of patriarch by Moscow (1589).

The process leading up to this covers almost the whole of the fifteenth century. This was the century of the awakening of the national consciousness of the Russians and the efforts of the Muscovite state to attain political autonomy. As in the case of the Franks, this awakening was accompanied by an aggressive anti-Hellenism—weaning itself away from dependence on the Greeks (from dependence on the Greek cultural body of the ecclesial event) perhaps demanded recourse to some kind of parricide.

The same fifteenth century also saw the fall of Constantinople (1453), the subjection of Hellenism to the harsh Turkish yoke, and its near disappearance from the historical scene. In many minds (not only of the Greeks), this event had the character of a "sign" of apocalyptic or eschatological significance. In Russia it was interpreted as a punishment visited on the Greeks because they had betrayed the Orthodox truth of the Church at the unionist (even if ineffectual) council of Ferrara-Florence (1438–45).

Within such a climate there was conceived in Russia in the fifteenth century the idea of *Moscow the Third Rome*: "For two Romes have fallen, a third stands and a fourth there cannot be."[65] For Russian nationalism the idea was striking and extremely suggestive that the Russians had been chosen by divine providence to form

---

64. F. Miklosich and J. Müller, *Acta Patriarchatus Constantinopolitani* (Vienna, 1860), 1:437.

65. Georges Florovsky, *Ways of Russian Theology*, vol. 5 of The Collected Works of Georges Florovsky (Belmont, MA: Nordland, 1979), 11.

a new "Orthodox" empire and therefore a patriarchate with a primacy among the Orthodox churches.

In 1589 Patriarch Jeremias II of Constantinople came to Russia to organize the collection of alms. The Russians then managed ("by force and through guile"[66]) to exact from him the promise that the metropolitanate of Moscow would be raised to patriarchal status. Four years later, in 1593, Jeremias II convoked a great council at Constantinople, with the participation of the Orthodox patriarchs and many metropolitans, that put the promise into effect. It recognized Moscow as a patriarchate, the first national patriarchate, and assigned it sixth place in the honorary hierarchy after Jerusalem.

The Russians believed that the Third Rome was not simply a continuation of the Second but replaced it. The Third Rome was committed not to promoting or conserving but to replacing and re-creating the Greek Constantinopolitan tradition, to building up from scratch the new (Third) Rome in order to oust the two older Romes that had fallen. The victory of the Hagarenes (the Muslims) over the Greeks signified to the Russians a manifest punishment of the Greeks for the betrayal of their faith. It rendered the Greeks thoroughly unworthy, because they lived under the yoke of the Hagarenes, the absolute sovereignty of the "pagan tsar's realm of the godless Turks."[67]

There thus began in Russia a frantic effort (of exactly the same nature as that of the Franks some centuries earlier) to differentiate Russian believers from the Greeks in one way or another in the many external elements of ecclesial life—fortunately not also in matters of dogma (in the conciliar formulations of ecclesial experience) as in the case of the Franks. The Franks had accurately perceived that the break with the Greek East could be accomplished historically only if it was experienced as a manifest difference in popular practice. That is why, over and above the dogmatic innovations, they insisted on changing external forms. They insisted that the faithful should make the sign of the cross with five (not with three) fingers, that clerics should shave their faces and cut their

66. Konstantinos Sathas, *Biographikon schediasma peri tou Patriarchou Ieremiou B' (1572–1594)* (Thessalonica: Pournaras, 1979), 83ff.

67. See Florovsky, *Ways of Russian Theology*, 12.

hair, and that baptism should be carried out by sprinkling, not by immersion in water. They abolished communion by the laity of the wine in the Eucharist, and replaced the bread with the unleavened "host."[68] They imposed obligatory celibacy on the clergy, and so on and so forth.

More gently, but clearly by the same logic, the Russians insisted on differentiations that made their own national particularity immediately apparent: a Russian form of the cross (with three horizontal cross-pieces on the vertical axis), a Russian form of the cassock, a Russian form of headgear, a Russian veil for clerics, a Russian type of iconography (with an ethereal impressionistic element), a Russian ecclesiastical architecture (with an emphasis on the radically different and solely decorative onion-shaped dome). Of course, these are difference of an external and secondary nature that could very easily have gone unnoticed if it had not been intended that they should function as expressions of national particularity, of a thrust toward primacy.

The nationalistic fragmentation of the unity of the Orthodox churches was brought to completion unfalteringly in the course of the nineteenth and twentieth centuries, within the context of the culture of modernity, through the universal spread of the *nation state* as the only model for the political organization of communities. One after another, the Orthodox peoples of the Balkans rapidly threw off the yoke of subjection to the Turks and formed a state of the modern type. They demanded ecclesiastical independence, separation from the Ecumenical Patriarchate of Constantinople, and promotion to a national church and, usually, to a patriarchate.

A start was made with the establishment of a Greek state in a small portion of the territories where the Greeks had lived since ancient times. This tiny and insignificant state, governed for the first decades of its existence by Bavarians and dominated by an ideology of the aggressive pursuit of rapid and unbounded (imitative) Westernization, decided unilaterally to detach from the Ecumenical Patriarchate those bishops whose dioceses in the territories it

68. From the Latin *hostia*, which means "victim" or "sacrifice" and expresses the Western understanding of the Eucharist as primarily a sacrifice.

controlled, and by government decree to set up an "autocephalous" Greek church (1833).[69] This church remained schismatic for nearly twenty years and was only recognized in 1850 by an act of condescension on the part of the Ecumenical Patriarchate.

There followed, by more gentle processes, the Ecumenical Patriarchate's recognition in 1879 of the national Church of Serbia as autocephalous and its elevation in 1920 to a patriarchate. In 1855 the national Church of Romania was recognized as autocephalous, and in 1925 it too was raised to a patriarchate. After a long period in a state of schism, the Bulgarian national church was recognized as autocephalous in 1945 and as a patriarchate in 1953. In 1990 the Church of Georgia was proclaimed to be autocephalous, and the archbishop of Tiflis assumed the title of patriarch "of all Georgia." The national Orthodox Church of Poland has been recognized as autocephalous since 1924, the national Church of Albania since 1937, and the national Church of the Czech Republic and Slovakia since 1998. The last named has its seat either in the city of Presov in Slovakia or in Prague in the Czech Republic, depending on the nationality of the incumbent hierarch.

Thus *Orthodoxy*, while once having the same meaning as ecclesial *catholicity*, has come to be understood primarily as a national religion (the state's "prevailing religion," as the Greek Constitution tellingly defines it on quantitative and population criteria). Ecclesial Orthodoxy is identified with the historical particularity of each nation, with its political adventures and ambitions, and becomes essentially an expression of the official state ideology. It unavoidably becomes subject to the aims of the state's internal and external policies, supporting (or "sanctifying") the use of force in military confrontations.

If at one time the word *Orthodoxy* manifested the enduring presence of catholicity in each local church, and its defense; if at one time it raised the existential event (historically, culturally, in tangible embodied form) to the level of a globalized ideal, today the same word *Orthodoxy* refers to a useful tool employed by nation-

69. See further my *Orthodoxy and the West* (Brookline, MA: Holy Cross Orthodox Press, 2006), chap. 15.

alists to safeguard the existence and power of nationalism in the state. This is a bitter fruit, a very bitter fruit, of the religionization of the ecclesial event both in the East and in the West.

4.5. *Pietism*

Historically we use the word *pietism* within the context of religious traditions to refer to organized movements, or simply trends, that constitute perhaps the clearest expression of humanity's instinctive need for religion.

Pietism bypasses or relativizes "dogma" (the intellect's claim to investigate metaphysical enigmas) with a view to attaining the chief goal of religiosity: the securing of psychological certainty with regard to individual salvation. It aims at winning salvation through emotional exaltation, mystical experiences, or objectively measurable achievements of virtue, of practical fidelity to religious precepts—through practical reverence for the sacred, which is *piety*.

As a phenomenon of the religious life, pietism certainly preceded the ecclesial event. In the early years of the Church's appearance, the chief pietistic trend was that of *gnosticism*. Gnosticism derived its name from the fact that what it chiefly promised was unmediated knowledge (*epopteia*) of transcendent reality, a knowledge, however, only attainable by applying oneself as an individual to practical forms of piety.

These pietistic practices, like the theoretical teachings of the various groups or traditions that together made up gnosticism, were a typical product of religious syncretism—an amalgam of elements from the ancient Greek world, Judaism, and the religions of the Near East. With the appearance of the Christian Church, there immediately also arose (from as early as the days of the apostles themselves) "Christian" expressions of gnosticism. The most notable were the gnostic groups of Saturnilus (around AD 130) in Syria, Basilides (in the same period) in Alexandria, Valentinus (after 160) in Rome and Cyprus, Marcion (around 150) in Sinope of Pontus and in Rome (with organized groups of Marcionites spreading throughout the Middle East), and Mani (around 240), a Persian whose teaching (*Manichaeism*) spread with astonishing success, reaching as far as China in the East and Spain in the West.

All these trends or manifestations of gnosticism had a number of points in common. The most characteristic of them may be summarized as follows.

The first point was ontological *dualism*. This is the belief that there are two causal principles for existent things: an evil God, who is pure matter and the manipulator of matter, who is the creator of the visible world and the author of evil in the world; and a good God, who is pure spirit, without any relation at all to the creation of the material world, and who has as his work the liberation of humanity from the bonds of matter, that is, of evil.

The second point was *docetism*. This is the belief that the good God sent his son, Jesus Christ, into the world with an apparent body (a body *kata dokēsin*) to suffer an apparent death on the cross in order to save humanity by his teaching and the salvific energy of his cross.

The third point, closely connected with the first two, was an *abhorrence of matter*, of the body, of any pleasure, and especially of the pleasure of sexuality, along with the rejection of images, holy relics, and the honor paid to the human persons of the saints. The gnostics believed that by a systematic practice of asceticism and by an intellectualist rationality they became capable of liberation from the demands of matter and attained likeness to God.

The Church fought against gnosticism from the first steps of its historical journey—most of the information we have about it derives from Christian writings produced to combat its opinions. Yet it survived historically in the Christian world with astonishing tenacity through the centuries. What survived were its basic points and the tendencies, views, and outlooks related to it, in collective forms, with different names at different times but with the same experiential identity.

It is worth noting in brief outline the main stages of this historical development.

The communities of *Marcionites* (the followers of Marcion) flourished until the time of Constantine the Great (fourth century) and remained active historically until the seventh century. They were then assimilated by the *Paulicians* in the East and by the *Manichees* in the West.

The Paulicians emerged from the Marcionites and also from the *Messalians* (or *Massalians* or *Euchites*), another branch of gnosticism that had appeared in the fourth century, mainly within the world of monasticism, and represented extreme tendencies of asceticism and enthusiasm. The Messalians survived at least until the seventh century in Syria and Asia Minor. They rejected or were contemptuous of the Church's sacraments and rites. They aimed at atomic union with God through atomic asceticism and atomic prayer or through dancing that led to the ecstasy of the atomic individual.

From the seventh century onward, the movement that continued the tradition of gnosticism in Asia Minor, Syria, Mesopotamia, and Thrace was now the *Paulicians*. They derived their name from the special honor they gave to the Apostle Paul and his teaching. They accepted Marcion's ontological dualism and Christ's docetic human presence, and rejected the Hebrew tradition and the Old Testament, together with the ecclesiastical rites, the clergy, the churches, the icons, and the veneration of the saints. The only people they called "Christians" were themselves; those who belonged to the Church were simply called "Romans," bereft of grace and salvation. These are features that clearly point to the religious denial of the ecclesial event and its institutional expressions, and to its replacement by a pietistic individualism—the route of atomic access to salvation.

In the tenth century this gnostic-Manichaean pietism was transplanted by the Paulicians into Bulgaria, under the form of groups or communities that called themselves *Bogomils* (which in Bulgarian means "lovers of God"). They preserved all the doctrines of the Paulicians, developing in addition an extreme asceticism. They abhorred marriage, loathed sexuality, abstained from meat, and celebrated baptism without submersion in water, only by the laying on of hands. Within three centuries, from the tenth to the thirteenth, the Bogomils had developed into a powerful movement with an impressive expansion both toward the East (where they were usually called *Neomanichees*) and toward the West (where in the first half of the twelfth century they were given the name *Cathars*, or "pure ones").

The Cathar heresy, with all the above marks of a Manichaeistic pietism, presented not only a religious but also a serious social challenge to the peoples of the West in the Middle Ages—a real scourge. The heresy's aggressive opposition to the Church's institutions echoed the unhappiness of a large number of people about the worldly, authoritarian character of these institutions, the taxes that were imposed on the laity, the different life of the clergy and their provocative opulence. These anticlerical and antipapal tendencies favored the demand for an objectively assured and measurable "purity," which was easily identified with an aversion to sexuality and ended up as a fanatical dissemination of the rejection of marriage. Such facts created the feeling that the powerful Cathar trend threatened the cohesion and even the biological survival of the communities where they predominated.

Roman Catholicism, the prevailing authority in the West, reacted forcefully against the heresy of the Cathars, at first with banishment, confiscation of property, and excommunication; later with imprisonment and torture; and finally with death at the stake, inflicted on the heretics by the *Holy Inquisition*, an institution founded by Pope Gregory IX in April 1233.

The gnosticism of the early Christian centuries (and chiefly Manichaeism) was continued and spread historically by the Marcionites and Messalians. From the latter came the Paulicians, from the Paulicians the Bogomils, and from the Bogomils the Cathars. The historical succession is continuous, without gaps. There are historians who regard the Cathars as forerunners of Protestantism and see in the great religious trends generated by the Reformation, in *puritanism* and *pietism*, the continuation and survival of a Manichaeistic pietism up to our own days.[70]

70. See Vasileios Stephanidis, *Ekklēsiastikē Historia*, 3rd ed. (Athens: Astir, 1970), 571, 575; Vlasios Pheidas, *Ekklēsiastikē Historia*, vol. 2 (Athens, 1994), 452, 458ff.; Steven Runciman, *The Medieval Manichee: A Study of the Christian Dualist Heresy* (Cambridge: Cambridge University Press, 1947); E. Voege-

Puritanism is not confined to groups of English Reformed Protestants in the sixteenth century who wanted their Calvinism to be kept "pure," uncontaminated by any residue from Roman Catholicism—nor is Puritanism simply a verbal echo of the Cathar heresy.[71] It is the real continuation of their outlook and practice, manifest in a host of "confessional" groups and movements in the Protestant world to this day. Puritanism is the matrix that has formed the distinguishing identity of Presbyterians, Congregationalists, Anabaptists, Quakers, Baptists, and so on.

By an unyielding historical dynamic, pietism too, transplanted originally from Anglo-Saxon Puritanism to Holland and Germany, rapidly succeeded in crossing the boundaries of traditions and "confessions."[72] Today pietism appears to have imposed a Manichaeistic dualism and a moralistic individualism as a definitive element of Christian life in every corner of the world.

It is not by chance that Manichaeism was a syncretistic amalgam of elements of deriving from several religious traditions (Babylonian-Chaldaic, Zoroastrian, and Jewish). These are elements that primarily satisfied the demands of natural, instinctive religiosity: a war between light and darkness, between good and evil, between spirit and matter, and the participation of the individual in this war with the aim of acquiring purity, righteousness, and salvation as an atomic individual—the eternal perpetuation of atomic life.

This observation largely responds to the question: Why did Manichaeism, in its various forms and under various names but always with the character of individualistic pietism, constantly

---

lin, "Religionsersatz. Die gnostischen Massenbewegungen unserer Zeit," *Wort und Wahrheit* 15 (1960): 7; S. Lorenz and W. Schröder, "Manichäismus II," in the *Historisches Wörterbuch der Philosophie*, ed. Ritter, Gründer, and Gabriel, 5:715–16. But before the historians, Pascal had stated unequivocally, "Les Manichéens étaient les Luthériens de leur temps, comme les Luthériens sont les Manichéens du nôtre" (*Ecrits sur la Grace*, in vol. 11 of *Oeuvres complètes de Blaise Pascal*, ed. L. Brunschvicg [Paris: Hachette, 1914], 282).

71. *Puritanismus*, from the Latin *purus*, which means "clean."

72. On the dominant influence of Protestant pietism today on the life of the Orthodox churches in particular, see my *Freedom of Morality* (Crestwood, NY: St. Vladimir's Seminary Press, 1984), 119–36; and *Orthodoxy and the West* (Brookline, MA: Holy Cross Orthodox Press, 2006), 217–50.

shadow the historical development of the Church? The answer is clearly that this parallel development embodies in historical terms the constant temptation of religionization that manifestly battles against the ecclesial event. The temptation is that of an objectified individualistic pietism ever present as an alternative proposal that substitutes religion for the Church.

Chapter 5

Orthodoxism: The Religionization of Ecclesial Orthodoxy

5.1. *The Codified Fossilization of Our Heritage*

We have seen that the authenticity of the ecclesial event was defined in the early centuries as *catholicity*—in contrast to the fissiparous nature of *heresy*. Catholicity signifies the wholeness of the ecclesial *mode* of existence, that is, the dynamic indeterminacy of a shared (i.e., offered for common participatory verification) experiential endorsement.

The later definition of authenticity as *orthodoxy* clearly aims at objectifying this dynamic indeterminacy—at fixing authenticity as the measurable validity of an acknowledged apodictic proof. The word *orthodoxy* is formed from *orthē* ("correct") and *doxa* ("opinion," "view," "belief," "conjecture"). It immediately suggests the need for commonly accepted criteria of correctness. Moreover, an opinion/view/belief presupposes an atomic (subjective) holder and something definite (defined, settled) that is held (the content of the opinion/view/belief). Consequently, in contrast to *catholicity*, which is offered for shared participatory verification, *orthodoxy* clearly inclines toward the familiar polarity of subjectivism-objectivism (which leads to the formation of a large variety of "isms," that is, to the turning of collective goals into ideologies).

Ecclesial Orthodoxy (like every other later—political, ideological, or confessional—orthodoxy) has made fidelity to the "prototype" a criterion of *correct opinion*: fidelity to the original formulations of the primary experience. The past of the ecclesial event is regarded as a rounded whole, as a consummate value. The memorials of this past (in texts, liturgical forms, ascetical practices, organizational structures) acquire the status of infallible stereotypes. Of unquestioned authority for the Orthodox churches is so-called *apostolic* and *patristic* tradition. That is the location of the certainty and assurance that the individual possesses the correct faith, the correct teaching, the correct way of life—for the safeguarding of the ego.

Assuredly, the testimony both of the "eyewitnesses" of the historical "epiphany" of Christ and of the first "Fathers" of the ecclesial body has very great significance for the authenticity of the ecclesial event, seeing that these were the first to shape the linguistic, liturgical, and organizational semantics of the Christian gospel. The critical question is whether this very important testimony is approached with awareness of the dynamic relativity that belongs to the semantics of any shared experience, or whether it is subordinated to the instinctive need of natural individuals to wrap themselves up with "infallible" objectivity—to their need for idols.

For the Orthodox churches the guarantee of the authenticity of their teaching, their worship, their organization, and their way of life is not the experience (verified through sharing in it) of the operation of the eucharistic body—it is not the "common struggle" to change one's *mode of existence*. The "criterion of truth" is objectified: it is the texts of the Fathers, every tiny phrase in these texts, even if detached from the context that gives a phrase meaning. It is the prescriptions for the Liturgy precisely as laid down by the Fathers. It is the canons drawn up by the Fathers (even when they contradict each other, or even those that, if really applicable, would excommunicate all Christians as a body).

For many Orthodox churches (and for many more schismatic offshoots), a criterion of the ecclesial event's authenticity is still the calendar established by the Fathers, the insistence, as already mentioned, that the celebration of the Church's feast days should be tied to the astronomically faulty (i.e., useless for organizing life in a realistic manner) Julian calendar of the patristic age, the "Old Calendar." In the Greek-speaking world, it became the custom some time ago (for reasons that are obscure but are clearly coincidental and circumstantial) for the daily liturgical cycle in the paschal period of Great Week to be celebrated back to front: Orthros is now sung in the evening and Vespers in the morning, without anyone thinking (or daring) to question this absurdity. For even in the case of absurdity, once something has been established, for whatever reason, it becomes yet another "holy" tradition.

And if this occurs in the official "order" of ecclesial worship, one can imagine the host of irrational nonsensical "traditions" that naturally follow and are idolized by popular piety. The blessing of the waters (a service that strikingly reveals the cosmological dimensions of salvation) acquires a formal distinction between a "great" blessing and a "little" blessing, with rules about the separate use of each. The sacredness of objects used in worship is idolized by establishing an additional regulative deontology as a result of which the objects perform their miraculous work—vessels, vestments, or the space under the veils of the altar. Another matter concerns assurances about the fate of the "soul" after a person's death, assurances according to which eternity is measured by this world's twenty-four-hour cycle, and so the "genuine" Orthodox know precisely where the "soul" goes on the third day, where on the ninth, and where on the fortieth or in the interval between Easter and Pentecost! All this "objective" information constitutes ecclesial "tradition" for many religious people, even if it manifestly perpetuates elements of magical imaginings about the underworld.

Even when there is some vital contemporary problem that was unknown and unsuspected in the age of the Fathers because it has arisen as a result of later developments and conditions, Orthodox theologians and pastors seek a "solution" in snippets of patristic texts—just as the Communist faithful sought a "solution" in quotations from Marx and Lenin. The same need for objective security clearly motivates both the former and the latter—a need rather to safeguard the psychological ego with the armor of a specific biotheory. Christian truth (the gospel of the universal human hope for the freedom of human existence from time, space, decay, and death) is identified with a fossilized language, with idolized codified doctrines, with sclerotic liturgical forms, with unrealistic canons defining sins, with unchanging institutions. And the genuineness of all these things ("Orthodoxy") is an expression only of their historicity, of fidelity to the past—to the apostolic, the patristic, and even the recent past.[73]

Like the apostles, the Fathers of the Church gave their testimony to ecclesial experience in the language of their age. And the limits of language are the limits of what is knowable in each age, the limits of humanity's understanding of the world as shaped by the scientific knowledge available in each age. The linguistic expression of the Church's witness is tied to whatever worldview is current, but this is not the case with what is signified by this witness. The signifiers refer to the experience of the *meaning* of the world and of human experience, beyond the circumstantial nature of any particular worldview. They refer to the meaning established by feeling one's way empirically, that is, the meaning created by the effort to participate in a *mode of existence*. The signifiers change, but never the things signified.

Roman Catholicism, institutionally ideologized as it was, became alarmed at the time of the Renaissance that the new scientific worldview threatened to falsify Christian witness as expressed in the language of a geocentric cosmology. Roman Catholicism thus began a senseless counteroffensive against the modern sciences (one that still continues openly or under the surface). It is manifestly clear that Roman Catholicism was unable to distinguish between the signifiers and the things signified (an inability that accompanies the need to idolize the signifiers with a view to cladding

73. The West's decadent religious art has replaced the art of the Church's icons and dominates Orthodox churches today, without even a single bishop thinking actively of resisting this squalid alienation, which has now come to be regarded as "tradition." The same is the case with the lamentable religious baroque style (also of Western origin) employed in the architecture of churches and the construction of icon screens, and with the Western religious music that has replaced the Church's singing. Even the most obvious expressions of the alienation of the ecclesial event, once they have prevailed for a couple of centuries or so in Orthodox churches, are imposed as "tradition."

the individual in the armor of "objective" certainties). The Orthodox churches today take up a position that differs only superficially: they express the Christian witness in a language that is incompatible with contemporary scientific cosmology and anthropology, but they do not fight against the findings of the sciences, nor do they think of giving these findings a meaning on the basis of ecclesial experience.

Thus the language of scientific demonstration and the language of ecclesial experience present themselves today as asymptotic: with regard to the reality of the world and of humanity, the former refers to a version corroborated by observation, the latter to a version that is mythic—without this antithesis leading to conflict or creating the slightest problem to the theologians and pastors of the Orthodox churches. No one is bothered if the churches endow a mythic, unsubstantiated cosmology and anthropology with meaning. The ecclesiastical endowment of reality with meaning is asserted to be simply a psychological recourse to religious myth, a withdrawal from what is real and empirically accessible, an escape into fantasy, into the projections of instinctive desires.

This is the ultimate stage of the religionization of the so-called Orthodox churches.

There is no real (scientific) proof, not the slightest, that would allow us to suppose that there was an initial phase, period, or evolutionary stage of physical reality that resembled or was analogous to the so-called (in the language of the Fathers) *prelapsarian* state of the world. The possibility that the world was once material but not subject to decay, and that by the "fall" of Man it became material and subject to decay (as almost all the Fathers claim), has no support in what has been scientifically established to date.

Millions of years before the appearance of Man, the phenomenon of life on earth was governed by the same laws of birth, development, reproduction, decay, and death that govern us today—the same laws of the evolutionary ascent of the multiplicity of species, of complementary mutual annihilation, of the instincts of self-preservation and pleasure, and of the multifaceted manifestations of sexuality. The possibility that "death came into the world through

Man," or that sexuality is a result of the "fall" of Man, or that toil, decay, pain, and pleasure are also products of Man's disobedience to God's commandments has no corresponding verification in the reality of our known physical universe.

Given the findings of scientific research that have formed the image and understanding of physical reality that we possess today, it is difficult for us to accept the sudden appearance of Man as a fully developed rational subject. The maturing of powers of speech, the formation of a linguistic code, the development of intellectual and critical functions, the facility of toolmaking, the rise of a creative imagination, and so on must have required a long evolutionary process. At any rate, it is impossible for us to envisage a stage in this very slow evolutionary process in which we could locate "Adam," if we suppose him, as is often done in the patristic texts, to have been a historical person.[74]

In the apostolic and patristic period, people had an understanding of *time* and *number* rather different from that which we have today. Chronological periods and their duration were accessible to empirical comprehension. Man's first appearance on earth was set then at seventy-four generations, at the most, before Christ (cf. Luke 3:23–38), that is, at 1850 BC. And the end of the world was expected in the near future—Paul appears certain that he himself would still be alive at Christ's second coming (cf. 1 Thess 4:15–17).

People today know that from the genesis of animate matter to the appearance of rational beings a billion years were needed. They know that the findings of geologists, paleontologists, and geneticists have dated the appearance of the human species as we know it today (*Homo sapiens sapiens*) to about 40,000 years ago. They know that our solar system has still about five billion years to run. People today hear about distances of stars or galaxies from the earth measured by the speed of light and expressed arithmetically in terms of billions of light years. They hear that our galaxy contains a hundred billion suns like our own and that in the visible

74. For a fuller discussion of the difficulty in reconciling the language of the Church's past with the findings of modern science, see my *Relational Ontology* (Brookline, MA: Holy Cross Orthodox Press, 2011), chap. 17.

universe there are another ten billion similar galaxies. People today know that the earth's population exceeds six billion and consequently that the total number of human beings who have lived up to now on the earth's crust and have been buried in its soil comes to many billions.

Such enormous temporal, spatial, and numerical values change the assumptions of modern people in comparison with those of people who lived in the apostolic and patristic periods. It would therefore be natural that there should also be significant instances today of changed assumptions in the language of ecclesial witness. If in the past, for example, the expression "unto the ages of ages" evoked a sense of wonder, today the measure of time's infinity is more likely to create a sense of duration threatening to intelligent life. It does not in any way seem a gift or charism to human beings that they should still continue to exist after five hundred billion years in a time without end and with no prospect of ending—the thought of it creates panic rather than hope and consolation. It is incomparably more consoling that death should lead to oblivion rather than to "eternal life," or to existence "unto the ages of ages." The gift and charism of God's love would be a *mode* of existence free from succession of time, free from the measure of the "ages," from a temporal measure.

Ecclesial "Orthodoxy," however, is concerned in its forms of expression to maintain the stereotypes of the past without any change. It is not concerned to preach to people the gospel of hope and consolation. It seeks its identity in the idolization of the signifiers, not in the struggle to lay hold of the things signified.

Ecclesial "Orthodoxy" seems to be thoroughly imprisoned in the language of the quantitative version of time and the dimensional version of the infinite. It correspondingly relies on the language and outlook of what in other periods were chiefly juridical priorities: on the psychological syndrome of master-slave relations. This is why it also insists on an excessive repetition of supplications (to the point of satiety) for the "pardon," "forgiveness," "purging," and "purifying" of people from "sins," "transgressions," "crimes," "faults," and "failings," and for their "washing clean" from "dirt," "mire," and "filth." People perhaps find it difficult to identify such a burden of specific culpability in their personal lives. The priority given to the individual's guilt, however—the remission even of an individual's imaginary, nonexistent sins—is more a response to instinctive religious need.

In the practice of ecclesial "Orthodoxy," the primary and dominant demand is not for a *relationship* with God, for the struggle of love as a eucharistic *mode of existence*. The desire does not predominate that a person should live with God at least the fullness and rapture that he lives in the experience of love with another person—a fullness and rapture that are uniquely personal, unlike and unrepeatable, and mutually exclusive: that is, free from any comparison with any erotic relations whatsoever of other persons with the same person of God. Nothing of this kind predominates. The primary (prevailing) demand in the language of ecclesial "Orthodoxy" today is for "mercy," for forgiveness of indeterminate guilt, of unspecified offenses.

5.2. *Confessionalism*

In the language of the early Church, the word *confession* (*homologia*) meant the public declaration of an attestation based on experience, the bearing of witness to certainties arising from the direct experience of personal *relationship*.[75]

Against the background of this early meaning, the word *confessor* during the centuries of persecution became synonymous with the word *martyr*.[76] By sacrificing their life the martyrs witnessed/

75. Cf. Peter's confession in Matt 16:16: "You are the Messiah, the Son of the living God" and in John 6:68–69; cf. also Matt 10:32: "Everyone therefore who acknowledges me before others, I also will acknowledge before my Father in heaven"; 1 Tim 6:12: "You made the good confession in the presence of many witnesses."

76. Cf. Justin Martyr, *First Apology* 11 (PG 6:341B): "Confess they are Christians, knowing that the penalty for confessing this is death"; *Historia monachorum in Aegypto* 19.1–2 (PG 34:1171A): "There was a monk called Apollonius . . . During the persecution this father encouraged the confessors of Christ and succeeded in making many of them martyrs" (Norman Russell, trans., *The Lives of the Desert Fathers*, chap. 19 [Kalamazoo, MI: Cistercian Publications, 1980], 103).

confessed/confirmed that their *relationship* with Christ was more precious to them than biological survival. The martyrs were called "confessors of the faith"; their martyrdom attested to and revealed their faith/trust in the gospel of Christ—and trust is only possible as a result of a personal *relationship*. When the meaning of the word *faith* (that which corresponds to it in actual experience) changes, then the sense of the word *confession* is also altered. If faith ceases to signify the struggle to attain trust, if it comes to be identified with the acceptance by the individual of theoretical/intellectual formulations (an acceptance synonymous now with conviction and psychological certainty), then confession too still remains a public proclamation but not one of testimony from experience. It becomes a proclamation of private convictions, individual acceptance of "principles" or "theses," and individual assent to psychological "certainties." Thus confession ends up by being defined as "official and public proclamation of the acceptance of religious dogma,"[77] or an "official statement by someone of the dogmas of the religious or more generally ideological faith accepted by him."[78]

The codification of the formulations of ecclesial experience was attempted with the decisions of the ecumenical councils. Even the First Ecumenical Council (325) drew up a *confession of faith* with a view to safeguarding the expression of this experience from signifiers that were deceptive or capable of various interpretations. However, the confession that was then codified functioned (and we have clear indications of this) as a *definition* (*horos*, a fixing of boundaries around common experience) and not as a substitute for experience. Confession functioned as *symbol*: an occasion for putting together (*sym-ballein*), for coordinating personal approaches to the common struggle of ecclesial experience, without the signifying occasion being made independent of the signified (and presuppositional) experience.

Given humanity's instinctive religious need for "objective" metaphysical certainties, however, one can understand how easily

77. Georgios D. Babiniotis, *Lexiko tēs neas Ellēnikēs glōssas*, 3rd ed. (Athens: Kentro Lexikologias, 2008), s.v. *homologia*.
78. Ibid.

the use of definitions and symbols of common experience can become independent of experience. The codified symbolic formulations in their linguistic form and in their semantic content come to be identified with "truth." Whoever relies on the form and understands the content of the formulations "possesses" truth in a private fashion; such a person is the master and owner of truth. Thus the ego of natural individualism is clad in the armor of dogmatic religious certainties (of supernatural authority), and the ecclesial struggle of the empirical sharing of truth is forgotten even as a standard for identifying alienation.

The confession of faith as a declaration of personal (intellectual and psychological) convictions and an acceptance of institutionally guaranteed, infallible formulations is a symptom of alienation that follows the historical journey of the Church. The most extreme cases of the symptom occur dramatically within the context of the underdeveloped world of medieval Western European Christendom. But with the gradual change of the cultural paradigm, the Orthodox East too became firmly if unconsciously subject to the now dominant ideologized understanding of faith.

Ideologization reached its apogee in both the West and the East with the advent of the Protestant Reformation. Having depreciated the institutional expressions of the ecclesial event in the highest degree, the Reformation favored in the highest degree (i.e., took to its extreme consequences) the religious individualism inherent in the Roman Catholic West. It did this through its emphasis on the personal faith of the individual (*sola fide*), on the objective validity of that faith (*fidei ratio*), and on the need to guarantee its objectivity by official (codified) "confessions" of faith.

From its outset every Protestant movement was based on a *confession*. In the confession were set down the movement's convictions: a specific way of interpreting the Christian gospel (and of applying this interpretation in practice). All who accepted these convictions constituted the members of that reformed church—the convictions expressed in that specific confession were the definition and presupposition of membership. For that reason the words *church* and *confession* came to have the same meaning in the Protestant world—the words functioned as synonyms.

Luther's followers (Lutheranism) defined their faith by the *Augsburg Confession* (*Confessio Augustana*, 1530). Zwingli's followers based themselves on the confession called the *Fidei ratio* (1530), which Zwingli himself had drawn up. The Protestants of the cities of Strasbourg, Constance, Memmingen, and Lindau expressed their faith by the *Tetrapolitan Confession* (*Confessio Tetrapolitana*) of Bucer and Capito (1530). There followed in chronological sequence the *Confessio Basiliensis* (1534), the *Confessio Helvetica* (1536), the *Confessio Gallicana* (Paris, 1559), the *Confessio Scotica* (1560), the *Confessio Belgica* (1561), and the *Westminster Confession* (1646).

The alienation of ecclesial faith in codified confessions of convictions was also immediately adopted by Roman Catholicism with a view to combating the Protestant Reformation on the ideological level. The Council of Trent (*Concilium Tridentinum*), which was held from 1546 to 1563, issued as its reply to Protestantism the *Professio Tridentina* (1564), whose eleven articles every Roman Catholic must accept as his personal convictions. On this confessional basis are summarized the *dogmas* of the Roman Catholic Church, that is, what any Roman Catholic is "bound to believe" (*die Glaubenspflicht*), the authentic, absolutely authoritative, and infallible proclamation of the word of God (*die authentische und authoritative, unfehlbare Verkündigung des Wortes Gottes*).[79]

To this fundamental core are added all the papal pronouncements on matters of faith, whose ideological/confessional character was clearly manifested by the character attributed to them by the First Vatican Council (1870). The concern here is not for formulations of the experience of the ecclesial body but for "revealed truths" (*Offenbarungswahrheiten—doctrina et veritas divinitus revelata*),[80] infallible in themselves (*ex sese*)—"not through

79. J. R. Geiselmann, "Dogma," in *Handbuch theologischer Grundbegriffe*, ed. H. Fries (Munich: Kösel-Verlag, 1962), 229.
80. Ibid., 230.

the consent of the Church"—when the Roman pontiff makes pronouncements *ex cathedra*.[81]

The idolization of formulations—making the intellectual and psychological reception of the signifiers autonomous, and detaching this reception from the (always shared) experience of the things signified—was an original mark of Roman Catholicism. Protestantism took this idolization to its logical conclusion, also dragging Roman Catholicism, the originator of the symptom, with it into a hardening of the ideological version of the Church's gospel. The conflict between the two expressions of the Church's religionization in the West was conducted on a level of abstract theoretical "convictions," "principles," and "doctrines" drawn up in codified "confessions."

What lies behind the form of the "confession" is manifestly the common individualistic demand for religious certainties wrapped up in institutional authority. That is why the challenging of these certainties becomes a battle between institutions. And so we have long periods of armed conflict—the Thirty Years' War (1618–48) and religious wars that still endured at the end of the twentieth century (e.g., Ireland)—that have set the stamp of their indelible horror on Western European Man.

The Western conflict was dramatically "decanted" into the Orthodox East. The Greek areas ruled by the Turks, along with Russia, became a theater of competition between Roman Catholics and Protestants as to who would win the support of the Orthodox against their rival—or who would manage more quickly to assimilate the Orthodox populations to their own doctrine. To defend themselves the Orthodox had to adopt the practice of "confessions" with the aim of defining their difference from both Roman Catholics and Protestants.

Four Orthodox confessions of faith were drawn up, by authors who gave their name to them, all of them in the seventeenth century.

81. "Infallibilitate in magisterio, vi muneris sui gaudet Summus Pontifex quando ut supremus omnium christifidelium Pastor et Doctor, cuius est fratres suos in fide confirmare, doctrinam de fide vel de moribus tenendam definitivo actus proclamat" (Canon 749, § 1, *Codex Iuris Canonici*, 1983 ed.).

The first (1601) was composed by Mitrophanes Kritopoulos, later patriarch of Alexandria, while he was still a young man studying in Helmstedt in Germany, in response to a request from his teachers. The second (1629) was written by Cyril Loukaris, patriarch of Constantinople, and raised a storm of controversy throughout the Orthodox world. In refutation of the Confession of Cyril Loukaris, confessions were drawn up by Peter Moghila, metropolitan of Kiev (1643), and by Dositheos Notaras, patriarch of Jerusalem (1672).

Of these four confessions, the most typically Orthodox was that of Mitrophanes Kritopoulos, in spite of his adopting the systematic academic style of theological expression and the religionized version of the ecclesial event. Loukaris's confession is a Calvinistic document without any attempt at a pretense of "Orthodoxy"—it remains an open historical question whether Patriarch Cyril was the real author of the confession (he himself neither condemned it nor adopted it). Because the confessions of Peter Moghila and Dositheos of Jerusalem are intended to refute Loukaris's Calvinistic theses, they are led into adopting Roman Catholic criteria, language, and arguments. They are typical examples of a Western type of "Orthodox" confessions—examples of *Orthodoxism*: the transformation of the Church's gospel into an ideology.[82]

The most important historical legacy of the "Orthodox" confessions of the seventeenth century was precisely the tradition that they created by making the alienation of the Church's gospel into an ideology a self-evident matter of "modernization." Among both the Slavs and the Greeks, the concept and practice of "catechesis," of "dogmatic theology," and of "symbolical texts" borrowed the character that the internecine religious wars in the West had given them—the Orthodox theology of the last few centuries offers itself without clear standards and criteria for distinguishing ecclesial witness from the proclamation of religious convictions and ideological principles obligatory for the "faithful."

---

82. See the longer discussion and relevant bibliography in my *Orthodoxy and the West*, chap. 9, "The 'Confessions of Faith.'" See also the very striking historical monograph by Gunnar Hering, *Oikoumeniko Patriarcheio kai Eurōpaikē politikē, 1620-1638* (Athens: MIET, 1992).

The Orthodox version of the Church's catholicity seems now to have been replaced by an ideological and radically religionized understanding of Orthodoxy.

5.3. *The Reversal of Ecclesial Criteria and Objectives*

The difficulty of distinguishing the ecclesial event from a religion subject to the instincts is also the mark of Orthodoxism. With the appearance or pretense of relying on traditional Orthodoxy, one portion of the Christian world seeks (or presents itself as possessing) the most correct convictions, in comparison with other religious "isms"; the most consistent morality (i.e., the most austere or "spiritual"); and the richest liturgical tradition (i.e., the most effective in arousing psychological emotions, in producing a sense of exaltation and individualistic well-being).

The criteria for distinguishing the Church's mysteries from magical acts, for distinguishing the Church's vital and life-giving communion from a sense of ideological solidarity, seem to have been lost. It is impossible to separate preaching (i.e., witness) from propaganda, ecclesial ascetical practice from private morality, pastoral care from psychological counseling, the compassionate service of "binding and loosing" from the grim exercise of authority. The eucharistic event and the ecclesial worship that it entails are regarded simply as a religious rite.

Both the pivotal operations of ecclesial life and its goals have manifestly been transposed from the common struggle to attain relations of faith/trust (from life as love) to the pursuit of personal guarantees—of salvation, justification, reward, and the unending existence of the ego. Consequently, no one is bothered with whether the *parish* functions properly: the eucharistic community, the body of the communion of persons. No bishop of the Orthodox Church comes forward to show in a practical way that he regards it a denial of the Church and its gospel that "parishes" exist with tens of thousands of "parishioners," that parish churches have been transformed into "branch offices" serving the religious needs of the faceless mass.

When the Eucharist is transformed into a religious rite (and sometimes repeated on the same day within the same church so as to be of service to a greater number of parishioners) without the slightest active participation of those "attending," it is clear that we must look for the Church elsewhere, not in the eucharistic community, not in the body of parishioners. For then not only the *mysteries* of baptism, marriage, unction, and confession but also funeral services, memorials, and blessings are merely "rituals" detached from any reality of the Church, self-standing "magical" benedictions of moments in one's private life.

Thus inevitably the Church is identified with its professional employees, that is, with the clergy, and chiefly with the "higher" clergy (the bishops) and with the buildings and offices where the institution is based. And ecclesial "Orthodoxy" will be identified with the elements of an idolized tradition, which is objectified in external features of liturgical dress, forms of worship, and pious customs. Some, the more "demanding," will also seek the "Orthodox" character of the Christian life in what has been received in a codified ideological form, such as the stipulations of canon law.

When the orthodoxy of the ecclesial event is alienated into a religious Orthodoxism, it is no longer of any concern (either to the clergy or the laity) that a body of living communion of the members/partakers of the struggle should exist, that the kingdom of God should be imaged "on earth as it is in heaven": the triadic mode of existence. It is of no concern that parish communities should exist, that the bishop should be a father and not an administrator or manager. The only concern is that each person should accept individually the ideological pronouncements and canonical precepts of Orthodoxism, and should regard all the patristic citations and snippets that support these pronouncements and precepts as "infallible." For every perplexity and every problem, answers should be sought in the past, because the Church is "Orthodox" only like a museum piece (as the historical continuation of a typology) without any contemporary living experience capable of illuminating perplexities and problems.

In Orthodoxism, monasticism becomes the "guardian" of the typological heritage, the guarantor of a fossilized authenticity. In this context monasticism is no longer about leading the way in the vanguard of the Church's existential struggle. It is no longer the ascetical discipline of stripping away the ego so that existence may be shared as loving self-offering. Nor is it about mourning as the anticipation of death, a mourning that liberates from conventions or half measures and confirms the joy of self-abandonment to divine love. It is none of this. Monasticism in Orthodoxism assumes the role of a prosecutor. The dress of *anachoresis*, or withdrawal, becomes the uniform of a policing authority.

Monks police the fidelity of clerics and laypeople to the letter of patristic passages and phrases, the letter of Orthodox dogma and "sacred canons." They hunt out and denounce every suspicion of infringement of the precepts of canon law, every deviation from a canonically defined "Orthodoxy." They accuse, reprimand, and castigate patriarchs, synods and archbishops, bishops and presbyters grown old in service, teachers who profess their faith, preachers, evangelists, and others pursuing lives of restraint. Monks claim in practice to be superior to all ecclesiastical hierarchy, to be an infallible source of authenticity within the life of the Church. It is these who decide whether the local bishop should be commemorated in the Eucharist (a commemoration that constitutes visible participation in the eucharistic community of the catholic Church). That is, they replace the conciliar bond (the guarantee of the living unity of the whole body) with their own ideological estimates of orthodox thinking and their own canonical assessments of orthodox practice.[83]

In the Church the institutional expressions of its life function precisely as possibilities of participation in the struggle of rela-

83. It is painful to see how far the monastic struggle has declined in comparison with the standard set by St. Isaac the Syrian in one of his exhortations: "You should know, brother, that the reason why we need to shut ourselves inside our cells is this: that we should not know the evil things that people do. We shall then regard them all as saints and as good through the purity of our minds. If we become people who censure, chastise, judge, examine, retaliate and complain, what difference will there be between our settlement and that of the towns?" (*Discourse 58*, in *The Ascetic Writings of Our Holy Father Isaac the Syrian*, 239).

tions of communion, possibilities of withdrawal from individualistic comparisons of abilities, charisms, or gifts. By contrast, in an ideologized Orthodoxism the institutions are ignored or held in contempt, and trust is transformed into judging the merit and authenticity of individuals. If, for example, some new teaching should arise, the adherents of Orthodoxism would not appeal to a synodical institution that would give judgment, on the basis of the experience of every eucharistic body, on whether the teaching was heretical. They would resort to some famous "elder" and to his individual charism—and he would offer them "objective" certainties that are ideologically (i.e., psychologically) guaranteed.

There is no limit to the quest for "objective" religious certainties—the need for individuals to safeguard themselves is insatiable. For the so-called "zealots" of Orthodoxism (those who boast of their religious zeal), the title of "Orthodox" is insufficient. They form sects of the "genuine" Orthodox, and these sects further fragment in the constant search for "more genuine" manifestations of the atomic zealotism of the "genuine." The search takes on the character of rivalry in asserting ever more extreme positions of conservatism: a pathological insistence on the letter of dogmatic ideological statements, regulative principles, and customary forms.

The idolization of the past, of tradition, and of "authenticity" kills the appetite for the search (the dynamic of the struggle involved in the search) that differentiates the ecclesial event from an established religion. A sign of this deadening effect is also the fact that Orthodoxism does not engender any art but only passively copies the art of the past, understanding art merely as the decoration of liturgical space—a decoration that is didactic or evocative of pious sentiments.

Historical experience confirms that a metaphysical search has the same significance as culture: it engenders art; it engenders celebration; it engenders the communion of persons. By contrast, every kind of "certainty" and "conviction" (religious or even nihilistic) alienates art into a commodity for psychological consumption; alienates celebration into a trade in sentiments and emotions, even to the extent of being incorporated into the profit cycle of the commercial year; and alienates the sharing of relations into a trade-off with regard to interests, a contractual safeguarding of egocentric concerns, a frigid loneliness.

Christian experience (always *ecclesial*—never unshared) has always denounced sentimentality, moralism, and the authoritarian idols of truth as the most fundamental undermining of the metaphysical quest. "This is what it means truly to find God: to seek him without ceasing, never to satiate your desire," wrote that wise interpreter of ecclesial experience, Gregory of Nyssa.[84] Truly to find God is to seek him not because he is useful to you in your private concerns, not so as to guarantee your "salvation," not so that your ego should exist in happiness "forever," not so that you should be rewarded according to the merits of your "virtues," but to seek him only because he is He Who Is.

Isaac the Syrian, another giant of experiential wisdom, adds, "Blessed be the honor of the Lord, who opens a door in front of us, that we might have no desire except to do his will."[85] Whatever metaphysical gift we ask for ourselves puts us in a real quandary, an asphyxiating nightmare. If eternal life is all about an endless prolongation in time of atomic existence, it brings us to a panic-stricken cold sweat. Atomic salvation can only be a torment if people we love very much are excluded from it. The only metaphysical request that grants us peace is "that we might have no desire except to do his will."

It is evident that in view of the reality of the Orthodoxism prevailing today (or of any other religionized version of the ecclesial event), if we are to recover once again some echo of joy from a shared exploration of metaphysical hope, we must be delivered of a heavy load of ballast, difficult to shed, consisting of fixed preconceptions, psychological preferences, and instinctive need, or else we will not find the remedy for the panic of death. Even the language of the

84. "This is truly to find God, always to seek him, never to find our desire satisfied . . . For it is not one thing to seek and another to find" (H. Musurillo, ed., *On the Life of Moses*, in *Gregorii Nysseni Opera*, ed. W. Jaeger and H. Langerbeck [Leiden: Brill, 1964], vol. 7, pt. 1, p. 116; and *On Ecclesiastes, Homily 7*, in vol. 5 of the same edition, pp. 400–1).

85. *Discourse 35*, in *The Ascetic Writings of Our Holy Father Isaac the Syrian*.

ecclesial tradition sometimes reflects the temptation of religious self-seeking, of religious individualism—for only at the harvest will the wheat be separated from the weeds sown in the same field.

In the ecclesial event the participants continuously spell out again, always starting from the beginning, the "honor" of the desire for God alone. It is an "honor" because the uniqueness of the desire signifies a charism of erotic self-offering and self-abandonment to the "manic yearning" that God has for each human person. Only a truly erotic desire is freed from self-interest, that is, from the insecurity of being mortal. And when erotic love gains a foothold in the experiential exploration of reciprocity, then freedom from death-dealing egocentrism is an "open door" and "blessed honor."

Ecclesial experience speaks of God as *Bridegroom*, as lover of humankind, not in a symbolic or metaphysical fashion. A realistic starting point for this empirical assertion (a tangible trace of what transcends us) is beauty. The metaphysics of ecclesial experience is not derived from apodictic syllogisms, or from some psychological investment in *a priori* ideological arguments. Only the beauty of the world, a beauty interwoven with the astounding wisdom that constitutes it in every minute detail, can function as an invitation-to-relation with a personal Causal Principle, Word, and Meaning of the world.

We accept the world with our logical capacity as a rational given—as a rationally activated *how*, not as a fixed static *what*. And the world is rational for us not only because of the astounding wisdom of every minute detail but also because of its character of being invitatory to *relation*, because of the aesthetic pleasure by which it attracts us—colors, shapes, sounds, tactile quality, smells: qualities of the strength of the invitatory *logos*, or rational principle, a principle that points to the existential otherness (to the unique, dissimilar, and unrepeatable Person) of the one who invites us. The world's beauty points to its Creator just as a painting (potentially, not obligatorily) points to the artist, a piece of music to the composer, or a poem to the poet. It does this in the way we recognize the personal otherness of an artist not by reading biographies of him but by our personal relationship with his work, by the qualities of the invitatory rational principle.

The language of ecclesial experience—the language of Orthodoxy—is poetry. Moral precepts, ideological stereotypes, and saccharine sentimentality are the language of instinctive religiosity—the language of Orthodoxism. They bear no relation to the ecclesial event, the struggle of a joyful metaphysical quest.

5.4. *The Popularity of the* Philokalia *in the West*

The *Philokalia* is an anthology of passages from the writings of thirty-six Fathers and ascetics of the Eastern Church tradition, the tradition of Greek Orthodoxy, from the fourth to the fifteenth century. The texts selected for the anthology all refer to the assumptions, practice, and aims of the ascetical life. In particular they refer to ways of prayer and especially the so-called *noetic* prayer (or "prayer of the heart"). These are ways of guiding the ascetic to *dispassion* (*apatheia*, freedom from the necessities of nature), to *watchfulness* (*nēpsis*, alertness and sobriety of the mind), and finally to *stillness* (*hēsychia*) and *contemplation* (*theōria*)—to a sense of divine pleasure "welling up out of the heart."

The first collection of this anthology was probably assembled by Metropolitan Makarios Notaras of Corinth (1731–1805); many similar anthologies of patristic texts circulated in manuscript in the eighteenth century. In any event, he handed it over to the monk Nikodemos of the Holy Mountain (1749–1809), who undertook to check the patristic texts against the manuscripts preserved in the libraries of the monasteries of Mount Athos and publish them.

The *Philokalia* was published for the first time in Venice in 1782 and again in Athens in 1893. In 1793, eleven years after its first appearance, it was issued in a Slavonic translation by the famous Russian monk Paisii Velichkovskii (1722–94). The Slavonic version of the *Philokalia* was a catalyst for the development of a dynamic movement among Russian intellectuals. This was named the "Philokalic renaissance." It was a movement with many branches, which, beginning at a provincial monastery (Optina) and an early group of Slavophile scholars who met there, later influenced great Russian writers and intellectuals, such as Tolstoy, Solovyov, and, chiefly, Dostoevsky.[86]

The most fruitful consequence, however, of the "Philokalic renaissance" occurred in the mid-twentieth century with the Russian theologians and scholars who came to Europe and North America after the Bolsheviks seized control in Russia in 1917. This diaspora became the occasion for a dynamic awakening of the alienated Orthodox conscience, the first since the fourteenth century, a real (and not ideological) confrontation of Orthodoxy with the West. The surprising unexpectedness of this awakening provoked important developments more broadly in Western communions, such as the active interest of mainly Roman Catholic theologians in the study of the Greek Fathers, Orthodox worship, and Orthodox art.

The "neopatristic" (as it was called) reorientation of Roman Catholic theologians found a hidden (but nevertheless encouraging) expression in the climate of the Second Vatican Council (1962–65), only to be stifled very rapidly by the conservative reaction of the Vatican. The influence of the Russian diaspora was much more fruitful in Orthodox countries (chiefly in Greece, Serbia, and Romania, and also in Lebanon), inaugurating the so-called "theological spring" of the 1960s.[87]

The third edition of the *Philokalia* was published in Greece in 1957 in five volumes,[88] and has been frequently reprinted. A Romanian translation by the Reverend Professor Dumitru Stăniloae began to be published in 1946 and was completed in ten volumes in 1981. But the most astonishing success began with the first publication of the *Philokalia* in the West and its enthusiastic reception by a broad readership in every Christian confession.

Indeed, in 1951 the highly respected publisher Faber and Faber issued a two-volume anthology of the *Philokalia*, translated by E. Kadloubovsky and G. E. H. Palmer. The publisher's reser-

86. See C. Motchoulsky, *Dostoïevsky* (Paris: Payot, 1963), 529.

87. See my *Orthodoxy and the West*, 211, 273–308.

88. Published by Astir and edited by Archimandrite Epiphanios Theodoropoulos.

vations about issuing a work of such "specialized interest" (with an extremely doubtful financial return) were overcome thanks to the warm support of Faber's publishing advisor, the Nobel Prize–winning poet T. S. Eliot. The work[89] met with unexpected success and went through eight reprints in ten years. Later the project was completed by the translation of the entire Greek original through the collaboration of G. E. H. Palmer, Philip Sherrard, and Kallistos Ware. The complete text (still in progress) has also been published in paperback.

Two years later, in 1953, the first French translation of the *Philokalia* was published, as a selection of texts in a small pocket edition translated by Jean Gouillard, under the title *Petite Philocalie de la prière du coeur.* This anthology betrays the religious interest of the anthologist in the techniques of mysticism. The success of the publication, however, and its repeated reprinting over several years were also in this instance a matter of surprise.

In 1979 the Abbaye de Bellefontaine began a new French version of the whole five-volume Greek text of the *Philokalia*, which was completed in 1986. The translation was made by the French poet Jacques Touraille, an Orthodox, and the theological supervision of the edition was undertaken by Protopresbyter Professor Boris Bobrinskoy. The work was originally published in eleven fascicules, which in 1995 were issued in two volumes by Desclée de Brouwer.

Concise versions of the *Philokalia*, in a single volume, were published in Italian (*La Filokalia: Amore della bellezza*, translated by Giovanni Vannucci and published by Libreria Editrice Fiorentina in 1998), in Spanish (*La filocalia de la oración de Jesús*, published in Salamanca by Sígueme in 1998 [7 reprints] and in Barcelona by Claret in 1986 [1 reprint]), and in Portuguese (*Pequena Filocalia: O livro clássico da Igreja Oriental*, translated by José Comblin, Carlos Mesters, and Maria Emília Ferreira and published by Edições Paulinas, Brazil, 1984).

89. *Writings from the Philokalia on Prayer of the Heart*, translated from the Russian text *Dobrotolubiye* by E. Kadloubovsky and G. E. H. Palmer (London: Faber and Faber, 1951).

A striking sequel to the broad interest shown in translations of the *Philokalia* is also the extensive literature on Philokalian topics published in European languages.[90] This is in addition to specialized articles and scholarly references in a wide variety of publications.

The most significant result, however, is probably the introduction to Western communions of a new language: words, expressions, and even themes drawn from the texts of the *Philokalia*. "Watchfulness" (*nēpsis*), "dispassion" (*apatheia*), "noetic prayer," "divine illumination," the "contemplation of God," the "contemplative mind," the "spiritual senses," the "vision of God" (*theoptia*), and a host of similar terms and expressions entered into the language of religiously minded people in the West. One could perhaps attribute this fact to the more general interest that people imbued with Western modernity (and satiated with a legalistic and intellectualistic religiosity) have in various forms of "esotericism" deriving from the (chiefly Far) East. Or one might attribute the interest in the *Philokalia* to some kind of resonance or affinity of the texts with the long habituation of Western people to the individualistic pietism and quietism that historically have prevailed in the West.

At any rate, the approval and enthusiastic reception of the *Philokalia* by religious Westerners raises an important question: If the critical difference between Orthodoxy and the West is the ecclesiocentric character of the former and the institutionalized religionization of the latter (the individualism of natural religion that historical circumstances imposed on the West), then the West's enthusiasm for the *Philokalia* is not a contradiction in terms. Might not the wisdom and experience of the holy Fathers of the Church, anthologized in the *Philokalia*, be coordinated with the individualistic, religionized version of Christianity that has formed the West's criteria and mental outlook?

The need for a critical response to these questions is an urgent one for an overriding reason: because the imperceptible (and as a rule unconscious) slide of ecclesial Orthodoxy too into

90. For an informative discussion on the influence of the *Philokalia* in Western Europe, see Fr. Placide Deseille, *La spiritualité orthodoxe et la Philocalie* (Paris: Albin Michel, 2003), vol. 3, pt. 4, p. 249ff.

religionization, into a religious Orthodoxism, had to a large degree already been accomplished when the *Philokalia* was compiled and published for the first time. Consequently, a properly critical approach will also examine the reasons why the Orthodox too approved of the *Philokalia* with such enthusiasm in a period when their priorities were chiefly religious and individualistic. We should control the likely resonance of the texts of the *Philokalia* with the religious individualism of Orthodoxism—not so that we should cast any doubts on the patristic texts themselves (the record, so precious for the ecclesial struggle, of the Fathers' witness) but perhaps on the reasons for their selection, the aims or criteria that governed the isolation of specific passages from their original context.

A control of this kind leads one immediately to a surprising fact: the reader is astounded to discover that nowhere in the five volumes of the complete Greek edition of the *Philokalia* is there any reference to the ecclesial event, to the presupposition of the gospel's *salvation*. The word *church* appears thirty-six times in the five volumes, but only to indicate the institution or the building for liturgical worship—never to indicate the eucharistic body, the struggle to image the loving communion of the Triadic prototype: "When you leave the church, go and pray in your cell"; "Afflicted by indolence, he absented himself from the church and the canon"; "As a wise theologian, deliver a discourse within the great church"; "Some praised the outlook and teaching of the Church"; "He who seeks the Lord will utter good words in the church of the faithful for the benefit of many"; "The Church founded from the beginning by the apostles"; "We are bound to accept the Church's dogmas by a sure faith and by questioning those who are experienced"; and so on and so forth.

Participation in the ecclesial event (in the eucharistic body, which realizes in a dynamic fashion the Triadic *mode of existence*) is totally ignored in the pages of the *Philokalia*—there is not even a hint that it is this *participation* that constitutes the gospel's salvation. The goal/mode of the *Philokalia*'s contemplation and practice is presented as purely individualistic: if the *mind* descends into the *heart*, with the persistent individual (psychosomatic) practice of asceticism, a person has been *saved*—nothing else is needed.

There is no need for participation in a body of relations of loving communion. The aim is not to share in existence and life. Individual ascetical practice is sufficient to lead a person to dispassion, to the vision of God, to immortality, and to deification—all that is needed is an athletic striving to attain personal achievements ranked axiologically by order of merit. What is proclaimed without any disguise whatsoever is love of self (*philautia*). "The good love of self" is explicitly extolled: "that which is true worship, genuinely pleasing to God, the careful cultivation of the soul through the virtues."

The reader will look in vain in the five volumes of the *Philokalia* for even an indirect hint that the only possibility of entry into the kingdom, the only path toward realizing the Christian gospel, is participation in the Church. On the contrary, the reader is persuaded on every page that salvation is won by an exclusively private effort: the keeping of the commandments, the guarding of the intellect, noetic prayer.

> By such spiritual and intellectual work, and also with the successful practice of the commandments and the rest of the moral virtues, when through the invocation of the all-holy Name warmth is engendered in the heart and its accompanying spiritual energy, on the one hand the passions are consumed . . . and on the other the intellect and the heart are cleansed and united with each other . . . Without the deification of the intellect, which is not the same as being sanctified, a person cannot be saved.[91]

Of course there are references in the *Philokalia* to the Church's Eucharist. But communion of the eucharistic bread and wine is not

91. I do not give here precise references (identifying which texts the passages are from) for one overriding reason: I have no wish to perpetuate the apparently arbitrary character of the "Philokalic" selection—perhaps the authors of the phrases I have quoted refute or correct the views noted here in other texts that have not been chosen for the *Philokalia*. I therefore refer to the *Philokalia* as a whole, not to the particular authors represented in it.

referred to as participation in, and engrafting onto, the "dominical body." Communion does not lead "those who eat together into a sameness of way of life." The point of communion here is the individual "reception" of a supernatural "grace" and "unfading power." The *grace* and the *power* are located in the distributed "species"—they are discussed in a manner that clearly reflects the idea of the "transubstantiation" (*metousiōsis*) of the bread and wine.

The logical conclusion to be drawn by the reader is that the Church is a useful institution for the Christian only because it (the institution and its Liturgy) administers the transmission to the individual, through the *sacraments*, of a supernatural (ontologically indeterminate, as also in the language of the West) grace. The Eucharist, together with baptism, is presented in the *Philokalia* as a help to believers to pursue their individual ascetical effort, on which (chiefly, or even exclusively) their salvation depends.

Individual asceticism, of course, is also a presupposition in the Orthodox (i.e., ecclesially centered) perspective for the *salvation* proclaimed by the gospel. But it is a presupposition as an actual *participation* in the common effort of the existential *mode* that constitutes the body of the Church—not as a private struggle. Individual asceticism is not a value in itself; it does not constitute its own end. It is the practical realization/manifestation of the individual's free will to participate in the ecclesial communion of existence and life—a communion that consists of a participated struggle for self-transcendence and self-offering. The *Philokalia*'s perspective lies at the opposite pole to this. There the asceticism of the individual is not only necessary but is a sufficient condition of salvation. It possesses clear characteristics of an athletic struggle seen as an end in itself, whereas participation in the Church, identified with a private drawing of grace from the sacraments, is simply supportive of the individual's struggle.

Broadly speaking (in too abstract a fashion), it may be said that in the *Philokalia* passages have been selected (anthologized) from patristic texts in a manner that is cut off from what is ontologically signified by ecclesial language. The word *salvation*, for example, in the language of the Church means that a person should exist in terms of freedom of *relation* rather than in terms of the necessities of nature. In the *Philokalia*, however, the chosen passages presuppose that "salvation is received through attentiveness and the guarding of the intellect"—that is sufficient—and that "the life of virtue is the short path to salvation." Everything is judged on the level of individual achievement.

The same is the case with the word *love*. In the language of the Church, it signifies *relation* as the mode of the Trinity's freedom from any existential finitude, existence as self-transcendence and self-offering. In the passages chosen by the *Philokalia*, love is the "metropolis" of individually possessed virtues—"love, self-restraint, and prayer [always of the individual] are capable of delivering from the passions."

In the Church's language the "principle and hypostasis" of existence "was the creative command" of him who called "out of nonbeing into being." "Eternal" life for human beings (i.e., freedom from time and space) is their loving response to the creative command of Christ the Bridegroom's love. In the language of the *Philokalia*, however, it is stated that "virtue begets immortality" and for humanity's theosis what suffices is "the descent of the intellect into the heart." Immortality is an attainment of the individual, and theosis begins and ends within the boundaries of ontic atomicity.

The stark distinction adopted (anthologized) in the *Philokalia* between two kinds of faith is revealing: the faith of the Church is one thing, and the faith of (individual) contemplation is another.

"The common faith of the Orthodox, namely, correct dogmas concerning God and his creatures, both intellectual and sensible, as, by the grace of God, the Holy Catholic Church has received, is one thing; and the faith of contemplation, that is, of knowledge, which in no way is opposed to the faith that generates it, but rather makes it more certain, is another."

The distinction is very clear, in spite of the denial of any opposition or the assurance that the second, the faith of contemplation, strengthens the first, the faith of the Church. The faith of the Church manifestly refers to the common *convictions* of the Orthodox because faith is identified explicitly with the "correct dogmas":

the codified formulations that the institution "received" and that the faithful are obliged to accept as "dogmas." This is a version of truth precisely as ideology, which each person must internalize individually as a totality of *a priori* axiomatic principles guaranteed by the authenticity of the institution—just as the West, after Augustine, understood faith and proclaimed it.

And this individualist, intellectualist, and psychological approach to the collective convictions by the "faith of contemplation," which is experiential but also individualist, emerges from an individual ascetic discipline (and not from participation in the *mode* of the Church) as a reward for meritorious attainments. It has a charismatic character ("supernatural" in an unexplained way) and comes to confirm individual convictions with greater certainty.

We Orthodox like to accuse the West of institutional rigidity and of imposing religionization on the ecclesial event, of submitting it to intellectualism, moralism, and legalism. But the case of the *Philokalia* proves rather that the West is "within us"—its historical outgrowths dwell in an obscure way in the "inward" instinctive need of every human being for individualistic self-protection and assurance.

The ego likes to be self-sufficient. The urge for autonomy is built into our nature (is an existential presupposition). We want the provenance of faith, of knowledge, and of salvation to come from *within us*, to be our own achievement. Hence the historically decisive change of direction with Augustine from eucharistic participation to the "interiority" and "spirituality" of the individual (in a closed self-referential autarky) is repeated as the supreme realization of Christian authenticity in every age.[92] Thus, in the absence of the ecclesial gospel, the human person continues to be divided, separated into interiority and exteriority, which means we interpret the human person with the *mode* of a eucharistic approach and "reference" radically reversed.

---

92. See also Ilias Papagiannopoulos, "From Augustine to Kant: The Oedipus-like program of Western metaphysics," in pt. 4, chap. 9 of *Epekeina tēs apousias* (Athens: Indiktos, 2005).

The religionization of the ecclesial event, then, signifies the (voluntary, of course) withdrawal of Christians from the desire and goal of life and their settling for a minimum level of survival. At least in a broad historical perspective, Christianity shows itself to be obviously individualistic and unaware of its ecclesial dimension—unaware of the existential goal of *relation*, unaware that its task is to image the Triadic model of life in the Church.

Even love is proclaimed as an atomic virtue, an achievement of moral behavior, a consequence of egotistic "interiority." This implies that the other, every other, does not exist for me as a real unique person standing opposite me, a call to love that person with a view to knowing him and thus coming to know my own otherness. The other exists only as an occasion for activating my own "interiority," the self-referential achievement of my "love"/virtue. It is thus possible for me to have a clear but illusory sense of certainty that I love that person even when my distancing of myself from the existential otherness of his presence is complete—when, for example, sex or race obliterates for me the other's personhood. In the *Philokalia* we read the following commandment: "Quickly expel from your heart the memory of wife, mother, sister, or other devout women . . ."

The great publishing success in the West of the translations of the *Philokalia* is a strong indication of the Western reader's sense of familiarity with the outlook, criteria, and order of priorities expressed in these anthologized passages. A separate detailed study could also demonstrate the similarity (or identity) of outlook, criteria, and order of priorities between the texts of the *Philokalia* and St. Nikodemos of the Holy Mountain's books on canon law (the *Exomologētarion* and *Pēdalion*) or his pastoral handbooks (the *Chrēstoēthia* and the *Handbook of Counsel on Guarding the Five Senses*).

Nikodemos of the Holy Mountain lived in a period when the Westernization of Greek ecclesial Orthodoxy constituted, in the apt expression of Fr. Georges Florovsky, a "Babylonian captivity," of which the Orthodox at that time were entirely unaware. The most important ecclesiastical figures battled against the "deviations" and "unorthodoxies," as they called them, of the West, but they battled against them with assumptions that were entirely Western—as if the points at issue were entirely ideological and concerned fidelity to the letter of codified formulas or legal precision about a "canonical" order.

The Orthodox East had no inkling that the West for centuries had been in the grip not of a *heresy* or a *schism*, as the Church understood these from its historical past, but of something radically different: the religionization of the ecclesial event, the reversal of the terms of the Christian gospel. Thus, although the East fought against the *Filioque* and papal primacy, it nevertheless adopted the practice of issuing indulgences and the institution of titular bishops. And it admired the "religious culture," the individualistic piety, the intellectualist discipline, and the ethical/legal "consistency" of the West as something noble to be emulated.

It is only within such a context that one can explain how and why Nikodemos, while living on the Holy Mountain (the "bastion of Orthodoxy"), was able to translate and publish as "most edifying" for the Orthodox two typically Roman Catholic handbooks, the *Spiritual Exercises* of Ignatius Loyola, founder of the Jesuit order, and the *Invisible Warfare* of Lorenzo Scupoli, a Theatine. It is only thus that one can explain how and why in his writings he adopted the teaching of Anselm and the Council of Trent "on the satisfaction of divine justice through Christ's death on the cross," how and why (and indeed with the authority of a conservative monk of Mount Athos) he imported into the Orthodox East the legalism and codified religionization of the Latins' presuppositions for participation in the Church—a veritable nightmare.

In the person of a saint, the Church recognizes the manifestation of the fruits of the "kingdom": marks of the realization of the catholic hope of its eucharistic body—it does not reward individual achievements or historic roles. And the critical pinpointing of aspects of Westernization in the works of St. Nikodemos of the Holy Mountain is meaningful because it serves the Church's hope—what other aim could it have?[93] Naturally the question also arises whether the official canonization of a person (a canonization made during the years of Orthodoxy's "Babylonian captivity" to religionization) grants amnesty to aspects of the saint's works that are flagrantly dominated by the language, criteria, and outlook of natural (instinctive) religiosity.

It does not come within the competence or power of a historian, intellectual, or writer, however, to pass judgment on the terms of institutional canonization. One can only offer the observation (obvious to all) that when a historical person is canonized, he does not cease also to be a child of his age, to have expressed himself in the language and in accordance with the assumptions of his social and cultural environment.

If we pass over in silence the religious individualism that governs the selection of the *Philokalia*'s texts, or the reversal of the ecclesial perspective in the *Pēdalion*, the *Chrēstoēthia*, and the *Handbook of Counsel*, we are abandoning the hope of the Church's gospel and throwing away the compass that shows us the difference between the Church and a religion.

93. For a more detailed discussion, see my *Orthodoxy and the West*, chap. 12. See also the refutation of my position offered by the Sacred Community of the Holy Mountain, "Anairesis tōn peplanēmenōn theseōn tou k. Chrēstou Giannarā peri tou en hagiois patros hēmōn Nikodēmou tou Hagioreitou," in the periodical *Orthodoxē Martyria* 40 (1993): 1–10, published in Nicosia, Cyprus.

Chapter 6

Can the Ecclesial Event Accommodate Natural Religiosity?

The ecclesial event is operative (constitutes an active reality) when it continues the *mode* (the vital dynamic) of the incarnation of God, when it assumes the flesh of the world (matter, the scientific knowledge of matter, the sense of the beauty of matter, and human culture in its changing current forms and with its historical products: language, art, and technology). For the ecclesial event to assume the flesh of the world means that it detaches it from the autonomy of individual use and transforms it into a shared reality of loving/eucharistic relation.

If this takes place with the "catholic" flesh of the created world that is subject to decay and death, if mortal flesh can be transformed into a *mode* of the realization of a free and uncircumscribed life, why should we not infer that this assuming can also include natural religion? If the ecclesial transformation of death into life is not simply an intellectual construction, a convenient occasion for individualistic psychological certainties; if it is the hope that as shared trust constitutes the *hypostasis* of what is hoped for, an experiential ratification ("control") of "things not seen," then why should we exclude humanity's instinctive religiosity from this assumption and transformation?

Religiosity is a natural urge, an instinctive need of human nature, that is often not subjected to rational control and judgment. It may be compared to hunger, the need for self-preservation (the central pivot of biological existence) through the taking of food, or to the sex drive, the instinctive operation of self-perpetuation.

Participation in the ecclesial event does not make the taking of food redundant; it does not abolish hunger or the pleasure of taste—just as it does not make the pleasurable coupling of a man and a woman redundant, the joy of sexual love and the begetting of children. It is participation in a common struggle that aspires to changing the atomic event into a shared event: the taking of food in the context of sharing food, a procreative mingling in the representation of Christ's relation to the Church—a participation that aspires to changing atomic survival into a mutual indwelling of life, the individual's need of self-preservation and self-perpetuation into self-transcendence and loving self-offering.

This is the sacrament of the Eucharist; this is also the sacrament of marriage. Within the Church the word *sacrament*, or *mystery* as it is called in Greek, signifies every event that (in the language not of concepts but of ritual, of participatory drama) manifests the ecclesial *mode of existence*, any event that manifests (as the *hypostasis* of what is hoped for) that "the terms of nature are overcome": the terms/necessities of nature are changed into the freedom of the loving sharing/communion of life.

If, then, the Eucharist is the mystery that grafts the natural need of self-preservation onto the ecclesial *mode* and marriage, and the mystery that grafts the sexual need onto the same *mode*, then which is the mystery that would be able to graft humanity's natural need for religion onto the Church?

In the language of Christian literature and worship, the whole ecclesial event—the Church in all its manifestations—is also called a *mystery*: it is a realization and manifestation of the Triadic mode of existence. This mode is realized and manifested by the synaxis of the "body" of the Church in every particular sacramental practice, above all, however, in the supper of the Eucharist, where the realization and manifestation of the body is accomplished by active participation in eating and drinking of the one bread and the one cup. The eucharistic reception of humanity's food/life summarizes the *mode* of referring to the Father every aspect of life and is every aspect that is grafted, as a loving reference, onto the ecclesial event.

Consequently (taking as given the inadequacy of language to signify the existential experience with any fullness), we may be so bold as to say that the Church is a *mystery* in the measure in which it extends the *mode* of the Eucharist into every partial aspect of its life. A gathering of bishops becomes (is not by definition) an ecclesial *council* when it functions as embodying the *mode* of the Eucharist. A painting becomes an ecclesial *icon* when its style and subject matter allow it to facilitate the "passing over" of the beholder "to the prototype," that is, to a personal *relationship*. The administrative organization of the activities and needs of a diocese becomes ecclesial when it serves a loving self-offering (not when its priorities are simply those of practical effectiveness).

From the above, one should be able to conclude that the "mystery" that grafts humanity's natural need for religion onto the Church is the Eucharist: the *mode* constituting the whole of ecclesial life. That is why in the space in which the Eucharist is celebrated, as in the celebration of the rite itself, it becomes immediately obvious (before anything else) whether there happens to be any religionization of the ecclesial event. It is very evident whether the icons, the ritual, the singing, the poetry of the hymns, and the illumination of the space are "referential," as the bread and the wine are, or whether they become autonomous so as to impress the individual, arouse an emotional response in the individual, and facilitate the individual's search for "salvation."

The Church (the lay body that constitutes it) has not hesitated to appropriate elements of religion and graft them onto its own *mode* of existence and life. It has appropriated a certain religious vocabulary, terms such as "revelation," "worship," "law," "commandments," and "sacrifice"; practices such as fasting, prayer, continence, genuflexion, symbolic types such as baptism in water, anointing with oil, incense, liturgical dress and vessels; and a host of other things. It has assumed them by reversing the meaning and function of what it has borrowed, transforming terms of use into terms of *relation*, an individualistic intentionality into the priority of loving communion, a legal character into a call to self-transcendence and self-offering. Scattered in the earlier pages of this book are various attempts to identify and discuss the new content that many of the above words and practices have acquired within the Church.

Church and religion are two realities that are incompatible and irreconcilable, like life and death, freedom and necessity, love and self-interest. There is no room for compatibility; the one reality abrogates the other. The Church, however, proclaims the abolition of the insuperable antitheses. It affirms experientially that "the dividing wall" has been demolished. For death to be transformed into life, for necessity to bear the fruit of freedom, it is sufficient to struggle to withdraw from self-interest. The catalyst for the transcending of every antithesis is *ek-static* love, the *real eros* that is also the mode of *real* (Triadic) *existence*—the Causal Principle of everything that exists. If human beings withdraw even from claiming existence and life for their atomic selves and abandon themselves to the love of the Father, then the antithesis between life and death, necessity and freedom, is also abolished.

Religion is an instinctive self-interest and the Church a struggle to attain freedom from self-interest. Without the self-interest that is an instinctive drive in nature, there would be no awareness of the struggle to attain freedom from nature, no awareness of the *person* as the hypostasis of freedom. And this means that without the instinctual need for religion, the ecclesial struggle to withdraw from religion would remain without any hypostasis. We are speaking here of a struggle, and consequently of the inevitability of failure, of missing the target of the struggle. It is rather for this reason that not only the possibility but also the dynamic of religionization follows the ecclesial event in its historical journey—a permanent temptation and scandal, but also a testing ground of freedom.

The weeds grow together with the wheat until the harvest. Every attempt at "cleansing" contains the danger of pulling up the wheat as well as the weeds. Only at the harvest will self-interest be separated definitively from eros, that freedom might be inalienable.

Bibliography

"Akolouthia tēs Theias Metalēpseōs." In *Hiera Synopsis*, 279–300. Athens: Kampana, n.d. Translated by Holy Transfiguration Monastery as "The Service of Preparation for Holy Communion" and "Thanksgiving after Holy Communion," in *A Prayer Book for Orthodox Christians* (Brookline, MA: Holy Transfiguration Monastery, 1987), 321–65.

Alivizatos, Hamilcar. *Hoi Hieroi Kanones*. Athens, 1949.

Babiniotis, Georgios D. *Lexiko tēs neas Ellēnikēs glōssas*. 3rd ed. Athens: Kentro Lexikologias, 2008.

Bashevis Singer, Isaac. *The Slave*. London: Secker and Warburg, 1963.

Birt, Theodor. *Das Römische Weltreich*. Berlin, 1941.

Caruso, Igor. *Psychoanalyse und Synthese der Existenz*. Freiburg: Herder-Verlag, 1952.

Chadwick, Henry, trans. *Saint Augustine: Confessions*. Oxford: Oxford University Press, 1991.

Clément, Olivier. *Hē theologia meta ton "thanato tou Theou."* Vol. 7 of the Synoro series. Athens: Dōdōnē, 1973.

Concise Encyclopedic Dictionary [in Greek]. Athens, 1935.

Deseille, Placide. *La spiritualité orthodoxe et la Philocalie*. Paris: Albin Michel, 2003.

Dostoevsky, Fyodor. *The Brothers Karamazov*. Translated by David McDuff. London: Penguin Books, 2003.

Dyovouniotis, K. *Ta mystēria tēs Anatolikēs Orthodoxou Ekklēsias*. Athens, 1912.

Florovsky, Georges. *Creation and Redemption*. Vol. 3 of *The Collected Works of Georges Florovsky*. Belmont, MA: Nordland, 1976.

______. *Ways of Russian Theology*. Vol. 5 of *The Collected Works of Georges Florovsky*. Belmont, MA: Nordland, 1979.

Freud, Sigmund. *Mourning and Melancholia*. In vol. 14 of Strachey, ed., *Standard Edition of the Complete Psychological Works of Sigmund Freud*.

______. *The Ego and the Id*. In vol. 20 of Strachey, ed., *Standard Edition of the Complete Psychological Works of Sigmund Freud*.

Geiselmann, J. R. "Dogma." In *Handbuch theologischer Grundbegriffe*, edited by H. Fries. Munich: Kösel-Verlag, 1962.

Goldberg, B. Z. *The Sacred Fire: The Story of Sex in Religion*. New York: Grove Press, 1962.

Gregory of Nyssa. *On the Life of Moses*. Edited by H. Musurillo. In vol. 7 of *Gregorii Nysseni Opera*, edited by W. Jaeger and H. Langerbeck. Leiden: Brill, 1964.

______. *On Ecclesiastes, Homily 7*. Edited by J. McDonough and P. Alexander. In vol. 5 of *Gregorii Nysseni Opera*, edited by W. Jaeger and H. Langerbeck. Leiden: Brill, 1962.

Grupp, G. *Kulturgeschichte der römischen Kaiserzeit*. Regensburg, 1921.

Harding, Celia. "Introduction: Making sense of sexuality." In *Sexuality: Psychoanalytic Perspectives*, edited by Celia Harding, 1–17. New York: Brunner-Routledge, 2001.

Hauck, Friedrich. "*Akathartos, akatharsia*." In Kittel, ed., *Theological Dictionary of the New Testament*, 3:427–31.

Hauck, Friedrich, and Siegfried Schulz. "*Pornē, pornos, porneia, porneuō, ekporneuo*." In Kittel, ed., *Theological Dictionary of the New Testament*, 6:579–95.

Hering, Gunnar. *Oikoumeniko Patriarcheio kai Eurōpaikē politikē, 1620-1638*. Athens: MIET, 1992.

Isaac the Syrian. *The Ascetic Writings of Our Holy Father Isaac the Syrian*. Edited by Nikephoros Theotokis. Leipzig, 1770. Re-edited by Joachim Spetieris (Athens, 1895).

John of Sinai. *The Ladder*. Edited by the hermit Sophronius. Constantinople, 1883.

Jones, Stanton L., and Heather R. Hostler. "The Role of Sexuality in Personhood." In *Judeo-Christian Perspectives on Psychology*, edited by William R. Miller and Harold D. Delaney, 115–32. Washington, DC: American Psychological Association, 2005.

Kadloubovsky, E., and G. E. H. Palmer, trans. *Writings from the Philokalia on Prayer of the Heart*. London: Faber and Faber, 1951.

Kittel, Gerhard, ed. *Theological Dictionary of the New Testament*. Translated by Geoffrey W. Bromiley. 10 vols. Grand Rapids, MI: Eerdmans, 1966–76.

Laarmann, Matthias. "Transubstantiation." In Ritter, Gründer, and Gabriel, eds., *Historisches Wörterbuch der Philosophie*, 10:1349–58.

Léon-Dufour, Xavier, ed. *Dictionary of Biblical Theology*. 2nd ed. London: Geoffrey Chapman, 1995.

Lorenz, S., and W. Schröder. "Manichäismus II." In Ritter, Gründer, and Gabriel, eds., *Historisches Wörterbuch der Philosophie*, 5:715–16.

Migne, Jacques-Paul. Patrologia graeca. 161 vols. Paris, 1857–86.

Miklosich, F., and J. Müller. *Acta Patriarchatus Constantinopolitani*. Vienna, 1860.

Moltmann, Jürgen. *Praedestination und Perseveranz*. Neukirchen: Kreis Moers, 1961.

Motchoulsky, C. *Dostoïevsky*. Paris: Payot, 1963.

Nygren, Gotthard. *Das Prädestinationsproblem in der Theologie Augustins*. Lund: printed dissertation, 1956.

Papagiannopoulos, Ilias. "The correlation between God and interiority." In *Exodos theatrou: Dokimio ontologias me ploēgo ton "Moby Dick" tou H. Melville*. Athens: Indiktos, 2000.

______. "From Augustine to Kant: The Oedipus-like program of Western metaphysics." In *Epekeina tēs apousias*. Athens: Indiktos, 2005.

Pascal, Blaise. *Ecrits sur la Grace*. In vol. 11 of *Oeuvres completes de Blaise Pascal*, edited by L. Brunschvicg. Paris: Hachette, 1914.

Pheidas, Vlasios. *Ekklēsiastikē Historia*. Vol. 2. Athens, 1994.

Pfister, Kurt. *Der Untergang der antiken Welt*. Leipzig, 1941.

Philippidis, Leonidas. *Historia tēs epochēs tēs Kainēs Diathēkēs*. Athens, 1958.

Reckermann, A. "Idol, Ido(lo)latrie." In Ritter, Gründer, and Gabriel, eds., *Historisches Wörterbuch der Philosophie*, 4:188–92.

Ritter, J., K. Gründer, and G. Gabriel, eds. *Historisches Wörterbuch der Philosophie*. 13 vols. Basel: Schwabe-Verlag, 1971–2007.

Runciman, Steven. *The Medieval Manichee: A Study of the Christian Dualist Heresy*. Cambridge: Cambridge University Press, 1947.

Russell, Norman, trans. *The Lives of the Desert Fathers*. Cistercian Studies 34. Kalamazoo, MI: Cistercian Publications, 1980.

Sacred Community of the Holy Mountain. "Anairesis tōn peplanēmenōn theseōn tou k. Chrēstou Giannarā peri tou en hagiois patros hēmōn Nikodēmou tou Hagioreitou." *Orthodoxē Martyria* 40 (1993): 1–10.

Sathas, Konstantinos. *Biographikon schediasma peri tou Patriarchou Ieremiou B' (1572–1594)*. Thessalonica: Pournaras, 1979.

Shafranske, Edward P., ed. *Religion and the Clinical Practice of Psychology*. Washington, DC: American Psychological Association, 1996.

Sherrard, Philip. *Christianity and Eros*. London: SPCK, 1976.

Söderlund, Rune. *Ex praevisa fidei: Zum Versfändnis der Prädestinationslehre in der lutheranischen Orthodoxie*. Hanover: Lutherisches Verlagshaus, 1983.

Stephanidis, Vasileios. *Ekklēsiastikē Historia*. 3rd ed. Athens: Astir, 1970.

Strachey, James, ed. *Standard Edition of the Complete Psychological Works of Sigmund Freud*. 24 vols. London: Hogarth Press and the Institute of Psycho-Analysis, 1953–74.

Taft, Robert. "The Pontifical Liturgy of the Great Church according to a Twelfth-Century Diataxis in Codex *British Museum Add. 34060*." Pt. 1, *Orientalia Christiana Periodica* 45 (1979): 279–397; pt. 2, *Orientalia Christiana Periodica* 46 (1980): 82–124.

Vasse, Denis. *Le temps du desir*. Paris: Seuil, 1969.

Vergote, Antoine. *Guilt and Desire*. New Haven, CT: Yale University Press, 1988.

Voegelin, E. "Religionsersatz. Die gnostischen Massenbewegungen unserer Zeit." *Wort und Wahrheit* 15 (1960): 5–18.

Weber, Max. *The Protestant Ethic and the Spirit of Capitalism*. London and New York: Routledge, 2001.

Yannaras, Christos. *Hē eleutheria tou ēthous*. 3rd rev. ed. Athens: Ikaros, 2002. Translated by Elizabeth Briere as *The Freedom of Morality* (Crestwood, NY: St. Vladimir's Seminary Press, 1984).

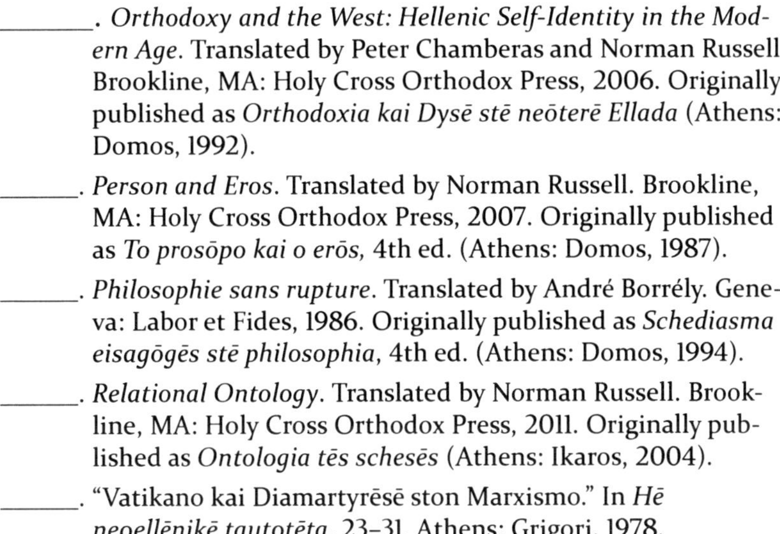

______. *Orthodoxy and the West: Hellenic Self-Identity in the Modern Age*. Translated by Peter Chamberas and Norman Russell. Brookline, MA: Holy Cross Orthodox Press, 2006. Originally published as *Orthodoxia kai Dysē stē neōterē Ellada* (Athens: Domos, 1992).

______. *Person and Eros*. Translated by Norman Russell. Brookline, MA: Holy Cross Orthodox Press, 2007. Originally published as *To prosōpo kai o erōs*, 4th ed. (Athens: Domos, 1987).

______. *Philosophie sans rupture*. Translated by André Borrély. Geneva: Labor et Fides, 1986. Originally published as *Schediasma eisagōgēs stē philosophia*, 4th ed. (Athens: Domos, 1994).

______. *Relational Ontology*. Translated by Norman Russell. Brookline, MA: Holy Cross Orthodox Press, 2011. Originally published as *Ontologia tēs schesēs* (Athens: Ikaros, 2004).

______. "Vatikano kai Diamartyrēsē ston Marxismo." In *Hē neoellēnikē tautotēta*, 23–31. Athens: Grigori, 1978.

Index

CPSIA information can be obtained at www.ICGtesting.com
Printed in the USA
BVOW07s2236150114

341688BV00001B/4/P

9 781935 317401